It's Worth Doing

Perspectives on the Japan Pharmaceutical Industry

it's WORTH X doing

Perspectives on the Japan Pharmaceutical Industry

P. Reed Maurer

Order this book online at www.trafford.com
or email orders@trafford.com

Most Trafford titles are also available at major online book retailers.

Printed in the United States of America.

ISBN: 978-1-4120-3507-1 (sc)
ISBN: 978-1-4669-0520-7 (hc)
ISBN: 978-1-4669-0521-4 (e)

Library of Congress Control Number: 2011961096

Trafford rev. 12/16/2011

 www.trafford.com

North America & international
toll-free: 1 888 232 4444 (USA & Canada)
phone: 250 383 6864 ♦ fax: 812 355 4082

Contents

Chapter I
The Drug Industry in Transition 1989–1999

Chapter II
Reinventing Japan's Health Care System

Chapter VI
Wholesalers Consolidate to Survive

Chapter VII
Drug Company Image

Chapter VIII
Managing People for Success

Chapter IX
Mergers, Acquisitions and Alliances

Chapter X
Foreign Firms Struggle to Compete

Tributes

Mr. P. Reed Maurer has been an extremely good family friend of mine for over 20 years.

We have worked together on many projects in these 20 years in the field of merger and acquisitions, licenses, consulting, venture establishments, study groups et cetera.

Reed's exceptional ability to listen, and to focus on the essentials have been instrumental in the accomplishments of many projects in Japan which ultimately provided an infrastructure for the establishment of a healthy pharmaceutical industry."

Gensuke Tokoro
President & CEO
aRigen Pharmaceuticals, Inc.

Thank you for your enthusiasm, your dedication to the industry, your readiness to share your network and your efforts to help others keep abreast and read through the lines.

This has been invaluable information and guidance, especially to the many newcomers to Japan, year after year.

Bruno Rossi
Operating Officer
Bayer Yakuhin, Ltd.

I was competing with Reed Maurer selling a product in the same animal health area when I first knew his name. I then knew him and his family better after they came up to Tokyo.

While he was with U.S. PMA office in Tokyo, he told me he had to repeat to answer same questions from new comers and visitors from the United States. I proposed him to write down answers to common questions, which I translated and asked the late Ando san, president of Drug Magazine to include in his monthly magazine. After a year or so, I proposed his articles be made into a book, which Simul International materialized as *Competing in Japan*. Japan Times then published it in English also.

I believe what he has done helped non-Japanese pharma companies to understand the pharma market and business here, but helped Japanese companies understand the way non-Japanese companies behave in Japan and compete with them.

Jiro Hayashi
Representative
J.K. Hay Consulting

In a country that values continuity, but sees expat managers change every 2–4 years, Reed's advise and insight has been an anchor for the foreign and local pharma community for over 40 years. Despite his long and successful tenure, Reed's thinking is as fresh now, as it was 40 years ago. I am a faithful reader of his articles, which are always as insightful as they are entertaining.

Reed, thank you for your invaluable contributions over the year. I am delighted to see that your work is being preserved for generations to come.

Michael Goettler
Regional President Asia-Pacific
Pfizer - Specialty Care

I first met Reed Maurer a long, long time ago when he was running the PMA in Japan, and I was just making the transition to the human health business in Taiwan after starting my career in Animal Health.

Just last month I had reason to think of him again when I was asked to help a biotech company on its Japan strategy, and suggested instead the man who I knew could do the job much better, Reed.

Sandwiched into that 40-year period was my time working in Japan, when I had the chance to enjoy his wit and wisdom first hand, to say nothing of his art.

As we say down under, a pretty special bloke.

Alan B. Bootes
Retired CEO
Pfizer Japan

Regrouping in one volume the contributions of Reed Maurer to Pharma Japan is a rich idea. So many copies pile up in my drawers, and every time I resolve to clean them up, I end up sitting down and reading them with renewed interest.

Reed would probably not like to be called a guru but his lines inspired me more than once, at least to look beyond the news of our industry to elaborate on the trends that really matter in Japan, knowing where to place the line between what makes Japan different from the rest of the world, as much as what makes it similar in more than one way. Close and far altogether, that's what I learned.

Philippe Auvaro
GSK

Reed has always enlightened me with his unblinkered insight into the Japanese pharmaceutical sector.

Although I have worked in Japan on and off for the past 25 years, a chat with Reed invariably layers a new perspective that prompts me to challenge again old adages about Japan and Japanese business practice.

Most enjoyably, Reed always offers his observations with good humor and wry delivery.

Mark Noggle
President, Representative Director
Ferring Pharmaceuticals Co., Ltd

Is there another foreigner who has contributed more to Japan's pharma industry? I think not.

This book should be on the desk of every executive both foreigner and Japanese alike.

Reed, a quick wit and as sharp as a tack.

Philip Carrigan
Representative Director
Morunda KK

Reed Maurer is walking & talking dictionary about health industry in Japan, but more so in form of his incredible industry knowledge along with historical context, sense of humor that has stayed with him through all these years and an absolutely young and inquisitive mind.

Reed remains ageless in his enthusiasm and quest for knowledge.

Maulik Nanavaty
Boston Scientific Japan K.K.

Rarely in life do you come upon a character like Reed Maurer.
By character, I mean:
A man who is passionate about his cause in life,
A man who is fiercely proud of his family,
A man who always sees the bright side to everything,
A man who has been the glue for foreign companies operating in Japan for many years,
A Man whom I consider a friend.

Tom Dooley
President & Representative Director
Alcon Japan Limited

There is literally no one who can match Reed Maurer's breadth and width of experience and knowledge about the pharmaceutical industry in Japan. And, most importantly, there is no one who is more willing and eager to share four decades of his professional experiences with colleagues, friends, competitors, and strangers.

I can't imagine how much harder it would have been to learn about the industry in Japan without Reed's guidance and advice.

Ira Wolf

Japan Representative
Pharmaceutical Research and
Manufacturers of America (PhRMA)

Reed Maurer's reputation is praiseworthy. When our company initiated our presence in Japan, Reed Maurer was the first expert we consulted. We have had a strong relation with him ever since.

For me as a newcomer to Japan, Reed Maurer and his initiative—the Study Group—helped me tremendously. Through the Study Group I got a strong insight to our business and met fantastic people.

I have always enjoyed Reed Maurer's visits to our office. He is very open for ideas on topics for coming Study Group sessions and would have an enlightening story or two about the Japanese pharma situation or the country in general.

It is a pleasure to know you Reed Maurer.

Michael Vilhelmsen

Former General Manager &
Representative Director
Lundbeck Japan K.K.

For the foreign pharmaceutical executives Reed Maurer has unique status. Based on his long experience, wisdom, insight and credibility, Reed has the ability to demystify preconceptions and misunderstandings and replace it with respect for the market we serve. Reed facilitates that all perceptions are put into the right perspective, not only to the help foreign executives but ultimately to the benefit of the health care system as such.

Claus Eilersen
President, Representative Director
Novo Nordisk Pharma Ltd.

Upon my arrival in Japan, one of the first industry people I met was Reed Maurer. My predecessor was adamant that my life in Japan (personally and professionally) would be forever changed by knowing Reed, and I'll be damned if he wasn't right. I've since come to know and respect Reed's wit, wisdom and perspective on all things Japan. The man is one of a kind.

Gary Winer
President
Abbott Japan

I have coached executives to improve their leader competencies for most of my career. Reed stands out as an example of all that makes the best leader. He is humble, wise, a great listener who holds genuine empathy and care for others, all combined with his expert knowledge.

The only thing of value we can give each other is our time, having only a finite amount of it. Reed has always been generous of his time and has been a wonderful mentor. He is a coach's coach.

Thank you Reed for the gift of your time and the honor of your friendship.

Rob Schrull
President
Global Business Leaders Association

Reed's insight and deep understanding of the business and cultural aspects of healthcare and the pharmaceutical business in Japan, combined with his wonderful humility, integrity, and humor, are an inspiration for all who have met him. He is able to bring clarity to the most complex business issues in a way that is easy to understand and assimilate for a Western mind.

He is a wonderful listener, mentor, and coach. He does these in a way that leaves you motivated and inspired.

I am honored and privileged to consider him a friend!

Tony Alvarez
President
MSD K.K.

Chapter I

The Drug Industry in Transition 1989–1999

As the 1980s ended and the 1990s began, the Japanese drug market and industry were on a roll; only a matter of time before surpassing the United States and its companies invading the West. A decade later everything changed. The transition caused a "re-think" of cherished assumptions. Restructuring was inevitable. A remarkable era in which the rules of competition were rewritten. Winners positioned themselves for the future, and the losers searched for ways to survive.

New Year Wishes

Out with the old, in with the new! Year-end in Japan is a great time to clean house and complete unfinished business. "Forgetting the year" parties are so popular reservations in hotels and restaurants must be made months in advance. Everyone concentrates on what must be done to make next year better than this year. I have a few modest wishes for the New Year.

It would be a blessing if reporters who write stories about health care generally and the pharmaceutical industry specifically, did their homework to search for truth. Doctors do not dispense drugs to line their own pockets with yen. Patients are not overdosed with ineffective drugs. Pharmaceutical companies are not obscenely profitable. Medical representatives do not throw lavish parties for physicians, shine their shoes, or wash their cars.

I wish a story would be written about what it is like to be married to a doctor. We could recommend a friend who spends many lonely nights because her husband is looking after sick people in the hospital. I wish a story would be written about an ulcer patient who did not need surgery because drugs eliminated the ulcer. I would recommend my father who had two-thirds of his stomach removed a long time ago before these drugs were discovered.

I wish a visiting American CEO would meet the press and say, "We know Japan is a tough, competitive market, but we intend to beat our competition. Our products are better quality and cost less than those made by Japanese competitors. We intend to satisfy our customers like they have never been satisfied before. Our employees have benefts no one can match, and we are in Japan to stay."

I wish the pharmaceutical industry and the Ministry of Health and Welfare would find a way to stop talking about the "downward price spiral." This may be wishful thinking as the issue seems so polarized. Insurers do not want to reimburse providers more than they pay for drugs. Providers believe it is their economic right to demand discounts which lead to reductions in reimbursement prices.   Will this vicious cycle be broken by the introduction of a reasonable zone, weighted average calculation of prices, and the antimonopoly guidelines? Or will all these changes aggravate the situation? Your bet is as good as mine—let's wish for the best.

I wish I could talk to a Japanese executive who did not utter the phrase, "We Japanese". It is as though they have authority to speak for the entire race. There are so many differences between individuals and companies that it is naïve to speak as though everyone acts in unison. There may be a Takeda plan for internationalization, but there is no Japanese plan.

I wish Japanese patients would have the nerve to ask their physicians what medicines they are taking and why, instead of buying a book to read about them. An educated patient is the best customer for the pharmaceutical industry. Removing the mystery from therapy is a movement whose time has come.

Another movement whose time has come is harmonization of regulatory requirements. I wish government officials in Europe, America, and Japan would expedite this process. The end results will be positive for everyone. Harmonization has a broad base of political support in Japan, thus rapid progress is anticipated.

Finally, I wish businessmen, government officials, and politicians on both sides of the Pacific would make renewed efforts to establish unbreakable, trustworthy bonds of business and friendship. Our future is mutually inclusive, mutually synergistic, and mutually rewarding. Inexorably we are seeing the benefits of competition and collaboration. Inevitably 1992 will bring further evidence of this fact. Win/win efforts cannot lose.

Pharma Japan 1284, December 1991

Once Upon a Time

Yes, we should look ahead, but I can't shake the pensive reflection, or melancholy, that strikes during *shogatsu*. It is not for lack of trying. I burned my finger lighting a string of firecrackers that for five minutes blasted the evil spirits away. The noise was deafening, but the Chinese gods were awakened. In quiet Japanese style we had a private cleansing inside a shrine. The swish-swish of the *oharai* was relaxing as shrill music from bamboo instruments reverberated off wooden beams and was absorbed by the *tatami* floor.

I drank champagne and watched the Pope's Christmas Mass televised from Rome. I ate poi and lomi lomi salmon, an old Hawaiian custom. My German ancestry dictated a hearty meal of sauerkraut and pork on New Year's Day for good luck. In the American tradition I went to see the Aloha Bowl football game, drank beer and ate a hot dog.

My propensity to look back may be the result of fatigue brought on by trying to appease all the gods that insure a prosperous future. But there is something else jerking my psyche back in time. It is the realization that so much has changed in Japan since my own arrival on these shores in 1970.

There is frustration with those who long ago typecast the Japanese, and believe they are still the same. There is frustration with foreign "experts" who once upon a time knew the Japanese pharmaceutical market, and believe it hasn't changed. A cure for my problem is to burden you with what was and no longer is.

Once upon a time Japanese pharmaceutical manufacturers' compound average growth rate (CAGR) of sales was 15 percent per annum. Now it is 6 percent. All companies show a decline, although some reduced growth rates are less extreme than others. Below is a sample of firms.

The largest five companies accounted for about 20 percent of industry sales in 1990, down from a 25 percent share of the top five during the early 1970s.

Once upon a time Japanese companies spent 6 percent of their sales on R&D. In 1990 it was 10 percent, obviously on a much higher sales base. In the old days, no one reported about Japanese origin NCEs because there were none. You know what happened. Of 443 NCEs introduced between 1981 and 1989, 117 originated in Japan, 107 in the United States. The next largest source was Germany, with 36.

Once upon a time there were over 1,200 local wholesalers. Now there are about 300. A few Japanese manufacturers controlled most of the wholesalers; now the survivors are independent, full line dealers with regional coverage. They conduct price negotiations and employ 35,000 salesmen who know more about the prescribing habits of 80,000 doctors in the so-called GP market than most manufacturers' reps.

Once upon a time foreign companies were limited to joint ventures. Now there are no investment restrictions, no discriminatory provisions in regulatory procedures, no reasons to fail except those that are self-inflicted.

In 1970, every Japanese had lived in Japan longer than me. Now I have lived here longer than 26 percent of all the natives. What does that have to do with anything? Absolutely nothing at all, except a reminder that it is time to start looking ahead to this wonderful year and the big changes unfolding right before our eyes.

Company	CAGR (%) 1982/83–1990	CAGR (%) 1975/76–1982/83	R&D/Sales (%) 1990	Ratio (%) 1975/76
Takeda	3	7	9	5
Fujisawa	1	12	13	6
Eisai	7	20	14	8
Shionogi	2	10	11	7
Chugai	6	21	16	7
Toyama	2	11	12	4

Looking Back on the Past Six Years

I opened an office in Tokyo for the U.S. PMA (Pharmaceutical Manufacturers Association) in March 1987, and served as the PMA Japan Representative until February 1993. It was a unique opportunity to view the industry from "outside," the Ministry of Health and Welfare from "inside," and to be in the "Tokyo Loop" while revolutionary changes occurred in the health care system.

Outside the Industry

A corporate insider's view of the outside world is distorted by isolation, filtered by overconfidence, and interpreted by extraordinary egos. Public relations people easily convince their bosses the world is waiting for the latest pronouncement from inside the corporation. Reality is different outside the corporation.

Politicians and bureaucrats do not fear public wrath if they take on the pharmaceutical industry. No large constituency is willing to back the industry. Individual companies may enjoy a favorable image in the financial community; they may be highly evaluated by pharmacy school graduates; academia may respect their research achievements; but the industry is assailed by their regulators.

A single company cannot lobby for fairness in the debate. The only effective voice is a unified position as presented by an association of companies. Unfortunately, individual members endlessly discuss policy objectives, but do not give the association a clear mandate to execute. The head of an association is reduced to a highly paid secretary rather than a leader. His role is to articulate a watered-down consensus of opinion.

Japanese government officials easily divided and conquered the industry. That is, they played Japanese industry associations off against foreign industry associations, effectively neutralizing the opposition. This changed when the entire industry worked out a unified position. Not a U.S., or Japanese or European policy, but an "industry" policy. Individual country or company proposals are not taken seriously.

Policy debates within an association cannot be relegated to corporate affairs personnel. Line executives gain or lose the most from government-imposed price reductions and regulatory delays. Association policy decisions cannot be delegated to corporate staffers.

Although the Japanese government is the insurer for only 30 percent of the population, it establishes drug reimbursement prices and medical fees for all insurers.

During the 1980s the government systematically lowered reimbursement prices, often arbitrarily based upon non-transparent, complicated formulas. Bringing sanity into this economic policy required a unified industry approach to a variety of audiences.

In retrospect the results were positive. Price revisions are now less frequent and less severe. New products are price listed regularly on a three-month cycle. Reimbursement prices reward innovation. Patents are strong and post-marketing reporting requirements give innovators exclusive marketing rights up to 10 years. No single company or national association had the power to influence these changes. The advantage of unity was demonstrated in a decisive fashion.

Price is an important issue, but are we so consumed by it that the benefits of this industry go unnoticed? Everyone in Japan has medical insurance with drug coverage. Out-of-pocket costs are low. The public is insensitive to drug prices, but that is all they hear from the manufacturers. Association meetings I attended for six years were dominated by one issue, i.e., the pricing policies of the Ministry of Health and Welfare.

The public's number one priority is not price. The value side of the equation must be addressed with as much vigor as price. When every Japanese knew someone with tuberculosis, antibiotics produced by pharmaceutical companies were a blessing. Today the public hears more about deadly resistant infections caused by overuse or improper use of antibiotics than they hear about lives saved by new antibiotics that took years to discover and develop. The industry is not perceived as a solution—it is thought to be the cause of the problem. Appeals for price relief are ignored if the perception of value is low.

Books, not published by the industry, describing the most commonly used drugs in Japan are best sellers. Industry associations would be wise to turn their attention to public needs for value and information. Lest we forget, the public ultimately decides if their elected representatives bash or boost an economically viable, research intensive pharmaceutical industry.

Pharma Japan 1361, July 19, 1993

Japan Breaks Away from Its Past

Forecasting developments in the Japanese pharmaceutical market is akin to predicting the onset and outcome of pregnancies. Some occur as forecast; others are planned but never occur. Some are surprises, either pleasant or unpleasant. Some begin then end unexpectedly. A successful outcome cannot be guaranteed, and delivery is more of a beginning than an end.

Forecasts are not reality, but may be credible if not mired in the past. Visions of Japan's past reality fast forwarded into the future are likely to yield forecasts 180 degrees off course. The Japanese pharmaceutical market is not what it used to be. Significant changes are taking place in Japan which will impact increasingly on the structure of the industry and the factors which enhance competitiveness.

Japan Has Changed

Yet old attitudes are slow to fade, and despite an interval of over 50 years, perceptions of Japan still suffer from the Pearl Harbor syndrome. Many senior executives consider Japan a closed market, although investment restrictions were abolished 20 years ago. Foreign R&D executives consider Japan's regulatory review procedures to be slow, non-transparent and biased towards 'Made in Japan' drugs, although Japan is the number one first launch country for new drugs.

The problem may be that change in Japan is rarely dramatic. Rather, it is pervasive—small changes occur constantly and permeate the system. Over time, this results in a fundamental shift in form and function.

Consider, for example, some of the changes that have taken place in the past 25 years:

- *Discovery research* was non-existent in the late 1960s. It later focused on second generation new chemical entities (NCEs), and is now on the leading edge of a number of scientific/medical disciplines. There was a time when Japan only licensed-in, now it is licensing-out.
- *Development research* was limited to confirming results obtained elsewhere, in other words, registration research. It became very time effcient, and is now focused on improving the therapeutic potential of NCEs, e.g., drug delivery systems.
- *Manufacturing* was the core of a company, a training ground for senior executives. Labor was later automated out of the system, and now entire factories are moving off-shore. Japan is exporting its manufacturing know-how.
- *Sales* were 'pushed through' controlled distributors. Today, wholesalers are evolving from dependence to independence, from a localized infrastructure to a regional presence, and from a narrow product line to a full line of prod-

ucts sourced from many manufacturers. Sales are 'pulled through' distribution channels by sophisticated selling efforts.

- *The labor force* was young, poorly paid and locked into a single company for an entire career. Today, employees are older, highly paid and well educated. In the future they will be more mobile and committed to opportunities for self-development, wherever they may be offered and exploited.
- *Management* was family and its outlook did not extend beyond Japan. Today it is in transition to a cadre of professional managers with working knowledge of other countries.
- *Doctors* were politically powerful. Now they are not. They were, and still are, price sensitive, but the present climate demands patient sensitivity. Informed consent is no longer an exclusive Western practice.
- *Pharmacists* operated pharmacies that sold everything except prescription drugs. In 1992 the number of prescriptions filled in 'outside' pharmacies increased by 12 percent to represent 14 percent of the total. Separation of prescribing and dispensing is now proceeding apace.
- *Clinical trials* were not much more than pre-marketing trials. Today they are better controlled but widely dispersed with too few patients in too many institutions. The trend is towards consolidation and adherence to protocols that result in meaningful comparative data.
- *The Ministry of Health and Welfare (MHW)* was protective of domestic interests, non-transparent and intent on slashing drug prices. Today the door is open, regardless of nationality. The future will bring openness, deregulation and transparent pricing.
- *Patents*, some 25 years ago, were only available for processes. In the mid-1970s a product patent system was enacted, and in the late 1980s, patent term restoration was introduced. Now there is market exclusivity based on the time required for post-marketing surveillance. These changes were not made overnight, neither were they implemented as part of a dramatic healthcare reform package. Nevertheless, the cumulative effect is no less than a fundamental shift in the way business is done in Japan.

1994 Key Events

Undoubtedly, the most important event in 1994 will be reimbursement tariff revisions on April 1, which will cover drug prices and medical fees. Medical fee increases in the past were linked to drug price decreases; that is, save money on drugs to spend more money on doctors. This zero sum budget game was possible because of a significant (23 percent) gap between actual purchase prices of drugs and their reimbursement tariff prices.

However, during the past year this gap has narrowed to an average 20 percent. Furthermore, the new calculation method allows 13 percentage points as a so-called 'reasonable zone.' In other words, if a drug is not discounted by more than 13 percent off the tariff price on a weighted average basis, the reimbursement price will not be reduced.

In late 1992 manufacturers implemented a single invoice price system in their transactions with wholesalers because of new antimonopoly laws and Fair Trade Commission (FTC) guidelines. This action directly reduced the level of discounts. Also, new products tend to be discounted less in order to avoid reimbursement price revisions which shorten product life cycles.

The biannual tariff process artificially dampens demand as everyone in the system adjusts to new prices and a new fee structure. Products that were discounted to increase volume (more margins for dispensers) lose their appeal when tariff prices are reduced. Thus, the competitive mix is altered, particularly within drug classes where therapeutic substitution is a common practice.

Moreover, while an increase in medical fees should reduce the demand for discounts, the costs involved in running a medical practice or hospital are increasing. Medical fees must rise by more than 5 percent to lessen the thirst for discounts. In fairness, it should be noted that medical fees do not adequately cover operating costs.

In recent years, absolute increases in healthcare costs have been tolerated because they did not exceed the growth in national income on a percentage basis. The healthcare spend was static at 6 percent of gross domestic product (GDP). Allocation of growing funds is a nice problem but in 1994 the problem will turn nasty. National income growth rates are down, tax receipts will shrink, and GDP growth has stopped.

These dynamics have led to acrimonious debates between the medical association and industry. Doctor lobbyists have demanded lower tariff prices on widely used drugs even though their market prices fall within the reasonable zone. While the rationale is to make money available to increase medical fees, industry spokesmen have countered that such action would make a mockery of the price revision process. Self-interest prevails, making the outcome uncertain and difficult to forecast. The last word will come from the Finance Ministry which controls the purse strings.

Another key event in 1994 will be the application of Good Postmarketing Surveillance Practice (GPMSP) guidelines to all prescription products (including generics) in April. Side-effect reporting procedures in Japan are embarrassing by any international standard, and corrections are long overdue. An important facet of the new guidelines is a requirement to remove the management of GPMSP from the sales organization. In other words, make the reporting process a safety mechanism rather than a sales tool.

GPMSP will increase the costs of doing business, but the positive trade-off is market exclusivity during the reporting term which can be extended up to 10 years. At present, the maximum term is six years.

This will also be a critical year for labor—Japan has caught the restructuring bug prevalent in the West. Practically all new employees enter companies in April. The most interesting aspect to watch will be employment patterns as they relate to the number of medical representatives (MRs). Companies are under a variety of pressures (mainly economic) to reduce the number of MRs (there are now 40,000 in Japan). However, global numbers are misleading as some companies are under-staffed and others have a surplus.

Finally, government actions to streamline the regulatory review process will be implemented in 1994 and 1995. A commitment to deregulate is now policy at the political level—how fast it will percolate through the bureaucracy is a key question. The intention of the MHW to harmonise regulatory requirements is an important element of deregulation. Japan will host the International Conference on Harmonization in 1995, a good reason to exercise leadership in 1994 to move the harmonization schedule forward.

Impact of Change

In many respects, the changes in Japan are a threat to large domestic companies which have dominated the top 20 ranking (there are only four foreign companies in this list). These threats include slow growth at home, open distribution channels and a surplus of medical representatives.

At the same time as the home market is experiencing slow growth, Japanese majors have substantially increased their financial commitment to research. Ongoing investments in research facilities, people and programs cannot be turned on and off according to economic conditions in Japan. It is clear that the sales base which supports research must be expanded off shore, primarily to Europe and the United States.

It is thus reasonable to forecast that research driven Japanese companies will be reluctant to license-out the fruits of their research investments. They must add value by establishing a presence outside Japan, and the likelihood is that the United

States will be seen as a more comfortable target than Europe, with its multiplicity of cultures, languages and regulations.

Further expansion of research must also go off shore, not for economic reasons, but to tap a diversity of innovative ideas. No country has a monopoly on brain power, but in the emerging field of biotechnology the United States is clearly the leader. Access to technology need not be through a wholly owned presence, and there is likely to be a variety of investments in science, either through academia or in venture based start-ups. The Japanese 'lost face' with ill conceived research investments in the late 1980s. In the future they will be more focused on ideas that are synergistic with their programs in Japan.

That said, old habits in large companies do not disappear easily. Control over the distribution system is diffcult to give up—it was so nice for so long. However, wholesalers have consolidated and the survivors prefer to welcome business from any manufacturer—big or small, Japanese or foreign—as long as they have new products. Wholesalers have also grasped the responsibility for pricing in a remarkably short time. This will increase their power and access vis-à-vis end users, thus enhancing independence from their former masters.

The role of the medical representative (MR) has also changed—from a price negotiator to a purveyor of useful information. Many MRs are now redundant or are no longer attractive to doctors. MHW is preaching a philosophy of 'more research, less promotion.' Selling tactics are shifting from a human wall approach to selective targeting and innovative marketing. Thus, the majors have an expensive surplus of MRs. Labor practices in Japan make it difficult to downsize quickly. The end result is pressure on operating income, just at a time when additional financial resources are required to expand outside Japan.

A Challenging Future

Middle-sized Japanese companies, particularly those without a productive research effort (most of them), will find the new reality challenging to say the least. Forecasts for consolidation in this sector are surprise free.

Newcomers to the pharmaceutical market include Japanese outsiders, e.g., chemical, textile, cosmetic and beer companies, and foreigners who have not yet established critical mass in Japan. The changes should enhance their ability to enter the market. Buying-in is the most viable option, although conditions in Japan today do not preclude any form of structure. The door is open but will not swing easy for those unwilling to make commitments of time and money (primarily the former).

Multinational foreign companies with a presence in Japan have the best opportunity to take advantage of current conditions to optimize their position. To them, Japan is not an enigma. They need more people rather than less. The new sales approach is a familiar one. Their research is focused on the needs of Japan's aging population.

As seen from Tokyo, the only limitation on success in Japan is self-imposed. Management distracted by the healthcare reform debates in Washington and across Europe may not allocate their best people, money and time to exploit opportunities emerging in Japan. If so, Japanese majors will have breathing room to adjust and keep a lock on the top positions. This competitive battle in Japan has implications beyond these shores—in 1994 and beyond.

Scrip Magazine, January 1994

Restructuring the Japanese Pharma Industry

The English word restructuring has entered the Japanese business vocabulary. No one can clearly define the word, but it insinuates positive responses to changing conditions. It avoids admitting present structures will fail. It facilitates thinking the unthinkable—layoffs of people, known politely as downsizing.

A unifed defnition of restructuring is impossible. Investment bankers see restructuring in mergers and acquisitions. Financial executives restructure debt into equity, or vice versa. Sales executives see targeting or micro-marketing as restructuring. Everyone describes the beast by what part is touched.

Japanese executives do not see the logic of restructuring in actions by their U.S. counterparts. Buying into generics is not a strategy the Japanese feel compelled to emulate. Economic and political factors that created a generic market in the United States do not exist in Japan. Japanese believe "new is better than old," and generics represent old technology.

Recent actions by Merck & Co. are also perplexing. Not long ago Merck shut down its international division and organized pharmaceutical operations on a global basis, proclaiming the United States was just another market in their portfolio of markets. Recently the company restructured the United States and Canada under one executive, and the rest of the world under another executive. The international division is back. Geographical restructuring appears to be a function of executive personality rather than global logic.

Not unlike in the West, Japanese executives must restructure two corporate functions, however, implementing change will be different. It is a mistake to assume the direction of change will be toward U.S. or European models. Change occurs, but the assumption: "Japanese are becoming more Western," will prove to be wrong.

Changes in the external and internal environment drive restructuring efforts. I will review both prior to describing the company operations that must be restructured.

External Environment Changes Since 1990

The external health care environment has fundamentally changed, affecting pharmaceutical operations from research to distribution. Yesterday's list of key success factors is irrelevant in today's environment.

In yen terms, the ethical pharmaceutical market grew 6.1 percent per year from 1984 through 1993. Volume growth averaged 10.5 percent per year. In 1993 Japan represented 22 percent of the world pharmaceutical market, second only to the United States (29 percent). Per-capita drug spending of $254 per year exceeded the U.S. level of $179.

Given Japan's aging population, a demographic shift unmatched by any country in recorded history, per-capita consumption of drugs will increase, irrespective of demand restraints implemented by the government. However, it is unrealistic to forecast volume growth at double digit rates.

A basic paradigm shift is occurring that involves regulators, payers, providers, and the Japanese public. For 30 years policy makers focused on equality of care, or guaranteed access to health care. The low infant mortality rate (lowest in the world), and life expectancy (longest in the world) attest to the success of these efforts. Now the emphasis is on quality of care, or the well-being and satisfaction of patients.

Fee-for-service reimbursement policies reward providers for dispensing units of service. Therefore, doctors increased their use of inputs, i.e., drugs. Government mandated reimbursement price reductions resulted in increased demand because doctors prescribed more drugs to maintain income derived from the discount between reimbursement prices and purchase prices.

Low priced drugs, such as generics, are not in demand because the per input margin is low compared to higher priced drugs. New drugs rapidly gain acceptance because of "the more we do, the more we earn" system of reimbursement.

Providing the best outcomes for patients as efficiently as possible, is not measured, let alone rewarded.

In 1992 flat-sum reimbursement tariffs were introduced in medical institutions caring for elderly patients with chronic diseases. This year insurers will begin to pay treatment costs for psychiatric patients and dialysis patients in the same way.

Flat-sum reimbursements will dramatically change incentives within the delivery system. Because treatment revenues for certain patients are predetermined, drugs are an expense, not a source of income. The obvious way to reduce expenses is to cut back on drug consumption, exactly what happened in chronic care institutions. Drug expenditures were often reduced by two thirds, not by using cheaper drugs, but by cutting the number of prescriptions. The cost of each drug must be justified by benefits, or it is deleted.

As more patients are covered by flat-sum reimbursements, it will be interesting to observe if insurers begin to monitor outcomes. Cost control is an easy first step, but will the result be underutilization of drugs and services to optimize income? If so, restricted access to drugs will become a reality. Flat-sum reimbursements will not eliminate inefficiencies in the system unless doctors are rewarded for providing the best outcomes for patients as efficiently as possible. An example is the 39 day average length of stay in hospital. Psychiatric patients stay in hospitals 18 months. Drugs that reduce the length of hospitalization are enormously cost effective, but this efficiency is not encouraged by insurers.

The Internal Environment

Pharmaceutical firms have not changed their internal cultures fast enough to cope with external changes. One example, internationalization, is not a reality because there are too few managers who understand how to do business outside Japan. Family management, seniority driven promotion, and risk averse strategies have led to studies of foreign markets rather than acting in foreign markets.

There is an old-fashioned production mentality inside many firms. In research the result is an emphasis on screening, on modification of known molecular entities, on small step innovation, on producing anything new. In marketing, the result is an emphasis on the number of doctor calls, the number of salesmen, the number of wholesalers, "push" rather than the "pull" of sales. Dominance is achieved by too much force and not enough fnesse, a great way to win battles but lose the war for public respect.

Restructuring R&D (Again)

Japanese research changed its mission twice during the past 40 years.

1955–1974: The Anything Old Era

When Japan recovered from the devastation of World War II, R&D focused on "anything old." Discovery research did not exist in Japan. Molecules discovered abroad were licensed-in for development, so "research" was a function of the licensing department. The only way to secure a pipeline of new products was to tie up a foreign firm in a joint venture. Banyu lured Bristol and Merck, Dainippon got Abbott and Searle, and Takeda linked up with Bayer, Lederle and Geigy, Sankyo with Parke Davis and Sandoz, Fujisawa with Ciba and SKB.

The research mission was to find new ways of making old drugs. Product patent laws did not exist, and process patents afforded little protection. Sumitomo researchers found a unique way to make indomethacin, thereby enriching the corporate treasury with fees paid by Merck to keep their copy product off world markets.

Development labs fashioned new product forms uniquely suited to the Japanese market. This risk free game of license-in, develop, manufacture and distribute came to an end when the market was liberalized, when tight regulatory procedures were enacted, and when originators became reluctant to license away their rights.

1975–1994: The Anything New Era

The research mission shifted from anything old to "anything new" after the "oil shock" in 1973. New laboratories were built to house new equipment, to be manned by new people. The health insurance reimbursement system rewarded minor improvements of established drugs with higher tariff prices, driving the wheels of small step innovation. As a result, 282 new chemical entities were discovered, but only 44 were marketed in major foreign markets because they lacked benefits over existing drugs.

Licensing-out came of age. In 1985, the value of technology exports came into balance with the value of technology imports. Discovery research is now a reality, but financial resources are limited, so companies focus research on second and third generation products, and then utilize marketing muscle to drive out first generation drugs.

1995–2014: The Anything Unique Era

Japanese R&D must now restructure its mission to discover "anything unique." It will require diversification of research outside Japan because virtually all research is conducted in Japan by Japanese today. No country or company has a monopoly on brains, and no research program can pursue every therapeutic lead. Three options exist for diversification:

1. Establish wholly owned research centers in the United States and Europe. Examples include Yamanouchi (U.K.), Eisai (Massachusetts), and Otsuka (Maryland).
2. Form alliances with academic researchers. Examples include Takeda and Shiseido.
3. Make bets on emerging research in biotechnology start-ups. Examples include Chugai, Kissei, and Kirin.

How can restructuring facilitate pursuit of these options?

1. Focus on areas of expertise. Too often Japanese companies express interest in everything, every R&D collaboration, every research alliance, and every venture capital fund. This approach spreads limited resources too thin. Japanese must learn to say NO to proposals that do not fit their research objectives.
2. Conducting scientific due diligence. The right bets on outside research start with an evaluation of the science. In house scientists are the best filter for proposals, but they tend to resist the allocation of resources outside the firm. They have a bad case of NIH (not invented here) syndrome.
3. Managing intercorporate R&D. Japanese have not learned how to manage foreign researchers. Their culture of innovation is so alien: They refuse to wear uniforms, eat at prescribed times, and join colleagues for morning exercises. It is wiser to take minority interests in emerging companies and leave management to locals.

The new research mission will begin with a realistic vision of the geographic, functional and intellectual strengths inside the corporation. Few will build an independent global research presence. More will establish a mosaic of foreign alliances. Managing innovation in these relationships is a challenge the new generation of researchers are eager to accept.

Restructuring Marketing

The traditional environment of Japan's unique pharmaceutical market favored large sales forces and distribution coverage as key factors for success. As a consequence, the industry employs 50,000 medical representatives (MR), a ratio of four doctors per MR. The U.S. ratio is 14 doctors per MR.

Major manufacturers managed distribution through a relationship (*keiretsu*) network of wholesalers controlled through equity and "back margins" to guarantee profitability for "friendly" wholesalers. As a result, the industry has remained fragmented, relatively stable, but with modest returns.

Since 1990 regulatory changes and economic conditions accelerated structural reform of the industry. As a consequence:

- Wholesalers consolidated into regional but not yet national players. Mom-and-pop-sized wholesalers are no longer viable.
- Keiretsu relationships are breaking down. Successful wholesalers are not tied to one manufacturer, but carry a full line of drugs from many manufacturers.
- "Monolithic" sales strategies must be modified to a targeted approach to doctors. Value added services must replace the total reliance on personal relationships.
- The fully allocated cost of one MR is $150,000 per year, or approximately $120 per doctor call.
- Pricing responsibility was transferred from manufacturers to wholesalers, thus MR's must assume a different role in which new knowledge of their market and product is required.
- Independent pharmacies are emerging and patients are demanding more information on drugs. Contact with these audiences will require a direct marketing and merchandising capability.
- Wholesaler account management expertise must be developed to leverage influence over fewer wholesalers who have direct access to buying groups and pharmacies.
- Co-promotion with wholesalers is more economical than increasing the number of MR's to cover small hospitals and clinics.

Large sales forces (over 900 MR) are more a bane than a blessing. MR expense is only one aspect of the problem. Drugs without incremental benefits over existing drugs cannot be "pushed" through the system by offering financial support or services to doctors. Back margins used to secure wholesaler support are now illegal. "Product pull" strategies are required; hence, redeployment and retraining of existing MR rather than more MR. The discovery and launch of innovative drugs will accelerate this aspect of restructuring.

These fundamental changes dictate a necessity for strong bonds between R&D and marketing. Traditional me-too drugs require a large sales force but will not receive premium reimbursement prices, making them uneconomical to promote. Innovative drugs with higher prices, promoted by a properly deployed, smaller sales force using sophisticated targeting approaches will yield greater returns, thus enhancing the capability to innovate.

This is an enormous challenge not made easier by a mentality lock on the status quo. Many adages of the past must be changed to cope with the future:

- More MR's are better than fewer MR's.
- More calls on doctors are better than the right calls on target doctors at the right time.
- Cash incentives to doctors are more effective than the delivery of useful information.
- More wholesalers are better than selecting "winners."

Surveys indicate MR visits to doctors have decreased as a result of recent changes. But no one doubts the effectiveness of a well trained, skilful MR. Restructuring the mission of MR is a major headache for traditional companies, but yield a plethora of opportunities for companies willing to innovate.

A surprise free conclusion is that restructuring of the Japanese pharmaceutical industry will present opportunities for foreign companies. The new keys for success in Japan are not unfamiliar to marketing and research executives in other countries. Applying this knowledge to a more open Japan will create favorable odds for success. Japan is not a mystery or an enigma. A challenge—yes, but higher rewards for success than in other developed markets.

Scrip Magazine, May 1994

Lousy Results Sometimes Happen

It was Monday before Christmas and my spirits of goodwill toward all men were lifted by seeing the remake of an all time classic movie "Miracle of 34th Street." We exited the theater in Shibuya and joined crowds of people literally sprinkled with merry souls on their way home from *bonenkai* parties. I retrieved my car from the garage and parked it on a nearby street so we could enjoy a leisurely meal at my favorite restaurant that serves the best spaghetti in Tokyo.

At 10:00 p.m. there was a feeling of all's right with the world. I went out into the brisk, clear, cold air to my car for the short ride home, automatically opened the driver's door, and then noticed all the doors were unlocked. For a moment I thought I had failed to lock the doors. In the second moment I concluded that was impossible given my usual pattern of always locking the car day and night. I brushed aside the thought that someone had broken into the car; I was in Tokyo where car theft is not a national pastime.

Nevertheless, I checked the trunk where my briefcase was stored for "safe" keeping. It was gone. This fact was obvious after a third search, stupid acts considering you can't miss something as large as a briefcase in an otherwise empty trunk.

To make a long story short, I ended up in the Shibuya Station Koban (police box) until 12:30 a.m. with my wife, while grandma sat in the car with two sleeping children. We arrived home at 1:00 a.m. thoroughly depressed and convinced nothing was right with the world. My life was in the briefcase: passport, credit cards, driver's license, irreplaceable pictures, and a half finished article for this newspaper on the virtues of Japan. Three days were lost replacing credit cards and restoring my national identity.

A week later the briefcase was found by an honest man who turned it over to the police. The cash was gone, but everything else was intact. But I haven't finished the "Ain't Japan Great" article; it must wait until my confidence is restored.

Since 1970, I have had two briefcases stolen in Japan, the first was taken from a hotel room; my home was broken into twice, once while my family was sleeping; someone hit my car and gave me a fictitious name and company address. Don't tell me bad things do not happen; they do, even in Japan. A bumper sticker I saw in Honolulu said it succinctly. "S--t Happens."

In 1994 more than a few people in the pharmaceutical industry were stricken by the random onslaught of lousy results:

• Makers of IFN's and the HMG-CoA Reductase inhibitors.
• Makers, promoters, prescribers, and users of Sorivudine.
• Makers of products routinely used by patients who were included in flat-sum reimbursement schemes.
• Research teams who expected approval of a new drug, only to be turned back to answer dubious questions.
• Biotechnology companies who experienced less than favorable results in Phase III trials.
• People doing a good job, then cast aside by an acquisition or downsizing decision.
• Men who were making all the right moves in Japan, then someone in the home office questioned their loyalty or order of priorities.

Corporate planners demand a significant amount of time from line executives for profit plans, five year plans, contingency plans, expense saving plans, and head count reduction plans. At times it appears planning is more important than execution. Who is around to help when something lousy happens?

The pharmaceutical market in Japan is quite orderly, most of the time. Consider the following:

- The reimbursement price tariff effectively establishes a price umbrella for all drugs and medical services. Attempts to duplicate this arrangement for other goods is illegal, although the construction and food distribution industries do a good job of avoiding penalties.
- The reasonable zone is strong guidance for discount margins, although many companies persist in shooting themselves in their collective feet by going beyond the guidelines.
- Politicians do not convene secret task forces to propose health care reform laws.
- Access to new drugs is not dictated by buying groups, formularies, or MBA's running HMO's.
- There is no parallel import market or dramatic loss of market share to generics.
- Healthcare providers are homogeneous and concentrated in well-defined market segments.
- Overall market growth is predictable, particularly during odd number years when there are no price revisions.
- The top 10 Japanese companies are the same today as they were 25 years ago, and not one has merged or been acquired.

Japanese company presidents typically set objectives that lack numerical targets. Usually the opening sentence is, "We will do our best to . . . " Maybe they are more aware of the unpredictability of people and events, ready to roll with the inevitable punches or to take advantage of fortuitous circumstances. Perhaps specific plans are confining and inflexible. Western prognosticators with laptops state with certainty what will happen, while the Japanese suck air through clenched teeth and direct the conversation to what happened versus what will happen. Foreigners who adapt to this style of thinking are accused by their colleagues of eating too much rice.

No doubt in 1995, like every year before, we will be entertained by forecasts similar to the following:

- The Japanese pharmaceutical industry will consolidate through mergers and acquisitions.
- Generics will become a significant factor in the drug market.
- Price revisions in Japan will eliminate discovery research.
- Japanese companies will take over the U.S. biotechnology industry.

I hope there is a special place in hell reserved for those who claim to know what will happen in Japan and are disdainful of those who say they don't know. Meanwhile, we should lobby the immigration authorities to interview all businessmen and refuse entry to anyone who plans to stay for three days and tell the local people how, why and when specific events will occur.

Maybe someday, someone will explain why bad results appear to happen when we least expect them, and at the worst possible time. On New Year's day we went with friends to Asakusa to pay our respects, throw some coins into the shrine, utter a silent prayer, and get crushed by the crowd of people all wanting to do the same thing at the same time.

One minute our friend's two children were next to us, the next minute they were gone. We spread out to search for them, but they were nowhere to be seen. After 30 minutes, a sense of panic began to set in as we made our way to the Koban to report two missing children. As we stood in the doorway, a Japanese couple approached to ask if we were the missing parents of two children they escorted to a children's center. The police, via their portable radios immediately confirmed the location of the children and sent one of their finest to bring them to the Koban. Within minutes the children and parents were reunited. Police are more serious about missing children than stolen briefcases.

Who were the people that went out of their way to solve the problem? We don't know, as they just melted back into the crowd. We thanked the policemen and went off convinced bad and good results will ensue in 1995. Yes, bad results occur, but they may lead to unexpected favorable results. Guess it's time to go back to that unfinished article about why it is good to live in Japan.

Pharma Japan 1435, January 1995

The Rules Are Changing in Japan

Japan was never an easy market to crack by the multinational pharmaceutical industry. Many gave up after their initial forays racked up more expenses than income. Others took the path of least resistance by licensing-out the fruits of their research for instant income at the expense of long term participation in the market. Some preferred sharing the risks with joint venture partners only to realize they remained outsiders to value added inside the system. Those who committed to a fully integrated presence are reaping the rewards of persistence.

Every company with leading edge technology, and those with promising products in development, must factor Japan into their marketing plans. The race is on to rediscover the world's second largest drug market, but the rules are changing.

First time visitors are perplexed by conflicting advice offered by people who supposedly know Japan. Old Japan hands are stunned by the pace of change in a market they expected to evolve slowly. Both want to believe the changes are positive, but all the news is negative. The enigma of Japan continues to frustrate those who want to participate in the market.

There are two assumptions about Japan you believe or were told to believe, i.e.:

1. Japan is different, and
2. Nothing changes in Japan.

The first says nothing, but effectively stops all further dialogue of a reasonably intelligent nature. The second is blatantly false, but effectively stops discussion about change.

In this article, I will address two issues of fundamental change occurring at a pace so rapid Japanese pharmaceutical executives cannot predict the outcome and despair at their ability to cope. One issue relates to healthcare reform, the second to changes in the distribution sector.

Healthcare Reform

The national health insurance system evolved largely intact from its enactment in 1961. Several features stood the test of time and admirably serve society. Universal, mandatory insurance coverage guarantees every Japanese healthcare—no one is excluded. Access to healthcare providers is not restricted. Japan achieved equality of healthcare long before other countries considered it a problem.

The results were dramatic. Mortality rates of many diseases plummeted. Life expectancy at all ages increased and infant mortality per 1,000 births dropped from 60 in 1950 to 4 in 1993. Deaths due to all diseases dropped from 11 per 1,000 people in 1950 to 7 in 1993. Although health expenditures increased rapidly, they grew in parallel with national income. In short, the society enjoyed world class healthcare at an affordable cost.

However, as the statistics in Table 1 indicate, Japan is a very different country today than it was in 1961, notably the number of persons 65 years and older in the population mix. In 1961 the elderly accounted for five to 6 percent of the population; today it is 15 percent, and in 20 years hence it will be 25 percent.

The system was designed for a young population with acute diseases demanding access to healthcare. In 1997, policy makers must address the needs of an elderly population with chronic diseases demanding quality healthcare. The economic consequences of this shift are exacerbated by the slowdown of income growth.

To address these dual issues of quality at a higher cost, and a declining rate of income growth, the government initiated a national debate on healthcare insurance alternatives. Simple fine tuning of the basic structure is not a viable option for the future.

As is typically the case in matters of national importance, Japanese government bureaucrats take the lead in preparing "visions" for the future. Since healthcare is the responsibility of the Ministry of Health and Welfare (MHW), it presented a blueprint for healthcare reform in August 1997. Consensus must be achieved with politicians, the public and the powerful Ministry of Finance, but we can expect implementation to begin April 1, 1998.

The key elements of reform are:

- Substantial increases in the level of co-payments by recipients of healthcare. Government policy makers have put a stake in the ground to limit their liability for the costs of healthcare. In parallel, they believe the burden shift to patients will dampen demand for healthcare, thus restraining the growth rate of expenses.
- A clear separation between insurance programs for the elderly and other schemes. Present needs mandate a distinction between patients—old and young, acute and chronic.
- The fee-for-service system is on its way out, certainly in large institutions. "Flat-sum" reimbursement programs, similar to DRGs in the United States, will be expanded.
- The current system of reimbursing drugs is on its last legs. In the short term a reference price system ii unlikely, but generic drug listing is. A free price system, regardless of its merits, will require a broader political power base to be

enacted. On the other hand, the political will exists to lower drug consumption in value terms, if not in nominal terms through delisting of drugs.

• A concerted effort by payers, insurance societies and employers to drive inefficiencies out of the delivery of healthcare. This will effect everything from the number of days in a hospital bed to margins in the distribution system.

The "old" insurance system provided enough money to support inefficient suppliers, providers, manufacturers without new technology, and those who offered minor improvements on old technology. The new system will not support these participants.

Changes in Distribution

The distribution sector of the pharmaceutical industry gradually evolved through a predictable process of consolidation since the early 1970s. Most foreign companies began to establish their own distribution network in the 1990s, a long period of neglect that was costly in terms of lost margins and knowledge of customers.

Since 1970, 700 wholesalers disappeared. They ceased to exist through mergers and acquisitions. Today there are 260 wholesalers, but 100 of these account for 95 percent of the drug market. It is obvious that consolidation is not finished, but in 1997 it dramatically changed direction.

After World War II, U.S. occupation forces set up a wholesaler distribution network with the enthusiastic support of a few major companies. These companies had two missions, i.e., establish a production base to manufacture products licensed-in from foreign sources (they had no research of their own), and to build a lock on distribution.

All wholesalers were aligned with one of four manufacturers: Takeda, Sanyo, Shionogi, or Tanabe. Because wholesalers were often in shaky financial condition, the alignment took the form of equity participation, a quid pro quo for cash infusion. To hedge their risks, manufacturers dispatched employees to work in the wholesalers, further cementing their close relationships.

Control of the supply chain was a key success factor in the era of push sales. Manufacturers who relied solely on pull-through demand created by medical representatives (MRs), were outmaneuvered by the lack of shelf space. Furthermore, MRs set the purchase prices to dispensing doctors and pharmacies, then ordered wholesalers to comply. Without access to wholesalers, MRs could not consummate a sale. In 1992, MRs were prohibited from discussing prices with dispensers, a dramatic change in the relationships between manufacturers and wholesalers.

As wholesalers consolidated with the blessing of their major manufacturers, financial stability followed. Mergers were driven by the desire to achieve economies of scale over a wider geographical area. Wholesalers became regional rather than local. As the changes were gradual, manufacturers could adapt without altering their supply chain strategies; that is, until recently. In April, Suzuken, a regional wholesaler based in Nagoya, will merge with Akiyama, the major wholesaler in Japan's northern island of Hokkaido. Suzuken will achieve a presence that is shy of national distribution, but far beyond a regional presence. Sales of the combined company will exceed those of Takeda, Japan's largest pharmaceutical company.

It was a sudden, unanticipated change. At the same time, four regional wholesalers announced an "informal" tie-up to optimize their physical handling of merchandise. These were major discontinuities in the gradual evolution of wholesaler consolidation.

Manufacturers accustomed to gradual change were shocked. The "new" Suzuken will achieve independence from the pressure of a single manufacturer—a reality that will be the norm of all surviving wholesalers in the future.

Wholesalers are focusing on bottom line income rather than top line revenue growth. Merged entities will eliminate excess personnel that physically transfer goods, and add value to their proprietary knowledge of customers' needs.

The consolidation of wholesalers will continue until another 160 are merged out of existence or aligned into cost efficient business units. Manufacturers do not have the luxury of gradually reducing the number of wholesalers to whom they devote time and resources.

Wholesaler executives are changing the rules of distribution. Foreign companies can throw out old notions of distribution barriers that prevented their entry. Those who preach what cannot be done in Japan do not understand the reality of these changes.

Toward Understanding

Japan represents about 20 percent of the world pharmaceutical market. Most foreign pharmaceutical company executives admit their sales in Japan are not commensurate with the market size and potential. The more candid will confess their sales growth was not consistent with market growth, thus, their market share performance is poor. Talk of problems rather than opportunities dominates internal analyses, and the latter are forfeited.

Change in the Japanese market will not automatically make it easier to enter—competition will be fierce, particularly as more companies battle for survival.

Nevertheless, when rules change, new opportunities arise for those who dare to be different.

A few of the key success factors are:

- Do not organize Japan as part of a region—it is a region.
- A presence in three functions must be under 100 percent control, i.e.:
  - Development
  - Promotion
  - Distribution
- Utilize partners or alliances to supplement weakness, but never rely on them to build critical mass.
- Use distribution for competitive advantage.
- Access discovery research emerging from Japanese university laboratories.
- Never forfeit access to end users.

Inside the System

The end result, as some companies have demonstrated, is a position inside the system rather then a preoccupation with breaking down barriers. Japan is still different, but it can be predictable. It need not be a threat, but an opportunity.

Table 1

	1961	1997
Population (million)	94	125
Life expectancy at birth		
Female	70	84
Male	65	77
GDP		
Nominal ($ billion)	41	5,111 (1995)
Per Capita ($)	436	40,897 (1995)
Employed Persons (million)		
Total	45	65
Agriculture, Forestry, Fishery	12	3
Medical Expenditures		
Total ($ billion)	3	270
Percent of national income	2	7
For the Elderly ($ billion)	Insignificant	90
Ownership (percent of households)		
Refrigerators	17	99
Cars	3	80

How to Crack the Japanese Pharmaceutical Market

No foreign company can boast it cracked the Japanese pharmaceutical market. Merck and HMR are the largest, each with a mere 2.8 percent share. Two beliefs inhibit progress:

1. Japan is different.
2. Nothing changes in Japan.

The first says nothing, but effectively stops all further dialogue of a reasonably intelligent nature. The second is blatantly false, but effectively stops discussion about change.

Dramatic Change

Change occurs in Japan, but foreigners make the mistake of assuming nothing happened unless the direction of change was toward Western models of market dynamics. Japan changes, but at the end of the day, Japan will still be different. The key is to understand the differences and execute accordingly.

One dramatic change is the aging and inexorable decline of Japan's population. Within five years the population will peak at 127 to 129 million people. By 2050, the population will decline to a maximum of 100 million. This is due to declining births; in 1950, 28.1 per 1,000 population; in 1996, 9.6. Fertility rates drastically declined from 2.13 in 1970 to 1.37 in 1998, a level below what is required to maintain the population.

Japan's population is aging more rapidly than any other country in history. This is due to a declining number of newborns, and decreasing mortality overall. There were 10.9 deaths per 1,000 population in 1950, but only 7.2 in 1996.

Implications

First, disease patterns shift. In 1950 tuberculosis was the leading cause of death; in 1996, malignant neoplasms were number one, followed by cardiovascular diseases.

Second, national health expenditures increase rapidly. In 1950, Japan spent ¥2,700 per capita on health care, in 1996, ¥223,000, or 7.3 percent of national income.

Third, the pharmaceutical market exploded and diversified from treatments for acute disease to therapy for chronic diseases. Japan now represents 20 percent of the world drug market, as large as the combined sales in France, Germany, Italy, Spain, and Britain. The market is big, and cannot be ignored.

Change Cycles Are More Frequent

The pharmaceutical industry was forced to reinvent itself three times since the middle of this century, and the intervals between basic changes are getting shorter.

From the dawn of the 20th century, companies had 50 years of relative isolation to establish a foundation. Drugs were derived from herbs or simple fermentation processes. Regulations governing quality and effectiveness did not exist. The core competencies of companies were embodied in a founder who had the entrepreneurial drive to organize a business.

After the end of World War II, companies had to start over from scratch. Out/in investment was heavily regulated. Discovery research did not exist as laboratories were busy developing licensed-in products or devising new processes to make drugs not protected by product patents. The core competencies of companies revolved around their ability to work with government regulators. This phase lasted for 25 years, and ended in 1975 when investment restrictions were removed and product patent laws were enacted.

The next cycle lasted 15 years from 1975 to 1990. Companies innovated by discovering modifications of breakthrough drugs originated outside Japan. The economics of the reimbursement system rewarded anything new. During this period, 282 new chemical entitles were discovered in Japan, but only 44 were sold outside Japan. The core competencies of companies revolved around their ability to negotiate high reimbursement prices for second, third, or fourth generation drugs.

In the current 10 year cycle, unique drugs discovered in Japan are internationally competitive. Core competencies revolve around an ability to shift resources from what was appropriate for the old idea of the business to what is appropriate for the new.

This cycle is unique in one respect. Heretofore, all companies survived: First because of isolation, then protectionism, then because the reimbursement system rewarded the discovery of low risk, minor modifications of first generation drugs. Changes in the current 10 year cycle will not isolate, protect, or reward those who do not restructure their business. They must shift resources away from past practices or cease to exist.

Many factors are accelerating the pace of change. Three will have an impact on every participant in the hearth care sector.

Regulatory Reform

Economic incentives are in the process of reallocation. Some are listed below:

Incentives Change

From	To
Patient Inputs	Patient Outputs
Me-Too Drugs	Unique Drugs
Fee for Service	Flat-Sum Reimbursement
Standard Care	Personalized Care
Access to Healthcare	Quality of Health Care
Adding Personnel Resources	Refocusing Personnel Resources

These and other changes are beyond the talking stage—they are being implemented. The question is not, "What will change?" The question is "How do we refocus our resources to something new?"

Surprise Free Forecasts

1. Fewer NCEs launched each year, but longer life cycles and stable prices for unique drugs.
2. Fewer rewards for mc-too drugs, but lucrative incentives for unique drugs.
3. Supply side cost containment eased, but demand side restrictions enacted and enforced.
4. Timely approval of new drugs, but development process must meet harmonized standards.

Distribution Reform

The most dramatic change in the distribution sector is consolidation. In 1970 there were over 1,200 pharmaceutical wholesalers, all with coverage confined to a local area. By 1980 there were 584 wholesalers, and today there are less than 250.

As might be expected, market shares of wholesalers also consolidated. The leading 50 wholesalers now control 80 percent of the market, the next 50 have a combined 15 percent share, and the remaining 150 wholesalers a 5 percent share.

A surprise free forecast is for fewer wholesalers in the future. The winners will have regional influence and be independent of any single manufacturer.

Wholesalers currently employ 39,000 salesmen called MS. As is typical in Japan, consolidation reduced the number of wholesalers, but did not reduce the number of personnel employed. This is now a migraine headache as margins get squeezed by manufacturers on the supply side and by hospitals on the demand side.

One solution is to specialize MSs into higher value added functions. Fewer people will be required to satisfy demand by taking orders and stocking shelves. Specialized MS will create demand to justify higher margins. Supplying demand does not justify high margins.

Distribution is no longer a black hole. However, to create an efficient supply chain, manufacturers must reduce the number of wholesaler accounts. Money is wasted by receiving, picking, packing, and shipping too many orders; and time is wasted by maintaining relationships with marginal wholesalers.

Industry Structure

The industry is fragmented and unconsolidated; national not international. Nevertheless, Japanese firms dominate their home market and demonstrated an ability to innovate. New drugs are discovered in Japan, which is more than can be said about any other country outside the United States and Europe.

Implications of Industry Structure

1. Stronger R&D capabilities are a must, because unique products will drive growth.
2. Refocusing resources or restructuring the business is a priority because inefficient cost centers cannot survive health care reform.
3. Globalization is a prerequisite because research, development and marketing cannot be confined to one market.

Given the accelerated pace of change, consolidation within and between companies is the most logical response. The timing of consolidation is debatable, but it is inevitable.

Key Success Factor

The accelerating pace of change will be resisted by those who are comfortable with the status quo, particularly if it protects insiders. Outsiders embrace change because it creates new opportunities. And the only way to take advantage of new opportunities is to have a presence in the market.

The objective is to establish a presence sufficient to efficiently conduct product development in a timely manner; promote and market products to the right targets; and use the supply chain for competitive advantage.

Those without presence forfeit customer contact, knowledge of and influence with the key policy makers, relationships, and value added margins. Foreign companies must commit to compete with Japanese competitors on their home ground. If not here, the battle will be lost elsewhere.

The point is to get inside the system. Stop saying Japan is different and believe differences are predictable and manageable. Stop saying nothing changes and view change as an opportunity instead of a threat.

Market Letter, April 1998

The Old and New

Every facet of the pharmaceutical industry and the healthcare market is changing in Japan. Those who hold on to the status quo, and they represent the majority, are losing out to those who embrace speed and change.

Below is a pocket guide to the old and new.

Hospitals:

Old: Feudal management structure with less sensitivity to the needs of patients than a veterinary clinic.

New: Bedside monitoring of diagnosis and treatment available to both patient and doctor.

Old: Out-patient clinics where a three hour wait is the norm. Add an extra hour in front of the pharmacy.

New: Referrals by appointment. Prescriptions filled at an outside pharmacy.

Old: Beds occupied for 40 days.

New: Social hospitalization confined to chronic care facilities.

Old: Ward-like accommodations normal.

New: Privacy respected.

Old: Centers of mediocrity.

New: Centers of excellence.

Clinics:

Old: With beds.
New: No beds.
Old: One man.
New: Group practice.
Old: Dispense drugs.
New: Issue prescriptions.
Old: Doctor sees 85 patients per day but talks to none.
New: Doctor talks, sees fewer patients.
Old: Doctor is old.
New: Doctor is young.

Doctors:

Old: Learned skills in medical school—no further certification.
New: Lifelong learning with periodic certification.
Old: Profession dominated by men.
New: As many new women doctors as men.
Old: Shortage.
New: Surplus.
Old: Rarely work for a pharmaceutical company.
New: Movement between academia and industry routine.
Old: Politically motivated via the JMA.
New: Scientifically oriented through specialist societies.
Old: Most interested in the *yakkasa* (drug margin).
New: Focus on quality information useful for their patients.

Healthcare Policy:

Old: Equality of care and access to providers.
New: Quality of care.
Old: One basic insurance system for all.
New: Alternative insurance plans proliferate.
Old: Young patients with acute diseases.
New: Old patients with chronic diseases.
Old: Reimbursement fees modified within an established structure.
New: Fundamentally change the structure.

Old: Encourage the purchase of capital equipment.
New: Encourage intellectual property.
Old: Policy determined top down and highly regulated by "bosses."
New: Policy making distributed with less regulation and more public/private partnerships.

Drugs:

Old: Anything new received a high price.
New: Only uniquely new products favorably priced.
Old: Short life cycles.
New: Longer life cycles.
Old: Clinical development essentially a premarketing exercise with many sites and few patients at each site.
New: Clinical development controlled by new GCP guidelines.
Old: Marginal benefits rewarded in Japan, viewed as worthless outside Japan.
New: Me-too drugs not worth the cost of development.
Old: Antibiotics the leading therapeutic category.
New: Cardiovascular drugs dominate.

Pharmaceutical Manufacturers:

Old: Stressed manufacturing and control of the distribution system.
New: Stress R&D and efficient marketing.
Old: Everyone could make money and dream about an international presence.
New: A few make an adequate return on assets employed in the business, others retreat graciously.
Old: Not concerned with selling, general, and administrative expenses.
New: Drive down overhead expenses.
Old: Stayed in unprofitable businesses unrelated to their core competence.
New: Restructure to focus on areas of competence.

Wholesalers:

Old: Moved stuff from one physical location to another.
New: Provide and receive high value information.
Old: Many companies, all with local influence.
New: Few companies, each with a regional presence.

Old: Bound to a single manufacturer.
New: Independent from any one manufacturer.
Old: Push sales in response to short term rebate schemes.
New: Create demand through long term promotion partnerships.

Foreign Companies:

Old: Act as though they cannot make it in Japan without a partner.
New: Act independent.
Old: Treat Japan operations as a subsidiary in a region.
New: Consider Japan a region.
Old: Clone policies developed elsewhere.
New: Develop original policies with input from experience in other markets.
Old: Complain about barriers and discrimination.
New: Take risks, throw out the status quo, and reward employees who know how to make changes quickly.

Pharma Japan 1601, June 1998

The Japanese Pharmaceutical Market Model

The title of this article promises more than can be delivered. But then, I always run the risk of oversimplification because limitations on space are dictated by the editors of this publication. However, to their credit, they print what they receive—no modification or censorship to reflect the perceived opinions of conservative subscribers. (That's a nice way to say some people think I am nuts.)

It is not an exaggeration to say that the introduction of Western medicine in Japan was the medium for the introduction of Western culture into Japan. In 1641, one hundred years after the first foreigners arrived on the shores of Tanegashima, Japan closed its doors to all Western contacts except the Dutch at Deshima, where they were confined in virtual imprisonment. Even the gutters of their houses were serpentine to prevent secret exchanges with the outside.

In order to gain access to Deshima, Japanese were required to serve as menials, but that did not stop them from coming to study Western medicine and to acquire drugs. No ban could diminish the abiding Japanese curiosity for new ideas and innovations.

I am skipping a lot of history, but in 1840 all Western studies, except medicine, were banned. In 1861 formal instruction in Western medicine began at the Institute for Western Medicine in Edo. In 1867 Meiji was enthroned as emperor, the Shogunate overthrown, and Japan entered the world. Three years later a decision was made to adopt the German system of medicine—and for good reason. It was by all odds the best system in the world. In the ensuing decades all aspects of German medicine flowed into Japan. There has never been an instance in history where a country not under colonial domination so completely adopted an outside system.

In 1915, Count Okuma, the premier of Japan, explained: "The Occidental part of Japanese civilization had begun with the introduction of Western medicine."

A second factor that has shaped the Japanese pharmaceutical market model is the singular veneration that the Japanese people hold for medicine. During the Tokugawa Shogunate it was the companion sciences of inflicting wounds and healing them that attracted the attention of ambitious young samurai.

Self-medication was a custom in Japan for many centuries. Itinerant dispensers would go from door to door leaving a spectrum of medicines with the housewife. In a month they were back to be reimbursed for the medicines that had been consumed.

Historical trends help us to understand why the present-day Ministry of Health and Welfare is loath to restrict access to drugs. Thus, one aspect of the model is safety first, effectiveness second. Some drugs approved in Japan have not been approved in the West because they do not offer benefits over existing therapy, but they did pass rigid safety tests. Dosages tend to be lower than in the West because of the same concern for safety. Promotion programs focus on the reduction of risk.

A made-in-Japan label, so effective with many consumer goods, is not a good way to sell drugs. Few doctors are so nationalistic that they would shun drugs of foreign origin. Obtaining drugs from abroad is so embedded in the national psyche that a policy of self-sufficiency is farfetched. Charges of discrimination against foreign drugs in the regulatory review process are a form of xenophobia. Japanese companies dominate the top 20 ranking because of their presence—not their nationality.

As mentioned earlier, in the medical field there has been a historical passion for new ideas and innovations. Today, doctors from major medical centers travel to international meetings as often as most foreign executives travel to the home office. There are innumerable opportunities to influence these opinion leaders "off shore."

The overriding interest in innovation suggests another aspect of the model. This is not a generic market, never was and will not be. It is a brand name market that will reward innovation. Administrators of large buying groups do not restrict a doctor's preference for brand names. Pharmacists wouldn't dare substitute a doctor's order (it's against the law for starters). Thus, the model does not include centralized buying groups, mail order pharmacies, generic substitutions, or therapeutic substitution—and don't expect any of these in the near future.

The innovation factor will drive the build-up of a discovery research infrastructure. Efforts to harmonize regulatory requirements will proceed apace, but the model will reward those who innovate and develop in Japan.

Interest in new ideas results in rapid diffusion of new products. It also creates a fickle customer, resulting in relatively short product life cycles. Those with older product portfolios fight for relief, those with new products love the system.

Lessons of the past fail us when considering the impact of Japan's aging population on the market model. Providing health care for the aged is a recent phenomenon. Healing wounds inflicted on the young has given way to providing QOL (quality of life) for people with chronic illness.

Thus, we come full circle. We know where Japan was and is. Where is it going? I would love to answer the question, but as stated in the beginning, the editors restrict my space and I just ran out of room.

Pharma Japan 1382, December 20, 1993

Changing Japan

Westerners want to believe (hope?) the Japanese are becoming more like them. This assumption (utterly false) eases the pain of entry. Having devised a model for success in the U.S. market, it is annoying to modify it for the Japanese market. Minions of visitors attempt to implement strategies in Japan which were successful elsewhere. They are like teachers with lesson plans that justify the trip. Students who want to learn need not apply. Business is business. Teaching Japan how to change is more comfortable than learning how Japan is changing.

Differences between Japan and the West have been recorded since the Portuguese first arrived in 1543. With them came the Jesuits who prepared frequent detailed reports for their home office at Goa. One report, by Father Luis Frois, described the contrasting practices of Western and Japanese medicine in the middle of the sixteenth century. (Note: The original book published in 1585 contained 19 examples, five are quoted below.)

- "Among us the physicians prescribe through pharmacies; the Japanese physicians send the medicines from their houses." (Father Frois was the original proponent of *Bungyo*.)
- "Among us all abscesses are burnt with fire; the Japanese will die before using our harsh surgical remedies."
- "Among us wounds are sutured; the Japanese place on them a little adhesive paper." (Exactly the treatment my daughter received for a cut on her forehead this year. Last year my other daughter cut her forehead in Honolulu—it was sutured.)
- "Among us, if a physician is not examined, there is a penalty and he cannot practice; in Japan, in order to make a living, whoever wants to can be a physician." (The status of Continuing Medical Education is remarkably similar today.)
- "Among us pearls are used for personal ornamentation, in Japan they serve for nothing more than to be ground to make medicines." (Some things do change; however, a recent Otsuka launch of an OTC medication for dry skin bears the name of Urepearl Cream—old perceptions of effectiveness have historical roots.)

Teachers are prone to force their views upon students who appear reluctant to apply the experience and wisdom of others. This Western attitude toward Japan also has a long history.

On February 15, 1844, the king of the Netherlands, William II, affixed his seal to a letter addressed to the Shogun, Tokugawa Ieyoshi. Two centuries before, the Dutch had been granted permission to trade with Japan, but they felt frustrated because the country was not really open. (Does this sound familiar?)

Sentences in the letter would be familiar to present-day residents of Japan. Take this example:

"There are important matters worthy of communication. They do not concern the trade of our subjects with Japan, but the political interests of the Empire. They relate to matters worthy to be treated of between King and King." (Substitute "high level" discussions or a summit meeting and you have the modern day equivalent.)

Anyway, William II wanted action so he advised the Shogun that China had been forced to open five ports to European nations and that in the attendant conflict thousands of Chinese had been killed, cities devastated, and millions in treasure seized by the conquerors. The King inferred Japan might suffer a similar fate in this passage from the letter:

We know that the laws of Your Majesty's Serene Ancestors were issued with a view rigorously to restrict intercourse with foreign nations. But (says Lao Tse, a Chinese philosopher) 'when wisdom is seated on the throne, she will excel in maintaining peace.' When in the strict observance of old laws, peace might be disturbed, wisdom will succeed in smoothing difficulties."

"This, All powerful Emperor, is our friendly advice, ameliorate the laws against the foreigners lest happy Japan be destroyed by war. We give Your Majesty this advice with honest intentions, free from political self-interest."

In his reply the Shogun stated that any amelioration of the laws against the foreigners "cannot be, as of now, through the inconvenience of the county." The Shogun went on to add he personally would protect the Hollanders "who desire to trade with their shipping in my country (which is of little value and small)," in the same manner as his own subjects.

Today, Western missionaries (staff people) and Kings (CEOs) like to believe changes in the Japanese pharmaceutical market will inevitably follow the West. Mergers between large companies, a large generic market, HMOs or buying groups influencing drug selection, price increases (albeit in line with inflation), direct sales to end users, and OTC switches to name a few.

Japan will change, it always has, but not necessarily in a direction that will make life easier for teachers who have fixed ideas about the future.

There is a rite of passage for most foreigners posted to Japan for the typical three-year tour. At the beginning they strive to remake Japan in their own image. Somewhere in the middle they stop teaching and begin to listen. At the end, they admit they are just learning how to make meaningful contributions. It is unfortunate that the cycle has been repeated over and over again for the past 400 years.

But let me conclude on an optimistic note. After the Dutch had been in Japan (at Deshima) for 50 years, a high Japanese official of the Shogun's court said, "With the exception of medicines, we can dispense with everything that is brought us from abroad . . . other foreign commodities are of no real benefit to us." It's always nice to feel needed—if not wanted.

Pharma Japan 1375, November 1, 1993

Common Myths

Do not believe anything written beyond this first paragraph. It may sound reasonable; you may have seen it written or heard it spoken elsewhere; it may be in your company briefs on Japan; you may have heard it from senior Japanese executives. Be wary, none of the following statements is true. They do not reflect the reality of the market or government policy. If someone inside or outside your company tells you these things, reject them, as they are myths, not the truth of Japan.

- Cost containment is the major objective of government officials responsible for health care policy. They achieve this objective by lowering drug prices every other year.
- Doctors make most of their income by dispensing drugs. Therefore, they over-prescribe to make more money.
- Japanese companies discover lots of new drugs that cannot be sold in any other market.
- All American executives have short term objectives and all Japanese executives have long term objectives.
- The Ministry of Health and Welfare (Koseisho) has an industrial policy to combine many Japanese pharmaceutical companies into about 10 majors capable of invading the rest of the world.
- The Japanese will take over biotechnology in the same manner as they took over semiconductors.
- Wholesalers do not like distributing products for foreign companies.
- Wholesalers will force manufacturers to drop their selling prices, then lower prices to hospitals to capture market share. This will result in a drastic reduction of reimbursement prices.
- Japanese government initiatives to harmonize regulatory requirements are a plot to help Japanese companies invade the United States and Europe.
- Japanese money is buying out the U.S. lead in biotechnology.
- A Japanese company will buy Upjohn.
- Pharmaceutical research in Japan is directed by Koseisho.
- An acquisition is not a viable strategy to enter or grow in this market.
- Health insurers will permit Koseisho to stop cutting drug reimbursement prices.
- Japanese pharmaceutical companies will establish a presence in the United States comparable to Japanese automobile manufacturers. Or the opposite

scenario—Japanese companies will not establish a meaningful presence in the United States.

- Implementation of the antimonopoly guidelines will result in companies reducing the number of their medical representatives by half.
- Japanese longevity is not due to successful health interventions but rather to a "Darwinian" survival of the fittest which occurred in the post-WWII period in which the least healthy and most unfit were unable to survive the devastation, famine, and shortage of medicine and health supplies.
- Low infant mortality in Japan is not due to good preventive care but rather to aborting all questionable pregnancies.
- And finally—all generalizations about Japan and the Japanese are false, including this one.

Pharma Japan 1281, December 2, 1991

Change

Enter the word CHANGE into an electronic thesaurus and 30 synonyms appear on the screen, from alteration to unsex. The dictionary function has nine different definitions for CHANGE as a verb or noun. The word is versatile to say the least, and may be one of the reasons Japanese give up on the English language.

The perception of change is obviously a personal experience. Many foreigners believe the Japanese are becoming more Western based on their observation of more dresses than kimonos, and a McDonalds on every corner.

The chart below depicts change on the vertical axis, and time on the horizontal axis. Change in Japan is compared to change in the "West."

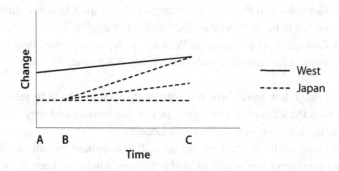

At point A, newcomers recognize differences between Japan and the West. This is the exhilarating, moving in stage when every statement begins with, "It's so interesting how the Japanese . . . " Add your own words in the spaces: eat with chopsticks; eat raw fish; take a bath; bow to one another; travel in groups; use the toilet.

At point B, usually after three months of living here, or sometimes after three days, foreigners split into two groups. Some people believe the direction of change in Japan is toward western patterns of behavior. This is usually expressed by the words, "Japan is catching up with the West." They view this as a compliment. Change is positive if Japan becomes less Japanese and more like us. At point C, differences between Japan and the West cease to exist.

Other people sink into a kind of pessimistic despair. "Japan will never change," they say. Over time they see Japan and the West diverging, each with its own culture isolated from the other. They lecture newcomers on how different the Japanese are from us. Interestingly, a sub-group emerges that become more Japanese than the Japanese. They lecture westerners on the value of Japanese business models, and want us to be more like them.

A few people recognize Japan is changing, but not toward a western model. Like parallel lines, Japan and the West change over time but never meet. Each society adapts in its own way to change. At point C, both have changed since Point A, but remain different.

This train of thought emerged because at the first two meetings of Pharma Delegates this year speakers from major consulting firms passionately talked about the pace of change in the pharmaceutical industry. If you were in the audience you might have had one of these reactions:

1. Change is occurring rapidly in the West. Some companies in Japan will copy these moves and catch up fast.
2. Companies in the West are changing so fast their Japanese competitors will be left in the dust because they will not change.
3. Change is occurring in the West and in Japan, thus providing unique opportunities for companies who are willing to act instead of wait.

One speaker dramatized how the internet changed his world by telling us how his wife uses the internet to order groceries on Wednesday and they are delivered by van to the house on Friday. This is in London.

It made me think what we can do in Tokyo without the internet. A phone call to any number of stores will prompt a delivery within the hour. A fax to National

Azabu in the morning will result in groceries arriving the same day. A fax to an orchard in Yamagata will get me apples the next day. Maybe London needs to catch up with Tokyo in terms of shopping time?

No need to look far to find differences between the pharmaceutical market in Japan versus the United States or Europe:

1. Generic drugs' estimated market share

(%)

	Share by value	Share by prescriptions
United States	35	40
Germany	31	38
Britain	15	44
Japan	5	8

If you believe Japan will change toward the western model, get into the generic business.

2. A wave of acquisitions /mergers has swept across Europe and the United States, but Japan has averaged less than one deal per year since 1983. The merged companies believe scale makes a difference in terms of research, cost structure, and their global reach. As of calendar year 1998, there were only eight Japanese companies in a global drug company ranking of 34 companies. But, in the same year only eight wholly owned foreign companies made the list of the top 34 companies in Japan as ranked by prescription drug sales. Mergers have not helped foreign companies increase market share in Japan.

3. Much has been written about excess prescribing of drugs in Japan. The authors insist Japan must change, i.e., use fewer drugs. However, the following data tells a different story.

	USA	Germany	Britain	Japan
Rx spending as a percent of GDP (1998)	1.6	1.2	1.1	1.4
$ expenditures per capita on pharmaceuticals	409	288	214	269

4. A knee jerk reaction is to think of major U.S. and European companies as international and Japanese companies as confined to Japan. The following data may be a surprise.

Estimated contribution to profit from overseas

Company	March 1999
Takeda	65%
Fujisawa	57%
Yamanouchi	40%
Sankyo	37%

The bottom line is that differences and similarities exist between the Japanese pharmaceutical market and the U.S. and European markets. Within Japan, significant differences exist between companies. Generalizations about the market and the players in the market are always false or at least subject to a long list of exceptions.

Change is a constant. Japan is very different today than when I arrived 30 years ago, but I still get culture shock when I travel to the United States. At the end of the day, sleep comes easy to those who try to understand how a business model works rather than why it works.

Pharma Japan 1674, November 1999

Chapter II

Reinventing Japan's Health Care System

Japan's health care system, established in 1961, provided accessible medical care to all. People were 100 percent insured, mortality rates dropped, life expectancy increased, and population demographics shifted to an aged society. Achievements were enviable. Equality of healthcare was realized. In the 1990s the focus shifted to the cost and quality of medical services. Economic growth slowed and chronic care supplanted acute care. Costs increased. The system had to be reinvented, but how was the question.

Medical History and Present Thinking

By historical standards, the foreign presence in Japan is a current event. The first Westerners to arrive were shipwrecked Portuguese seamen washed ashore at Tanegashima in 1542. In a twist of history, this is the same site that Japan now launches its rockets and satellites into space. On a more earthly note, the Portuguese left a lasting imprint on Japanese cuisine by teaching locals the wonders of boiling fish and vegetables in oil, voila, tempura. Not much else remains of note.

The Americans did not arrive until 1853, 311 years after the Europeans, when Admiral Perry blasted his way into recognition. His countrymen tend to use the same tactics to the present day.

Whatever the techniques, a common complaint of ambassadors and executives is that Japan is a tough market to enter. To be fair, the Japanese never told their visitors it would be easy. In 1691, after Westerners had been here for 150 years, a high ranking Japanese official commented, "With the exception of medicine, we can dispense with everything that is brought us from abroad." Many would agree that bureaucrats today, 306 years later, have the same attitude.

The good news is for those in the business of discovering and selling medicines, they are in a favorable position. Count Okuna, the premier of Japan in 1915, said, "The Occidental part of Japanese civilization had begun with the introduction of Western medicine." How this came about and its influence on present thinking is the rest of the story.

The reverence of Japanese society for medicine and medicines is acted out in samurai dramas everyday. The most respected samurai are either those skillful in inflicting wounds or those who heal them. Anyone who visits an outpatient clinic will note the veneration Japanese hold for medicine. Patient visits to clinics average 12.8 per year, compared with the U.S. average of 5.3 per year. It is a rare event for a patient to leave a clinic without medicine.

The first recorded outside medical influence on Japan was Chinese traditional herbal medicines introduced via Korea in the 5th century. Diagnosis, or chung-i, was based almost solely on meticulous palpation of the pulse at each wrist. Therapy was given via medicines, acupuncture, and moxibustion. Ginseng and powdered horn were the chief therapeutic agents.

These 1,300-year-old traditions influence present practices. In my doctor's office in Hawaii the nurse takes my pulse; in Japan, my doctor ponders the pulse much longer than it takes to count the heartbeats per minute. During the next sumo tournament look at the wrestlers on close up shots and note the small patches over acupuncture sites, or the red skin indicative of moxibustion. Check out any drug store to see the amount of shelf space devoted to various preparations of ginseng.

In the 16th century, indigenous schools of medicine emphasized the priestly role of physicians. Medical practices were closely guarded secrets.

The 17 rules of one school have been preserved. A few examples illustrate the point of secrecy and modern day similarities:

"The teaching of medicine should be restricted to selected persons."

"You should not tell others what you are taught regarding treatments without permission."

"You should not speak ill of other physicians."

"You should not establish association with doctors who do not belong to this school."

The Jesuit priests who arrived in Japan in the 16th century made detailed reports to their home office in Goa, many of them documenting medical practices. One report filed in 1585 is illustrative. It said in part:

"Amongst us pearls are used for personal ornamentation; in Japan they serve for nothing more than to be ground to make medicines."

"Amongst us the physicians prescribe through pharmacies; the Japanese physicians send the medicines from their houses."

"Amongst us, if a physician is not examined, there is a penalty and he cannot practice; in Japan, in order to make a living, whoever wants to can be a physician."

Skipping 300 years of history, in 1869 when the last Shogun left his castle and the Emperor Meiji was restored, Japan opened its doors. An Imperial Proclamation in that year stated, "Wisdom and knowledge shall be sought after in all parts of the world to establish firmly the foundations of the Empire." Missions were dispatched to foreign countries to assess government structures, military organizations, the courts, and other aspects of daily life.

To select a medical education system however, there was no need to dispatch a mission: the German system was the overwhelming choice.

During the ensuing decades, all aspects of German medicine flowed into Japan. One commentator remarked, "There has never been an instance in history where a country not under colonial domination so completely adopted an outside system." Every New Year is welcomed as a time of change, a renewal, a chance to shed the old and adopt the new. This year the focus is on deregulation, a new opening of Japan. A constant, well known to foreigners for 455 years, is Japan is a tough market to crack. But history has taught us one lesson worth remembering. Some people, some companies, and some institutions do succeed and have enormous lasting influence. There is no law, no edict, or rational reason why you cannot be one of these.

Pharma Japan 1533, January 1997

An Emergency Room on Saturday Night

All of the events described below occurred on Saturday, October 30, 1993.

6:30 p.m.
I was grilling the last of 100 sticks of yakitori (chicken) for a party of 20 adults and 13 children. The meal was "pot luck" and I was getting favorable reviews on my chicken from a group that included some great cooks. Earlier, the children went swimming and at 6:00 p.m. I was informed my eight-year-old daughter had slipped on the indoor pool deck and bumped her head. No blood, but a lot of crying. An ice pack was applied and I assumed the matter was settled.

Feeling very smug about my yakitori expertise I prepared to join the group, dig into the food, and talk with some interesting people. I was intercepted by my wife who was trying to keep an ice bag applied to the forehead of our crying daughter who has a very low threshold for pain. I carried her into a quiet bedroom and tried to soothe away the hurt. In times of stress young girls (at least mine) always want their papa.

7:00 p.m.
My little girl violently vomited into the toilet, fortunately sparing the bed cover and carpet. My brain flashed back 18 years to when my son fell into a window casement at the Kobe Club, hitting his head on the way down. I waited until the next morning to drive him through the Mt. Rokko tunnel to the Seventh Day Adventist Hospital. It was also a Saturday, and I was standing by the X-ray machine when the picture came through. On one side of the skull was an unmistakable fracture. Dr. Johnson immediately called a neurosurgeon at Kobe University Hospital who recommended close observation as an inpatient.

As the day passed, it became apparent there was no internal bleeding or damage, but a huge hematoma had formed between the skin and bone. This was treated by using a large barrel syringe to drain off the fluid. After a second day of observation we returned home feeling lucky and relieved the episode did not test our confidence in a Japanese neurosurgeon.

As this experience vividly came to mind, I immediately decided to take my daughter to a hospital. Great decision, but where? I had not been to an emergency room in Japan for 18 years. My wife, much wiser than I, called the Tokyo Metropolitan Hiroo General Hospital and we were on our way.

7:20 p.m.
Made a stop at our apartment to pick up my wife's health insurance identification card.

7:30 p.m.
Checked in at the emergency entrance. The sign at the entrance (in English and Japanese) said that all patients receive treatment but serious cases are given priority. I was contemplating the usual three-hour wait when my daughter urgently requested me to take her to a toilet saying, "I want to throw up."

7:40 p.m.
A nurse with registration papers clipped to a board talked with us in the hallway. She immediately connected with my daughter through a combination of compassion and sincere interest. But most of all, she evoked a strong sense of overwhelming confidence and efficiency.

7:45 p.m.
We were called to see a doctor. I was not impressed by his appearance: overweight, thinning hair, a nerdish look, at least 10 pens jammed into a small breast pocket, open back shoes that were a cross between a Japanese slipper and a Dutch wooden shoe.

Appearances were quickly forgotten when he went about his examination. It was quick but deliberate. Then he explained that children can take blows to the head much better than adults because their skull is not yet firmly fixed. In other words, it was still flexible, unlike the adult eggshell. Nevertheless, he wanted to take X-rays and a CT scan to be absolutely certain there was no damage.

8:00 p.m.
The X-ray technician was strapping my daughter to a huge machine while I tried to sound brave, uttering things like: they will only take a picture—no shots, no pain, just a camera.

The whole machine pivoted while the "bed" moved toward a circular opening. We were asked to wait outside.

8:10 p.m.
I listened intensely for screams to come from inside the room. None came and the procedure was over. "No problem," said the technician as he opened the door.

8:20 p.m.
We were called back to see the doctor who was standing in front of a brightly-lighted panel on which were mounted a series of pictures—at least five X-rays and eight CT pictures.

The doctor patiently led us through each picture. No broken bones, no internal bleeding. "If there was a problem you would see it here, or there, but all of this is normal," he said.

8:25 p.m.
We sat relieved at the news and listened to follow-up instructions, i.e., keep the child relatively quiet for two or three days, feed her easily digestible food, etc. Then my girl began to vomit. A nurse standing close by whipped out a plastic bag from nowhere, and the doctor sprang to his feet barking orders for an IV. He inserted the needle cleanly, then issued another order for a drug to be injected into the IV bottle.

The doctor explained he wanted to observe our daughter for the next two hours, the IV would prevent dehydration, and the drug would prevent nausea. We were back in the hallway behind a screen with our girl on a stretcher under a *futon*.

8:30 p.m.
During the next two hours our daughter's color returned, she slept, the doctor came by three times, nurses checked the IV every 15 minutes. Everything was under control so I observed the drama of a Tokyo government hospital emergency room on Saturday night.

Two young men were wheeled in from an ambulance, victims of a car crash. One was covered with blood from a bleeding arm, the other had severe chest pains. A black American entered gasping for breath because of an asthma attack. An old man with lower abdominal distress came via a taxi. A middle-aged woman, apparently in serious trouble, was attended to by a team of doctors and nurses, then wheeled into intensive care. A five-year-old boy vomited in his mother's lap. A young man coughed violently.

All were treated quickly with calm efficiency. I counted five doctors and four nurses coming and going. Several families waited outside the ICU, friends of the crash victims arrived to offer support. The nurses never walked—they ran.

We talked to the nurse who first met us. I asked if emergency room nursing was her speciality. She replied, "Yes, I have been doing this for many years, enjoy the action, but most of all, I like to help people when they need it most."

10:30 p.m.
We were ready to go home. My sleeping beauty did not complain when the needle was removed or the tape peeled from her wrist. My wife checked us out and paid ¥5,900 for the out-of-pocket portion of the insurance bill. Doctors, nurses, X-rays, CT scans, IV, drug, immediate access, attention—all for less than a taxi fare to Haneda.

10:45 p.m.
Picked up our younger daughter at a friend's home and returned home. I had not eaten, missed the party conversation, but had a, "learning experience." Like many aspects of Japan, the system works. Dedicated people cared, doctors were available, advanced diagnostic procedures were accessible, and a good drug was available. No health care system is beyond reform, but for my little girl with a bump on the head this one worked to perfection.

Pharma Japan 1378, November 22, 1993

Accessing Quality Medical Care on Demand

11:38 p.m.
My 3 1/2 year old son wakes up coughing, choking, gasping for breath, and crying his heart out. His stomach and chest muscles contract violently to force air into his lungs. The mucus buildup in his throat makes him vomit.

11:45 p.m.
We have our boy on the sofa in the living room with a nebulizer to his face pumping a mist of albuterol into his nose and mouth. In fear, he struggles to breathe. More vomit as he tries to clear his airways.

11:55 p.m.
Called the Municipal Hospital in Hiroo to tell them the problem and that we would
come to the emergency room. Get dressed, pick up the insurance card, put socks
and shoes on two kicking little feet, find my drivers license, make sure our two
older girls are sleeping, clean up more vomit, out the door and down to the garage.

12:02 a.m.
Drive down the hill, remind myself that safety not speed is the proper response
behind the wheel. Three traffic lights between the house and the hospital—all red.
In the back seat my wife calms our boy. Maybe the medicine is working, or maybe
the last throw up cleared his throat of mucus. But breathing is raspy and labored.

12:08 a.m.
Pull up to the emergency room door. Stop. Should I find a place to park? I decide
to leave the car where it is.

12:10 a.m.
Check-in takes a minute and in the next minute a nurse with a thermometer is
checking our son's temperature, just over 37°, a slight fever.

12:15 a.m.
Dr. Usui, a pediatrician, conducts a thorough examination, takes out a memo pad
and calmly describes his diagnosis in understandable words and pictures. The records show my son is allergic to many foods and has a history of asthma. But
what's going on here is Croup with dyspnea, probably triggered by a viral infection. He must be admitted to the hospital for close observation and therapy. We
understand and do not argue.

12:25 a.m.
I leave the examination room with the excuse to park my car. In reality I do not
want to watch the procedures: start an IV, take blood for tests, do a skin test for
allergy to antibiotics, take a sample of mucus from the throat, hook up a device to
monitor blood oxygen levels. There is loud crying as I exit.

12:35 a.m.
Dr. Usui interrupts my pacing in the corridor to assure me not to worry because
everything will be fine.

12:38 a.m.
We make our way to the elevators en route to the pediatric ward where four nurses are ministering to patients and preparing for our arrival. The doctor is at the nurses' station writing up the necessary orders. With quiet efficiency a bed is prepared with a mist, IV bags, and blood oxygen monitor pulsing with a green light.

12:45 a.m.
The doctor comes into our room which is shared with five other boys, all three to four years old, all with some respiratory problem, all sleeping. He talks about the therapy, assures us the oxygen levels are fine, and tells us the other boys will be good playmates in the morning, alleviating our anxiety because this hospital does not allow parents to stay in the room.

12:55 a.m.
We are still talking with the doctor as my son goes to sleep. Dr. Usui has infinite patience with a series of questions, all important at the time, all mundane in retrospect. Then we just sit and watch the green light and IV drip, drip, drip.

1:38 a.m.
Time to go home as there is nothing more we can do. The nurses' move in and out checking each child. We say good night to Dr. Usui who is reviewing case reports at the nurses' station.

1:45 a.m.
The three traffic lights are green on the way home.

2:30 a.m.
Who can sleep? I am reading all about Croup in the Merck manual and it is like reading a report of what actually happened. A textbook case: symptoms, diagnosis and treatment.

8:30 a.m.
Back to the hospital with a few favorite toys for Brett who is sleeping calmly and looks fine. The nurses are changing their shift; Dr. Usui is still on the floor. When does this guy sleep? A nurse tells us that earlier the boy next to Brett was talking to . him in Japanese and Brett was talking back in English. They seemed to know what each was saying as the "conversation" went on for some time.

I guess that pretty well sums up the evening. The doctors and nurses communicated by what they did, the words were unimportant except to calm and lend assurance. There were no hassles, frustrating delays, or lengthy administrative procedures. Just efficient service with a smile, and reconfirmation that the system works just as we have come to expect in a city where things get done and run on time.

My final thought as I leave the hospital for the office. What did people do before there were effective drugs to normalize acute respiratory distress? Once again, and it will not be the last time, I feel good about a decision made in 1964 to be associated with the pharmaceutical industry.

60 hours later
Dr. Usui calls our home to say the chest X-ray is clear and the IV was removed. We can take Brett home. Who said Japanese doctors don't talk to their patients (and parents); and hospital stays are too long?

Here's what I learned from the Merck Manual: Croup is an acute inflammation of the upper and lower respiratory tracts, characterized by inspiratory stridor, subglottic swelling, and respiratory distress that is most pronounced on inspiration. Dyspnea is shortness of breath, the sensation of difficult, labored, or uncomfortable breathing. Dr. Usui nailed the diagnosis in about three minutes.

Pharma Japan 1647, May 1999

A Cure for the Common Cold?

We know medical scientists and pharmaceutical companies have not found a cure for that miserable affliction known as the common cold. We also know the lack of a scientific cure does not inhibit those without a cold from telling those with a cold how to get rid of it. Therefore, I have no fear of offering advice.

First a bit of background: In a North Carolina rural town in my first sales territory a young doctor opened an office at the request of older doctors in the community. He had it made because there was essentially no competition for new patients.

During our first meeting he assured me he would not give shots or prescribe antibiotics for a cold. These medicines would not cure a virus infection and would only cause discomfort and a financial burden to his patients. Bed rest and plenty of liquids is an effective prescription.

For months his waiting room could have been called a no wait room. Then he was packing them in. I asked what made the difference. He replied, "I started giving shots." A lesson learned is worth remembering. When people go to see a doctor they want to be treated. Your mother can tell you to drink orange juice and chicken noodle soup. You want action from a doctor so there is something to talk about back at the office.

If you are looking for an aggressive cold treatment in Tokyo check out the Iwai Clinic on the 12th floor of the Kasumigaseki Building. There is also an Iwai Clinic in the New Otani Hotel Tower if that location is more convenient. The following routine is what you can expect, and believe it or not, I was in and out within one hour.

The first step is checking in. Once you establish a file this procedure takes five minutes and you go to a seat outside the ear, nose, and throat room. A nurse called my name and I was ushered to one of two chairs, about six feet apart, each with a doctor in front. No wall separates the two, so whatever you say to the doctor can easily be heard by your fellow patient, and vice versa. Doctor consultations in Japan are not private affairs.

My doctor and the one attending the adjoining chair were both women, young women. There are approximately 8,000 new medical graduates each year and 25 percent of these are women. I must admit that my cold symptoms were already abating as this soft voice asked me questions about my condition.

Next came a not so delicate probing of the upper regions of my nasal sinuses. This brought tears to my eyes. Next was the throat. After wrapping her fingers with a piece of gauze, she held my tongue and pulled it forward—at the same time exhorting me to say Aaaah! The reflex choke mechanism dominated my desire to maintain an executive calm.

I was then sent to the X-ray room to have pictures taken of my skull—particularly of the sinuses that could not be probed. Ten minutes later I was back in the chair and the pictures were on a back-lighted panel. I tried a lame joke about an empty skull; the young woman doctor was not amused. She pointed out the inflamed sinus passages and solemnly declared I had a sinus infection which required treatment.

I was directed to a device that is a glass blowers dream connected by a rubber hose to a panel with dials and gauges that would delight a computer engineer. Two small glass bulbs are inserted in the nostrils and connected to these is a larger bulb which contains medicine in liquid form. At the touch of a button a blast of air bubbles through the liquid and the vapor goes through a connecting tube into the small bulbs, and up my nose.

When this was finished a throat tube was substituted for the nostril bulbs and the vapor from a new reservoir of medicine was directed to my throat. The effect of both treatments was immediate. I felt completely relieved, opened and cleared.

Final instructions related to a series of prescriptions which I was told to take for one week. The orders were definite and compliance was assumed.

I left with a bag of medicine—four different kinds in their blister packs to be taken morning and night. By the way, the pharmacy was on the third floor. Probably *Bungyo*, a separation of the dispensing function from the doctor's room. However, I am sure that Dr. Iwai also controls the pharmacy.

It worked, in one week the cold was gone. Maybe chicken soup would have been equally effective, but who would be interested in reading about that?

Pharma Japan 1276, October 28, 1991

Medical Service via a Travel Agent

Hawaii's beaches and golf courses are not the only attractions for many Japanese who disembark at Honolulu's International Airport every morning. Armed with insurance cards, these people go directly to hospitals for scheduled appointments with doctors.

A receptionist at a Honolulu hospital assured me their check-in procedures are more convenient than a Waikiki hotel. She told me an insurance company established a local office to process medical claims by Japanese nationals. Their bilingual instruction manual is concise and clear. Payments are made quickly. "The system works well," she said, then added with a smile, "Business is booming."

Because my family has been on the receiving end of healthcare in Tokyo and Honolulu for many years, it is not difficult to understand the reasons why there is more money to be made providing Japanese with medical services than selling them pineapples. It is a short list that businessmen will recognize as customer focused service.

1. Doctors talk WITH patients, not to them.
2. An appointment at 9:15 am means exactly what it says. No waiting around until noon.
3. Laboratory results are available in 24 hours, not days or weeks.
4. Professional and efficient paramedical personnel are readily available.

5. Healthcare providers are rewarded on the basis of outcomes, not inputs such as tests, long hospital stays, and drugs.

This summer my wife and I took our infant son to a doctor in Honolulu. During the consultation he wrote a phone number on a piece of paper and said, "I am available at this number 24 hours a day unless I am dead." Difficult to say if the medical treatment was better or worse than in Tokyo, but my wife was delighted and relieved.

Japan's low infant mortality rate is enviable, but Honolulu obstetric wards are delivering Japanese babies every day. I once thought this was all about getting a U.S. passport for anyone born in the country. The truth, according to my Japanese friends, is in the service. Mothers are provided every conceivable support during labor in a room that resembles a resort suite. After delivery, mom and dad are treated to a candlelight dinner in the hospital.

At the other end of the spectrum is a Japanese company operating a nursing home in Oahu, and building two more. Why? They figure Japan will need lots of nursing homes, but haven't a clue how to build or operate them. They are learning how in Hawaii.

Excuse me, are the key policy makers in Japan listening to these fugitives from the system as they debate the issues of healthcare reform? The power structure within the Japan Medical Association appears to be intent on protecting its share of the pie while neglecting the needs of patients. Their study groups suggest lower drug prices, more generics and restricted access to new drugs. To help patients? No, to raise medical fees. They scold drug companies for too much promotion and not enough research, but do not implement meaningful continuing medical education programs for their own members.

Koseisho wants to revert to their previous bad practice of revising prices every year. They exercise the power to implement special price reductions on flaky assumptions, and want to slash prices of any drug on the market over 10 years. Meanwhile, the public whom they serve, cry out for less regulation, more options for healthcare, and unrestricted access to treatment.

The U.S. healthcare system has problems which Japan should not adopt. But it also has benefits which can be emulated. Why not:

1. Provide a variety of affordable treatment options for elderly care? The price of buying your way into one of the few but good nursing/retirement homes in Japan is close to one million dollars.

2. Get psychiatric care out of the dark ages of institutionalization and into the real world of rehabilitation?

3. Train emergency paramedicals to do more than drive a patient to the hospital? A few months back we called an ambulance for our baby. It arrived in five minutes, loaded up, then parked around the corner for 15 minutes trying to figure out which hospital to go to.

4. Enforce relicensing requirements for doctors who left medical school 30 years ago?

5. Foster collaboration between medical researchers in public institutes and those in industry?

6. Allow "for profit" businesses into healthcare delivery?

7. Reward doctors who talk with patients?

These things work in the United States, they can work here. Japan takes great pride in its healthcare indices, e.g., longest life span, low infant mortality, universal insurance coverage, and the low incidence of communicable diseases. These are achievements of the past.

People who believe the price of an airplane ticket to Honolulu is a small price to pay for good medical service; the hundreds of young doctors who want postgraduate medical training in the United States; and researchers who flock to the United States with dreams of a Nobel Prize are sending a message about the future of healthcare in Japan. Will anyone listen?

My friends in Honolulu tell me to shut up. This kind of healthcare reform in Japan would ruin their business, and they hate picking pineapples.

Pharma Japan 1517, September 1996

Knee Jerk Reactions

Talk to the average guy on the street and you are apt to get knee jerk reactions to questions about Japanese physicians. Normally reticent, well reasoned people do not hesitate to state very definite but unsubstantiated statements about the medical profession, and the people who devote their lives to practicing its science and art. Here is one that everyone has heard.

"Doctors depend upon the dispensing of drugs to provide their income: Therefore, they prescribe too much, and most of that is not effective, so one half ends up down the drain."

Stay with me for a moment to go through some arithmetic. In 1987 the total drug market was estimated to be ¥4.8 trillion at NHI prices. Koseisho estimates discounts average 24 percent. Therefore, about ¥1.1 trillion, "leaked" out of the insurers drug budget into the hands of someone, certainly not the manufacturers or wholesalers.

A trillion yen is a lot of money, but it must be spread around. In 1986 the government reported there were 219,623 doctors registered as providers of medical care benefits. Thus, we are talking about ¥5 million per doctor per year. I could not find out what doctors earn in one year but some people estimate they make 6 x the average salaryman in large enterprises. Pity the poor salaryman, everyone knows what he makes. In 1986 the figure was ¥5.7 million. Six times is ¥34.2 million, and ¥5 million is 15 percent of that. However, this is not a net number since we must assume significant costs are associated with dispensing drugs, i.e., the salary of a pharmacist.

Enough of the math, I think we may have made the point. Total elimination of drug income to the doctor would hardly put a dent in his pocketbook. Seldom does one mention the practice of patients giving doctors a "gift" of appreciation for his services. A friend of mine recently had an eye operation and he was told ¥250,000 in a plain envelope would be an appropriate way to say thank you. The doctor does eight operations in one day. I should think this income is far more important than what is derived from the drugs he prescribes. Everything is relative.

Secondly, how many drugs are too many? If a patient gets four different medicines, are two better? I prefer to rely on my doctor to make that decision versus some health economic bureau staffed by MBAs. The same applies for what is or is not effective for me. A few years ago someone close to me had cancer. I wanted the doctors to try anything, even though the odds were terrible. This is why I am troubled about "essential" drug lists. If something works for me I want my doctor to have it available even if it only works in 10 percent of the population.

Few of us go to doctors voluntarily. We stuff our own homes and bodies with all kind of useless items, but it is our decision. Taking a drug is typically dictated by someone we would rather not see in the first place. Are some drugs over-prescribed? Probably. Are some drugs ineffective for certain patients? Certainly. Do patients stop taking their medication when they feel better and trash the rest? Of course. Is the system and those that administer it all screwed up? Then tell me why the Japanese may be the healthiest people, by many measurements, on this earth. It's not all due to eating sushi versus red meat.

Japan's Health Care System

If I was a doctor, this article would focus on the diagnosis of disease in Japan. The first priority for doctors is a proper diagnosis. I would tell you about the diagnostic skills of Japanese physicians; that diagnostic procedures are not restricted in Japan; that any hospital can purchase exotic equipment to perform tests that are reimbursed by the insurance system; that this government does not allocate or ration diagnostic procedures. I would tell you that diagnosis is key—treatment is secondary.

If I was a Koseisho official I would cite statistics indicating that Japanese society is the worlds' healthiest. That life expectancy is the longest; that infant mortality is the lowest; that there are no outbreaks of preventable childhood diseases; that mortality rates for many diseases have progressively declined for many years. I would ask you to show me a better health care system for the money.

If I was an economist I would tell you that the health insurance system in Japan works because it makes money. I would ask you if another government administered health insurance system anywhere in the world is profitable. I would tell you companies are not burdened by insurance premiums that in other countries are out of control. I would tell you that this society has achieved equality of health care, universal access to health care, and compassionate treatment at a cost that does not exceed 7 percent of its gross national income.

If I was a lawyer I would cite the low incidence of malpractice suits and the absence of obscene liability judgements against providers of health care. I would tell you that doctors do not practice defensive medicine and obstetricians deliver babies without fear of being hauled into court because of a complicated delivery.

I do not have any of these specialized credentials. I can only speak to you as a user of the medical system for over 21 years. My message can be summarized in three brief statements:

1. Compared to other health care systems in North America and Europe, Japan's model is admirable and may be worth emulating.
2. Rapid demographic changes in Japan will fundamentally alter health care.
3. Because Japan is becoming the richest country in the world, it will have the resources to provide universal quality care at an affordable cost.

That's it—an admirable model that is changing to meet future needs, with enough money to try anything, but only the best will be accepted.

This does not mean the system is ideal. Waiting times to see doctors are but one of the reasons why Japanese are unsatisfied with the quality of their health care.

Ambulances do nothing more for patients than get them to a hospital. The traditional autocratic authority of the physician and his right to make all the therapeutic decisions for the patient is being questioned. Nurses are underpaid and overworked.

In addition to the medical needs of its aging population, the largest problems in Japan relate to social policy. You have seen the issues debated in *The Japan Times*: brain death, informed consent and patient rights, the ethics of living to living transplants, bioethics, and the overall quality assessment of health care. Patients visit their physicians three times as often as the average American. This is not entirely due to their medical needs, but relates to the point system for paying medical fees.

The demographics of diseases are changing. Japan is aging rapidly, indeed faster than any other society in history. People no longer live on the farm, dietary habits have undergone rapid change. The average diet is becoming low in fiber and high in fat content. Animal meat is eaten in preference to fish. Cholesterol levels of Japanese children are now as elevated as their U.S. counterparts. Heart disease is now the second leading cause of death, after malignant neoplasms. Maybe the Japanese are not becoming more Western in their thinking, but their diseases have become decidedly more Western.

The strengths of this system stem from efforts in public health screening, an historical preference for non-invasive diagnostic and therapeutic procedures (Japan has one quarter the number of surgical cases as the United States with one half the population), and an emphasis on primary care. The delivery system reflects egalitarianism in the society, with equal access to the same quality of services assured to all Japanese.

These basic strengths of health care in Japan are certain to get better. While other governments are trying desperately to cut health care costs, Japan increases its rate of spending in line with the growth in national income. While insurance societies elsewhere lose money, in Japan they make money. While some countries are rationing health care services, Japan has a system that encourages open access to medical care.

Japan's health insurance system is not a perfect model, but it may be the best around in relative terms. It certainly faces challenges as people demand quality to go with the equality already achieved. How Japan will allocate its wealth to provide quality health care is the current challenge.

It boils down to this. Japan has increased the years of life for its citizens. The objective now is to add life to these years. It is the quality of life that Japanese health care policy makers must consider seriously. Will they succeed? No one knows for sure, but as foreigners in Japan we have a ringside seat to perhaps the most dynamic health care system in the world. Will it turn out to be a model, or a mess? My bet is that it will be a model for providing quality health care at an affordable cost.

Pharma Japan 1286, January 13, 1992

Health Care Reform in Japan (I)

Health care reform is now an issue in Japan because the Japanese are older and richer. Quality of life is not a dream; it is demanded as a fundamental right. The Japanese have achieved the longest life expectancy in the world. Now their priority is not to live longer, it is to enjoy the years they have.

No one wants to be sick. We go to a restaurant and expect to have a good time. Women (and more men) buy expensive cosmetics, facials, and hair treatments because they expect to look better. When we go to a hospital we are angry and expect the worse.

But the Japanese visit doctors more frequently than people in any other country. On average, 12.8 times per year, or once per month. The U.S. rate is 5.3 visits per year. What's going on? Do the Japanese like to be sick?

One answer is access to health care—anywhere, any time. Rich or poor, old or young, self employed or salaried, housewife or executive—everyone has equal access to a hospital or clinic doctor. Equality of health care is a reality.

What about the quality of health care? Waiting three hours to see a doctor for three minutes is not fun. The duration of hospitalization for an average patient in Japan is 39 days, in the United States, 7 days. Hospitals are not fun, ask any overworked and underpaid nurse.

Quality of health care has many definitions. A mother with young children wants to get in and out of a doctor's office quickly. An older patient is quite content to linger in the waiting room, socializing with neighborhood friends.

Many patients want their doctors to communicate, to tell them what is wrong, and what can be done to correct the problem. They want to know what drugs they are taking, and why. Quality for these people equals information.

Health care in Japan is accessible and affordable. Out of pocket costs for diagnosis and treatment are relatively low. It is comforting to know that a major illness will not cause a personal financial crisis. Universal insurance coverage is a positive benefit of this system.

However, aging of the population has caused a problem between the type of health care facilities that are accessible, and those which are required. Japan has 2 million hospital beds, one-third more than the United States with half the population. These beds were created for acutely ill, younger patients. They are not suitable for chronically ill, older patients.

This is the quality of life issue. Duty to one's parents is alive in Japan, but it is simply not possible to administer sophisticated medical care within the limited confines of an average home. Few institutions provide quality care for elderly patients. Japan needs more nursing homes where patients can walk around and breathe fresh air. In high tech, intensive hospitals they are confined to beds, stuck with needles, given invasive diagnostic tests, and sedated with a variety of drugs. Japan has changed, but delivery of health care has not.

There are 212,000 doctors in Japan, and 8,000 new doctors are licensed each year. Because the population growth rate is declining, the number of doctors per capita is increasing. That is to say, more doctors are chasing fewer patients, thus increasing the power of the consumer, a positive benefit of supply and demand.

Unfortunately, the dispersion of doctors is not uniform. There are too many in urban areas and not enough in rural areas. A friend contemplating retirement would like to move to the countryside near Kyoto where he can enjoy trees and birds. However, he will stay in Tokyo because of the availability of health care.

Primary care physicians in small clinics are aging. Their sons opted for careers in financial services rather than medical services. Young doctors who prefer to practice in a clinic cannot afford the cost of land and a building. Thus, they become employees in large hospitals.

Out-patient clinics at university hospitals are crowded, impersonal places where each person has a number rather than a name. Will Japan restrict access to health care, or allocate patients to specific institutions? When governments restrict freedom of choice, quality suffers.

Pharma Japan 1355, June 7, 1993

Health Care Reform in Japan (II)

When you go to a restaurant, there is a choice of dishes displayed in plastic or in pictures, or listed on a menu, or written on banners hung on the wall. You feel good because you have a choice.

When you go to a hospital, the doctor prescribes drugs he believes will make you feel better. The prescription is written in a language you do not understand, the ingredients of each drug are unknown to you, and they are dispensed by a pharmacist not of your choice.

Books that describe drugs are best sellers. People want to know what they are taking and why? What are the risks and benefits?

Over 900 companies in Japan manufacture prescription drugs. About 450 companies have 14,500 drugs listed in the reimbursement price list, or *yakka*. Japan does not restrict the availability of drugs if they are safe and effective. Therefore, the doctor has unlimited choice, which is not the case in many countries.

Drugs are delivered to clinics, pharmacies and hospitals exclusively by wholesalers. When I first came to Japan there were over 1,000 wholesalers; now there are 240. Any patient, anywhere in Japan, can get drugs immediately, and because they are covered by insurance, the out-of-pocket costs are low.

More new drugs are launched first in Japan than any other country. This is a result of an efficient regulatory review process and the absence of restrictions on usage. Government policies have fostered innovation, which has made Japan a leading country in the discovery of new drugs. Society benefits when new technology is welcome regardless of national origin; when the risk of discovery research is rewarded with patents; and when regulations are transparent and fair.

Do the Japanese consume too many drugs? Do doctors over-prescribe? The evidence for and against this question is anecdotal. Critics cite patients who consume 25 drugs every day, but never identify patients who should take drugs but do not. No hard evidence exists to prove the Japanese suffer from a drug overdose problem. The bottom line may be the cost of health care in Japan. Expenditures are 6 percent of national income, roughly comparable to European levels, and less than half the U.S. rate. Health care expenditures have increased at a lower rate than the growth of national income. The system is not out of control.

The pharmaceutical industry in Japan is small. It employs about 200,000 people, which represents 0.3 percent of the total work force. However, it does employ 50,000 medical representatives (MRs) to call on doctors. The United States has the same number for twice as many doctors. MRs primarily call on the 130,000 doctors who work in hospitals with more than 100 beds. Wholesalers employ 35,000 marketing specialists (MSs) who focus on clinics with 99 beds or less. U.S. wholesalers employ one-tenth this numbers.

Should the total number of MRs increase? The full annual cost of one MR is ¥15 million. Considering the number of doctors called on, this translates into a cost of ¥12,000 per doctor call. The call must be beneficial for the doctor, that is, a transfer of valuable, objective information on the benefits and risks of drugs. The quality of MRs is now more important than the number of MRs.

Efficient utilization of MSs is also critical. Japanese wholesalers must upgrade their sales staff because information on drugs is a crucial element in the process of ensuring safety and proper usage. Wholesalers who survive in the future will accept this responsibility.

Health care providers must strike a delicate balance between technology and compassion. To date, the results are admirable. Regulations have not stifled creativity, the system is financially sound, affordable, accessible, and safe. However, the health care needs of this society are changing rapidly.

Pharma Japan 1356, June 14, 1993

Limits on Patient Focused Health Care

Koseisho and the pharmaceutical industry are jumping on the bandwagon to empower consumers of health care. They believe well informed, out of pocket paying consumers, not the medical profession, should dictate the supply and demand of medical services. They argue the end result would be higher quality health care at a lower cost.

Market-driven, or consumer-driven scenarios suggest the decision to select a course of therapy for a specific medical problem is no different than buying a car or a personal computer. In essence, a decision based on a simple equation of value and convenience as a function of time and money.

Is this the real world? I think not.

Insurers, Koseisho included, would like to strip away the veil of god-like aura enjoyed (undeserved?) by Japanese doctors. Informed consent, access to medical records, the spread of *bungyo*, pharmacist-provided drug information, and significant co-payments are proposed to give educated patients more control. Then, insurers believe, patients will not take home five bags of medicine, endure unnecessary tests, or stay in hospital beds for 40 days.

If this behavior pattern becomes a reality, insurers' bank accounts will overflow with cash. Am I too suspicious to believe this is their real motivation? Will patients feel better about their treatment if they get one drug rather than three?

Industry executives, prodded by a new breed of consumer marketing managers, are itching to contact patients directly through print media, television, and the Internet. The number of "hits" on a drug company home page is tracked as avidly as doctor calls.

No doubt the manufacturers are responding to an insatiable demand for more information on drugs—their benefits and risks. It is also a fact that many prescriptions are redundant, if not dangerous, when taken concomitantly. Am I too suspicious to think direct consumer approaches are a cheap substitute for an intelligent detail by a medical representative? Will patients feel better if they tell a doctor how to practice medicine?

The pendulum is swinging toward a focus on consumers. There is an acute need for free-market systems in Japan. As the patient population ages, there is an absolute necessity for cost-consciousness in the market.

The Japan Medical Association cannot retain its position as guardian of a system that is outdated in terms of consumer convenience and burning cash faster than it is coming in.

The airline industry is an interesting analogy. In its early days, pilots were in control of everything from maintenance, to schedules, to passenger check-in, to the cabin, to the cockpit. In essence, they ran the business. By and by, consumers demanded efficient reservation services and convenient route schedules. They wanted first class seating with all the frills as well as, cheap, economy class seats. Market-driven managers added club rooms, frequent flyer miles, and other amenities for discerning flyers. The consumer, not the pilot, is now empowered to make choices.

Nevertheless, no sane person would advocate anything but a qualified pilot in the cockpit while passengers are strapped safely in their seats. We also want a strong regulatory authority to protect us from maintenance deficiencies and breaches of security. A free but regulated system.

If only medicine was as straight-forward as an airline. Consumers have a very difficult time comparing medical treatments. Short of a cure, what will satisfy the patient? Unfortunately, most of our ills do not lend themselves to mathematical, either/or solutions. There are no simple answers and few absolute cures, just a world full of trade-offs.

I was diagnosed at the age of 31 with a melanoma. It was a shocking experience, the survival rate is low. So I read every medical publication on the subject to become a well informed, educated patient. On the eve of my operation, the surgeon said there were two options. He could excise the tumor with a shallow incision, do a biopsy, and close me up in a matter of minutes. Or, he could go deep and take skin off my hip to close the hole, a major, time consuming procedure more expensive than the first option. Mr. Maurer, he said, ''What is your decision?''

I was speechless, but not for long. I said. "Doc, you are in charge, do what you think is best: the next day he went deep. Did I regret his decision and the expense? Not for 29 years.

Patients are not as eager to control their medical care as much as consumer-driven proponents would have us believe. We prefer to trust doctors to make the difficult decisions on our behalf.

Nor do we want doctors restricted by spread sheet wielding administrators who generate cost-effectiveness outcome analyses on treatment options. Or by a restricted drug list devised by academic pharmacologists.

Health care can be improved through patient participation. New technology will allow patients to monitor their conditions in the comfort of their own homes. Drugs, wisely used, can eliminate the need for surgery or long hospital stays. Market-driven competition will improve the quality of care. Waiting three hours to see a doctor for three minutes is stupid, and a waste of time.

Keep in mind drug companies and Koseisho do not deliver health care. Doctors do that within the context of a process that is as much an art as it is a science. Empower consumers, but when the plane is ready to roll, make sure a qualified pilot is at the controls.

Pharma Japan 1561, August 18, 1997

Japan's Response to Rising Health Care Costs

Payers of health care expenditures in the United States, Europe and Japan share a common problem. The cost of providing universal health care exceeds the capacity to pay for it. In simple accounting terms the formula is: costs minus income equals deficit.

Remarkably, the Japanese response to the problem is diametrically different from actions by policy makers in the West. This has profound implications for manufacturers of products prescribed by health care providers. At the very least, it suggests that corporate or government strategies toward Japan cannot be building upon the Western model. Keys for success inside Japan are not those that open locks in other advanced economies.

This article will first define the common causes of rising health care costs: secondly, elucidate the different responses by Japanese and Western policy makers to the problem; and close with suggestions for achieving competitive advantage inside Japan's health care delivery and reimbursement structure.

The Problem—Rising Health Care Costs

In the United States, Europe and recently in Japan, the growth rate of medical expenditures is higher than the growth rate of national income. The surprise free result is a global debate on health care reform, and budget debates inside governments, corporate boardrooms, hospitals, and families. It has provoked a bitter political struggle in the United States, increased the tension in bilateral trade negotiations, and created cross border disunity in Europe.

The escalation of health care costs is driven by three factors, i.e. excess capacity, excess demand, and new technology.

Excess Capacity

Japan has two million hospital beds, one-third more than the United States with half the population. To make the comparison worse, recent studies in the United States indicate a surplus of hospital beds. At least one-third of U.S. hospital beds are unoccupied on any given day. Every community wants a modern hospital staffed with professional personnel and equipped with state of the art technology. The desire for access to proximate, convenient health care is imbued in Western and Japanese society. Indeed, it is considered a basic right.

Facilities, once in place, are self perpetuating. Politicians, administrators, and doctors strive to optimize utilization rates lest they be deemed redundant. Closing or downsizing may be a rational economic decision, but political and ego factors interfere in the process. Hence, fees are increased to cover deficits and/or government (tax payer) money is solicited.

Eight thousand newly qualified doctors enter the medical profession each year in Japan. Since the population growth rate is almost nil, the per-capita number of physicians has increased. There is now a surplus of doctors in urban areas, all desirous of generating fees and earning an above average standard of living. Other countries have an excess of specialists, but a shortage of general practitioners. All these factors create excess capacity of high value added services, thus driving up costs.

Excess Demand

Rising incomes directly correlate to the demand for health care generally and for high quality (more expensive) health care specifically. Private rooms, special meals, and auxiliary services may increase the quality of care, but come at a price, particularly when the availability of low cost labor is scarce, e.g., no one wants to empty bed pans.

Aging of the population is particularly acute in Japan. Since the intensity of medical treatment increase with age, an older population demands more health care. To compound the problem, treatment of chronic diseases may not result in cures, thus, expenses escalate until death.

Even among younger, healthy people there is a rising demand for "wellness" services. Health fads sweep through society. Diagnostic services are imposed on large segments of the population without regard to costs versus realized benefits.

In some countries the issue of liability for malpractice has increased the demand for defensive medical services. A caesarian child birth is much more expensive than a natural birth, but the latter is more risky in terms of liability. Heroic treatments are given to terminally ill patients although the outcome is a foregone conclusion.

In short, increased demand for health care does not recognize national boundaries. We want the best, and we want it now. Few of us want to make the decision to pull the plug, shut off the life support equipment, or cease treatment. These are not macroeconomic decisions; they are very personal, individual decisions.

New Technology

We are witnessing an explosion of hardware to diagnose and treat illness. Each new product promises to save lives, reduce the time in hospital, and get sick people well faster. But the promises of technology pale in the reality of increased costs. Payers of health care have become immune to cost/benefit analyses, and computer models prepared by consultants do not appear to generate real savings at the patient bedside.

It is an established fact that the cost of bringing new technology through regulatory hurdles has escalated. Demonstrating efficacy, quality and safety is a time consuming, arduous, expensive process. Regulators, understandably, want fail safe procedures, but the cost of implementing these procedures is beyond the means of many firms. Products that get through the maze must generate adequate financial returns to cover losses of products that fail to make the grade.

Payers often construct barriers to new technology. They come in many forms and stifle innovation where they are applied. Companies close down research programs, governments impose restricted lists, formularies slow the diffusion of new technology, and entire countries elect a beggar thy neighbor policy that relies on others to carry out discovery research.

Responses to the Problem

In all countries, health care payments have been transferred from individuals to third parties, both government and private. In the United States more than 50 percent of all prescriptions are now paid by third parties. Fewer payers result in greater buying power, most often applied to the supply side of the cost equation. Japan was not an exception to this phenomenon.

Supply side attacks are politically acceptable because they affect a limited number of stakeholders, typically politically inept corporations and their associations. Demand side cost containment affects all patients and politically powerful interest groups. It is no surprise these measures are used sparingly.

During the 1980's, Japan implemented supply side cost containment policies that were used in other countries, e.g., sharp reductions in drug reimbursement prices. Since 1992 the pattern changed. Japan is no longer playing follow the leader to the United States and Europe.

To illustrate this point in concise form, I have generalized the responses to rising health care costs below, combining the United States and Europe as the Western response, and comparing it to the Japanese response. The contrasts are thus pictured in stark relief when in reality there are numerous shades of gray in between. Furthermore, specific country policies are evolving and my comments are a static description of a dynamic process. Nevertheless, the trends are real and must be taken seriously by those who intend to compete successfully in Japan.

Western Response

1. Bash the pharmaceutical industry
2. Promote old technology
   a. Fast tract generic approvals
   b. Low prices for NCE's
   c. Restrict market exclusivity
3. Restrict market access
   a. Tough formularies
   b. Limited lists
   c. Slow approval
4. Force rebates and large discounts
5. Weaken patent protection
6. Cut basic research budgets
7. Increase bureaucratic review of new technology
8. Concentrate on the equality of medical care

Japan's response

1. Support a research intensive pharmaceutical industry
2. Promote new technology
   a. List generics infrequently
   b. High prices for NCE's
   c. Extend market exclusivity
3. Open the door
   a. Open formularies
   b. Expanded lists
   c. Expedite approval
4. Minimize discounts and stabilize prices.
5. Strengthen patent protection
6. Expand grants for research
7. Streamline regulatory approval procedures
8. Equality achieved—enhance the quality of care

At the same time, Japan is acting to reduce the demand for health care. These policies are unique compared to other countries because of the nature of health care delivery in Japan. A few examples are:

1. Promote the separation of dispensing from prescribing, thus removing the doctor's economic incentive to supply drugs.
2. Convert the treatment costs of certain diseases from fee for service to flat-sum reimbursements, or fixed daily reimbursable amounts. This forces providers to deemphasize patient inputs and emphasize patient outcomes.
3. Increase patient co-payment and eliminate reimbursement of certain services, e.g., hospital meals. These actions increase customer awareness of treatment costs.

None of the above policies are designed to reduce the absolute amount of health care expenditures. Fortunately for Japanese policy makers, health care costs are not out of control and represent a relatively low percentage, about 6.2 percent, of national income. Rather, the policy goal is to restrain the growth rate of health care costs within a range that does not exceed the growth rate of national income.

The bottom line is Japanese society can afford to pay more for quality health care, and is willing to pay if it is administered in an equitable manner. In other words, restricted access to treatment and rationing are not attractive policy options.

Achieving Competitive Advantage

Changes in Japan are proceeding at a pace unthinkable a few years ago. Change is a real problem for those who learned to compete under the old rules and either refuse to believe conditions are different today, or do not have the vision to manage change. This includes many well established companies who benefit from the status quo and try to keep it that way.

Conversely, change introduces new opportunities for yesterday's outsiders and those who do not have a stake in perpetuating the past. If the trends described earlier continue, the following strategies will create competitive advantages for the firms that implement them:

1. Selling via a discount strategy is not viable as a tool to increase volume. Companies must strive to create value. Three options are:
   a. Microsegmentation of target audiences with a high response capability to their needs. Human wave selling has priced itself out of the market.

b. Assist hospitals to lower costs by reducing patient inputs and providing tools to measure patient outcomes.

c. Axing product candidates early in the development cycle if they are unlikely to demonstrate significant efficacy benefits over established therapies.

2. Strategies that propel the firm into generics and vertical integration go against the trend. Fostering innovation, forming alliances with academic researchers, and reducing labor intensive overhead optimize the value added operations of the firm.

3. Take advantage of the government's desire to harmonize regulatory requirements and streamline the approval process. Use contract services to supplement peak demands for clinical research associates. Think of government officials as development partners, not as antagonists.

Summary

In historical and cultural terms it is perfectly logical for Japan to place a high value on new technology, to balance spending and income growth, promote businesses to become world class competitors, and consider equality and quality as complementary rather than mutually exclusive policy goals. These national traits are being brought to bear in health care issues for the first time.

This sounds like the ideal market for a. research intensive, high value industry with low labor, pollution control and energy requirements. Multinational pharmaceutical companies should see more opportunities than problems in Japan, assuming they haven't been too busy competing in Western markets, they forgot what made them multinational competitors in the first place.

Scrip Magazine, December 1994

Chapter **III**

Government Regulators Change the Rules

Government officials approve new drugs. How they do this has enormous consequences for the pharma industry. In the early 1990s they did it very well then later badly as a result of internal scandals and reorganizations. Industry suffered while the health ministry fiddled. Regulators also administer reimbursement rules of the health insurance system. Their actions affect the economics of health care payers, providers, patients, and drug industry. The rule changes caused turmoil for every participant.

Government Regulators Change the Rules

Drug Price Revisions in Japan

The *yakka kijun*, or reimbursement tariff list, is set for all prescription drugs in Japan by Koseisho. As of April 17, 1992 this list covered 13,589 preparations, 8,594 oral drugs, 3,138 injections, 1,754 topical drugs and 103 dental drugs. The tariff represents consumer prices because reimbursements to dispensing institutions are paid according to the official list by all insurance carriers and patients enrolled in Japan's national health insurance system.

Compulsory insurance commenced 70 years ago with the Health Insurance Act of 1922 which provided protection for workers against sickness and occupational accidents. The scheme was not put into force until 1927 because of serious disruptions to the administrative functions of government by the Kanto (Tokyo area) earthquake in 1923.

It is beyond the scope of this article to describe in detail the subsequent expansion of medical insurance schemes. Briefly, by 1961 Japan achieved 100 percent national health insurance coverage; since then improvements in the system paralleled Japan's economic achievements. For example, in 1927 there were 316 Health Insurance Societies; as of March 1991 there were 1,822 insurance societies providing coverage for employees in businesses employing 700 or more persons.

Government-managed health insurance covers 29.5 percent of the population; society-managed health insurance covers 25.8 percent of the population; and the remainder of the population is covered by a variety of schemes operated locally by municipalities and mutual aid associations. Fund income exceeds expenditures even though medical care costs per capita have risen from 2,700 yen in 1955 to 160,000 yen in 1989.

Because Koseisho establishes the tariff for all insurance carriers, they effectively set a cap on consumer prices. Koseisho does not act in isolation. Its actions are determined by an advisory body, namely the Central Social Insurance Medical Council, or Chuikyo, made up of representatives from the payers (insurance societies), providers (doctors, dentists, pharmacists, hospitals), and the public. Note the absence of suppliers such as the pharmaceutical industry.

The remainder of this article will focus on drug price policy, particularly as it relates to revisions of the reimbursement tariff. I will give a historical review of price revisions, note the changes under which this policy has been implemented, and conclude with the results of a survey conducted in April 1992 among 73 foreign and Japanese pharmaceutical firms on the impact of price revision procedures.

One of the most striking features of the Japanese drug price system during the 1980s was Koseisho's systematic reduction of the official tariff, now referred to as the "downward price spiral." While government control over drug prices is common throughout developed countries, Japan stands out internationally for the downward trend of its drug prices.

Price revisions have been carried out for two reasons; first, to bring the actual market price (wholesaler to dispensing institution) closer to the customer price and second, for cost containment reasons. The second purpose is the more important motivating factor. Koseisho has an implicit target to restrict the growth rate of medical care costs at or below the growth rate of national income. Medical care costs grew consistently at double digit rates through 1978, but dropped to single digit rates during the 1980s.

From 1968 through 1980, Koseisho did not take aggressive cost containment measures. During this 13-year period there were only five price revisions, each relatively mild. Taking the 1968 average drug price index as 1, in 1980 it was 0.8. This policy changed drastically during the 1980s.

From 1981 to 1990 the average reduction rate per year compared to the previous year was 7.1 percent. Thus, the index referred to above dropped to 0.4 by 1990, or a 50 percent reduction in 10 years. In 1992 average prices were reduced by 8.1 percent.

Price reductions were distressing enough, but other factors caused turmoil from 1981 through 1986 when there were five price revisions. The timing of each was a moving target, June in 1981, January in 1983, March in 1984 and 1985, April in 1986. Some price revisions covered every drug in the tariff, others were "partial revisions," affecting only some drugs. Confusion reigned, it was impossible to predict the timing of price reductions or the number of drugs to be revised.

An important watershed event occurred in 1986 when the MOSS Agreement was signed by Japan and the United States. Since then price reductions have occurred in April of every other year (1988, 1990, 1992), and partial revisions were eliminated. Koseisho also pledged to list new drugs in the tariff every three months. Prior to MOSS the timing of new drug launches was unpredictable, often a year went by without any new listings. These changes reduced much of the uncertainly in the price revision and price listing policies.

However, the old "bulk-line formula" for calculating drug prices remained intact. This formula, established in 1950, was poorly understood, openly manipulated, and non-transparent. In 1992 it was replaced by the weighted average market prices of all package sizes. A reasonable zone (R-zone) of 15 percent was also introduced. This meant that if a drug's actual weighted average market price was within 85 percent of the consumer price, the tariff price would not be reduced.

These changes were proposed by Chuikyo after intense industry lobbying. As we will see later, the result in 1992 was a more transparent process and a significant reduction in the number of price reductions. Nevertheless, the downward price spiral continued, an aberration by any international standard.

An overview of the 1990 and 1992 price revisions is presented below as an introduction to the industry survey. I initiated this price survey in 1990 to elucidate the price revision process in a representative sample of pharmaceutical companies. Because Koseisho only publicizes the crude reduction rate and a new tariff, it is hardly a public explanation or justification of their vowed intention to improve transparency.

Japanese industry associations, the European Business Council, and PMA member companies cooperated in this endeavor. The final tabulation included responses from 40 Japanese companies, 18 U.S.-based companies, and 15 European companies. The survey sample closely parallels the universe of companies and products, thus is representative of the entire industry.

In 1992 fewer drug prices were reduced, more prices were increased, and more drug prices were left unchanged. The average price reduction in 1992 was less than 1990, but this number has little or no meaning to individual companies, none of whom compete in the "average" market. Specific therapeutic category revisions are more meaningful. For example, antibiotic prices were reduced by 18.4 percent, but external optic drug prices were reduced by only 0.6 percent.

Price increases should also be put into perspective. 16 percent of the tariff drugs were given price increases, but the effect was a mere 0.4 percent overall increase. Note the selection of these products is at the sole discretion of Koseisho.

Below is a summary of the responses to specifc questions in the survey. These questions were answered in quantitative terms, thus the numbers are presented accordingly. Qualitative answers to other questions are summarized at the conclusion of this article.

	1990	1992	Survey
No. of Drugs	13,352 (100%)	13,573 (100%)	7,281 (100%)
Price Reductions	9,472 (73%)	7,681 (57%)	4,339 (60%)
Price Increases	1,700 (13%)	2,121 (16%)	1,153 (16%)
No Change	1,910 (14%)	3,771 (28%)	1,789 (25%)
Average Price Reduction	-9.2%	-8.1%	N.A.

	No. of Companies	No. of Products
Overall Price Reduction:	73 (100%)	
8% or more	36 (49%)	
Less than 8%	37 (51%)	
"Old" Product Prices Reduced by:		3,893 (100%)
R-zone (15%) formula		
Indexing method		917 (24%)
Unknown		776 (20%)
"New" Product Prices Reduced by:		328 (100%)
Actual market prices		164 (50%)
Indexing		164 (50%)
"Overall" Price Reduction:	73 (100%)	
Larger than estimated	26 (36%)	
Smaller than estimated	13 (18%)	
Close to estimate	30 (41%)	
No estimate made	4 (5%)	
Reductions by R-zone Formula:		3,417 (100%)
Larger than estimated		899 (26%)
Smaller than estimated		851 (25%)
Close to estimate		1,376 (40%)
No estimate made		291 (9%)

The companies split between those above and below the average price reduction of 8.1 percent. However, as I mentioned earlier, an average is not very instructive. Some companies had zero overall price reductions, while others had double digit price reductions. I have not correlated these differences with company size, product mix, or any other factor.

The R-zone formula was used most often to reduce product prices. Chuikyo proposed that Koseisho use this formula in revising 1992 prices. However, it is distressing to note that in 24 percent of the products an indexing method was used. Indexing is arbitrary, non-transparent and does not necessarily rely on actual market price data—the only rational basis for revising prices. Furthermore, in 20 percent of the products it was not clear what formula was used to reduce prices. This uncertainty casts considerable doubt on the credibility of the price revision process.

A total of 328 new products were launched after the April 1990 price reductions. Koseisho revised the prices of 50 percent of these products by indexing. This is an improvement over the 68 percent number we recorded in the 1990 survey. Indexing is arbitrary, and arbitrary price reductions neither encourage innovation nor encourage companies to maintain their prices within the R-zone.

Finally, company price reductions and product price reductions by the R-zone formula were either larger or smaller than estimated in 54 percent and 51 percent of the cases respectively. In 1990 the comparative percentages were 69 percent and 52 percent. This is a sign of improvement, but one would expect a much higher response rate in the "close to estimate" column if the process was well understood by all participants.

The final questions in the survey attempted to probe reasons for variances between actual price revisions and company estimates. Koseisho surveyed market prices in June 1991 and conducted interim surveys. Most companies believe variances occurred because Koseisho:

1. "Grouped" their products with others in the same class.
2. "Leveled up" prices by administrative judgement.
3. Adjusted their product prices to others which have a different brand name but the same active ingredient.
4. Adjusted their products to others listed in the tariff at or around the same time.

A total of 35 companies indicated "grouping" was the primary reason for variances. This was fewer than in 1990, but indicates Koseisho continues to reduce prices by factors other than actual market prices. These responses lend credence to the argument that price reductions are not based upon objective criteria.

Qualitative comments confirmed that the R-zone formula and weighted average calculations were a significant improvement over past practices. Constructively, many asked Koseisho to:

1. Reveal more details of their market price data.
2. Spend more time with each company (now 10 minutes) to resolve variances.
3. Rely on market data for the price revision rather than administrative, subjective procedures.

In conclusion, it is clear that many significant improvements have been made in the price revision process since the early 1980s. Nevertheless, downward revision of drug prices is an international anomaly, so at the very least it must be credible. Koseisho must give a clearer justification for this policy and improve the transparency of the process.

Pharma Japan 1304, May 25, 1992 & June 1, 1992

The Rites of Price Revisions

There is a special spot in heaven reserved for pharmaceutical executives who must cope with government-mandated, downward price revisions. To paraphrase an old Southern U.S. spiritual song, "Nobody Knows the Trouble They've Seen."

Consider the following scenario: a hospital is reimbursed 100 for drug X, and buys it for 80, yielding income of 20. After a 10 percent reduction in the reimbursement price, the hospital gets 90, but still needs an income of 20, so it wants to buy at 70.

	Current	After Revision
Reimbursement	100	90
Hospital Cost	80	70
Income	20	20

Manufacturer A makes a brave decision not to lower the selling price of drug X. Thus cuts the hospital income in half. It does not take a rocket scientist to predict the hospital will look for another drug.

Manufacturer B decides to maintain the same percentage discount on the reimbursement price, in our example, 20 percent. Thus, the hospital income drops 10 percent, which may or may not be acceptable. This is a tough sell because in the eyes of the customer the manufacturer has raised its price.

Manufacturer C went to Harvard Business School and learned the key to success is to satisfy a customer. Therefore, he decides the hospital should not lose income. To do so he must lower the hospital purchase price by 12.5 percent.

All of the above scenarios work in a "free" market where buyers and sellers are seeking to optimize value. For example, customers might be willing to pay more for a camera with a built-in automatic focus.

Unfortunately, pharmaceutical manufacturers do not operate in a free market—for two reasons.

First, unlike the camera maker, any change in the drug product is subject to strict regulatory procedures which require time and money. So what you say, it took Minolta time and money to develop an auto-focus lens. Yes, but Minolta can set a new, higher price in a free market that reflects a customer benefit, i.e., I will pay more because I get more.

Consider a drug that lowers high blood pressure. It is taken orally three times per day, is effective and safe. The reimbursement price is fixed at 100. Through pharmaceutical development, the same drug in a different form can be administered once per day. It is equally safe and effective. However, development took four years and the reimbursement price of the original drug was reduced two times. Since higher prices are not granted to a once-a-day copy, the improved version must be sold at a lower price than the original at the time of its launch.

Thus, regulated prices discourage innovations that provide customer benefits and enhance compliance to dosage regimens. Development lead times are lengthened, e.g., don't launch a camera until you develop an auto-focus lens.

Second, prices are regulated downward to refect market prices. So what you say, I pay less now for a camera than I paid four years ago.

Yes, but drug reimbursement prices are fixed and routinely reduced. In the example of Manufacturer C the customer was satisfied because the actual market price dropped from 80 to 70, but the discount went up from 20 percent to 22.2 percent. A higher discount will result in another downward price revision. To avoid this, the manufacturers must keep the discount fixed, as "B" did; then the customer is unhappy.

Now you know why there is a special place in heaven reserved for pharmaceutical executives. I need not tell you where the regulators will go.

Pharma Japan 1292, February 1992

Good Thing Japan Does Not Imitate

Visitors to these shores often cry out in frustration, "Why can't the Japanese be more like us?"

Etched in my memory is a classic example. It happened when I lived in Kobe and was responsible for the Eli Lilly operations. One of our Japanese employees invited a visiting executive to his home for dinner—a rare honor. He arrived at the small apartment on time, eager to be on his best behavior. After a drink and sensing dinner was about to be served, he asked to use the bathroom. Immediately husband and wife disappeared and left him alone for what became an unbearable length of time. Finally, they reappeared and triumphantly announced his bath was ready.

Needless to say our visitor learned that the bath is a separate function from the toilet.

In the drug industry we can count our blessings that the Japanese have not imitated some of our practices. To name a few:

- Dr Henry Grabowski and others at Duke University and UCLA have studied the availability of new drug introductions to poor patients in nine states in the United States over the period 1979 to 1985. Anyone with experience in Japan will find the results shocking.

In these states, a typical new drug took 20 months after FDA approval to gain acceptance to the Medicaid formulary. New drug introductions were available to poor patients less than 40 percent of the time during their first four years of market life.

In Japan there is rapid diffusion of new drugs after listing in the reimbursement tariff. No prefectural government restricts formulary listings; doctors are free to prescribe any of the 15,000 listed drugs; patients, rich or poor, have equal access to therapy, and are universally insured.

- The FDA required an average of 30.3 months to review the new drugs approved in 1991. Every proposal to expedite review time is met with outrage by citizens' groups who claim the government is sacrificing public safety on the altar of corporate greed. No Washington lawyer publicizes the number of lives lost because effective new drug therapy was delayed by bureaucratic "better safe than sorry" inaction.

In Japan the review time is down to 18 months, and no study has ever shown that Japanese society is at greater risk because of bureaucratic efficiency. There is a cultural bias toward new is better than old. Activists do not picket Koseisho to delay approvals. Diet members do not ask Koseisho officials to endlessly justify their review procedures.

- HMD's, state governments, insurance carriers, and Congressmen promote generics to allegedly save zillions of dollars. Research-based pharmaceutical companies establish new companies staffed by talented people to sell me-too drugs under labels that say "trust us." Old technology sells.

Generics in Japan are approved every other year, new drugs every three months. No government agency encourages doctors to prescribe generics, economic incentives are biased against their use. Old technology doesn't sell.

- Mail order pharmacies are a booming business in the United States. They encourage doctors to prescribe the cheapest therapeutic alternative. Call our 800 number for a six month supply.

Prescriptions in Japan are limited to a maximum 30 days, often two weeks. Patients must see a doctor to obtain a renewal. Yes, the waiting time is long and the consultation time is short, but the doctor looks at and touches the patient, takes a pulse and blood pressure reading, and may order a blood test. Time enough to monitor, calibrate, revise a dosage, and practice preventive medicine.

There are aspects of health care elsewhere that the Japanese would be wise to emulate, but fortunately they are not imitating everything. People need to learn the difference between a toilet and a bath. Bad practices should be flushed.

Pharma Japan 1321, September 28, 1992

Innovative? Clinical Superiority? Who Will Decide?

Koseisho classifies a drug as innovative and it receives priority review, then a premium reimbursement price. The FDA reviews a drug with the same principal molecular features as a previously approved orphan drug, but it is not approved for marketing for the same indication because it did not demonstrate clinical superiority. In each case the agency label can mean the difference between an economic bonanza or losses that include both time and money.

The drug industry is heavily regulated in most countries. Product claims and product prices are preapproved by government ministries. The last bastion of free pricing, the United States, is certain to experience some form of regulated pricing in the near future. It is difficult to imagine the industry will escape an assault on healthcare expenditures which surpassed 14 percent of Gross Domestic Product in 1992. Drugmakers will argue that their products account for only five cents of the healthcare dollar, and that spending on prescription drugs has remained substantially under 1 percent of GNP for the past 25 years. More companies will voluntarily restrain price increases to the overall inflation rate. But they also see the writing on the wall, and are moving to cut costs, set up generic-drug units, sell off low-profit, nondrug operations, and establish marketing alliances to save money and boost efficiency.

Possibly a few people who are half a bubble off plum (two cards short of a full deck), i.e., unrealistic, may argue for deregulation, but most assume regulation is a fact of life. Enlightened regulation should enhance creativity, ensure safety, and rely on market mechanisms to diffuse new technology at prices that are both affordable and rewarding.

I submit Japan's system of regulating price has not dampened enthusiasm for entry into the drug business, nor forced marginal performers out of the business. New products receive a price premium over older products. Since price increases are rare, the only way up the price curve is to launch something new. In other systems where the sole focus is on price suppression or formulary restriction, innovation becomes extinct.

However, the Japanese model coupled with severe price reductions, fostered small step innovation or minor improvements over existing therapeutic modalities. Safety was more important than efficacy. Now, Koseisho is taking a new approach.

Price premiums will not be given to look-alike drugs. Innovative drugs will be given significant premiums and a guaranteed market exclusive for up to 10 years. Orphan drugs, which are innovate by definition, will get priority review (fast track approval), and financial support. These incentives will shift R&D resources away from the "anything new" mentality.

So far so good. But, how will the regulators define "innovative"? A cop-out is to say, "We can't define it, but will know it when we see it." Do you think this is nonsense? Listen to what the FDA recently had to say about clinical superiority. They declined to give examples of it, saying they could be "misleading." The FDA admitted it cannot define clinical superiority "as precisely as some would like, but the agency believes it is a useful concept." They really said that. In this light Koseisho looked good—they suggested Tagamet and EPO were examples of Innovative drugs.

We are entering a new era in which government agencies will determine if a drug is innovative and clinically superior. No other industry is subject to such government intervention. There are many examples of products that were considered oddities in their discovery phase, only later to prove they were innovative and superior. The only real decision makers are users in the market. They ultimately decide what is useful. Koseisho would be wise to create an environment in which their decisions do not preempt consumer choice.

Pharma Japan 1342, March 1, 1993

What Is an "Important" Drug?

Licensing departments keep a data bank of "important" drugs to satisfy their bosses that they made deals on a signifcant number of the candidates. As you might guess, the list is short. Annual reports list drugs in the research/development pipeline. Each drug is reported to be a major advance in therapeutic efficacy that will make major contributions to future earnings. If you add up all the important drugs in annual reports the list gets very long.

Stock analysts classify important drugs as those with $100 million or more in sales. The "blockbuster" label is applied to billion dollar sellers. Regulatory agencies work back from life-threatening or "serious" diseases to classify drugs which are effective against these diseases as important. Some regulators would like to define an important drug as one which shows positive pharmacoeconomics (only a few people can define this word).

Certain sectors of society consider generics important because they are cheap. In Japan important drugs are expensive. In China herbal drugs are important. In certain situations a placebo is important if the patient is told he or she is taking a new, experimental drug. Mind over matter, beauty is in the eye of the beholder. Payers, providers and drug makers all have their own definitions of importance.

This would be a benevolent exercise for dictionary writers if it wasn't for the fact that the act of defining a drug important results in rationing access to health care.

A bureaucratic decision to label a drug important results in fast track approval. Presumably other drugs get on a slow track and are not available to patients for an extended period of time. Formulary committees decide a drug is not important and patients never get it. Japanese clinics decide that any drug discounted less than 30 percent will not be stocked. U.S. mail order pharmacies push cost effective (for the payer, not necessarily the patient) alternatives. In all these cases patients are denied access to therapy and sadly, never realize it.

THE drug for hypertension (pick any disease) has not been discovered nor is it likely to be discovered. My doctor tells me he gets good results with drug A in patient B, but lousy results in patient C, and both patients watch their weight, exercise and all that other good stuff. He doesn't like the prospects for his profession, but each person's hypertension may be unique. Thus, he wants as many different drugs as possible to systematically try each one until he gets the desired response. The present method of diagnosis, i.e., the pressure cuff, does not distinguish between different types of hypertension. It measures the result, not the cause.

If this anecdotal scenario is anywhere near universal truth, formularies, restricted drug lists, cost/benefit analyses, important drug definitions are all a sideshow. Every drug may be an orphan drug. It will not be enough to say a drug works most of the time, rather it should work every time for a specific person. No bureaucrat will be able to tell Mr. Suzuki that he must take the drug that works for Mr. Yamamoto. Suzuki-san will demand the drug that works for him.

A long time ago Henry Ford told the public they could have any color car, as long as it was black. This sounds familiar when we hear: "You can have any NSAID, any calcium antagonist, or any ACE inhibitor as long as it is the one permitted on the formulary." So-called standard cars are history; so-called standard therapy may be the next victim of progress.

Pharma Japan 1377, November 15, 1993

The R&D Paradox

During the 1980s drug prices were savagely reduced—yet more research laboratories were built than in the previous 30 years combined. Major pharmaceutical companies increased R&D spending and R&D expense to sales ratios. Is this another example of everything being backwards in Japan?

Price revisions occur every two years, and the net effect is a downward price spiral. These revisions shorten the economic life cycle of drugs and make it very difficult to establish a stable of cash cows.

Thus R&D spending is discouraged.

On the other hand, new drugs are approved relatively quickly and given higher prices than comparative, older products. Furthermore, new drugs are not restricted and diffusion into the market is rapid.

Thus, R&D spending is encouraged.

Since prices cannot be increased, the only way up the price curve is through a new drug. It will get a comparatively higher price, have a fast take off, but enjoy a relatively short life cycle. The system is cruel on those who fail to innovate.

Thus, R&D management is forced to freshen product portfolios.

So far so good—for the innovators. However, the system forces small-step innovation, or risk-free research. More serious is the R&D focus on a limited number of therapeutic categories where existing drugs enjoy high prices. The system drives innovation toward therapies with high safety profiles and low benefits. I call these drugs marginally beneficial placebos.

One answer to this paradox is under discussion, i.e., give higher prices for unique, innovative drugs, and lower prices for minor modifications of existing drugs. This has theoretical appeal as a way to encourage giant-leap innovation.

Consider this example. A company finds a cure for cedar pollen allergy, a problem that causes millions of Japanese to wear surgical masks on the subway and in their offices. The Health Insurance Bureau lists the drug at a high price relative to existing anti-histamines which only alleviate symptoms of the allergy.

However, the drug is only effective if given intravenously for three days. Since this requires a short stay in the hospital, other costs are incurred. Nevertheless, thousands rush to receive this miracle cure and throw away their face masks.

After two years another company finds a new molecule with the same efficacy, but administration is via a suppository. Six months later another company finds a molecule that can be dosed orally, but must be taken every two hours, or 12 times per day. Six months later another new molecule is discovered that can be taken orally six times per day. New discoveries continue until someone finds a molecule which can be given via a nasal spray packaged as a single dose. One inhalation per year.

Which product is the true innovation, the first or last? Who gets the carrot and who gets the stick? Defining or rewarding innovation via price reimbursement mechanisms is a delicate business. Particularly since prices are set by bureaucrats, not by the market in our regulated system.

I submit the present system rewards innovation. There is no need to fix it. The problem is with a system that penalizes market judgments of usefulness. If doctors find a drug useful they prescribe it more frequently and sales increase. This leads to requests for higher discounts to enhance hospital margins; price reductions follow which artificially reduce demand. This aspect of the system should be fixed.

Pharma Japan 1258, June 17, 1991

Postmarketing Surveillance of Drugs

Anyone who had half his brain matter free of beta amyloid deposits knew that postmarketing surveillance (PMS) reports were useless. Their noble purpose went unrealized. The data was worthless. Everyone knew that case card reports were ersatz sales gimmicks, degrading to the people who filled them out and demeaning to those who offered money to collect them. Fortunately, the Pharmaceutical Affairs Bureau (FAB) under the direction of Mr. Okamitsu is going to cleanse the system on October 1, 1993.

New Koseisho guidelines, known by the hard-to-remember acronym, GPMSP (Good Postmarketing Surveillance Practices), will fundamentally alter investigations carried out during the period of reexamination, which starts immediately after the launch of a new drug. Furthermore, Koseisho is considering a modification of the Pharmaceutical Affairs Law that will extend the reexamination period from its present 6 years to 10 years, and mandate that all drugs, including generics, fall under GPMSP guidelines.

The latter changes are significant for two important reasons. First, while a drug is under reexamination no copy product may be approved for marketing. Thus, regardless of a drug's patent status, it will have 10 years of exclusive marketing. Second, me-too product companies will incur the expense of postmarketing surveillance, eliminating the free ride they enjoyed on the innovators' market experience.

"Postmarketing surveillance" means the gathering of information related to the efficacy and safety of an approved drug, assessing and analyzing that information, deciding on steps to be taken based upon those results, and dissemination of the results to physicians. Several types of investigations are specified by the guidelines, all to be undertaken by those who hold an approval for manufacture or import of drugs, i.e., the "manufacturer."

Manufacturers must establish, prior to October 1, 1993, a PMSMD—you got it, a postmarketing surveillance management department. The kicker is that the PMSMD must be independent of the sales department, and the manufacturer must ensure that the responsible person heading the department "does not suffer any hindrance in the execution of his tasks." Sounds like a great job for a free thinking, independent person.

Each drug investigation must have a separate protocol and the guidelines ensure that the protocol is not a spurious exercise. Medical institutions that are capable of satisfactorily achieving the objectives of the investigation must be requested to do so in writing. Gone are the days when Dr. Sato in a five-bed clinic could have his high school graduate receptionist fill out case report forms. Indeed, postmarketing clinical studies, one form of investigation grossly abused in the past, must be carried out in accordance with Good Clinical Practices (GCP).

To nail down authenticity of the investigations, Koseisho used a rare note of understatement worthy of the British. They said, "The purpose of an investigation should be clearly defined, and each investigation should have its own purpose. Attempts to collect a variety of information in one investigation may end in ambiguous results."

The last but not least article in the guidelines permits a manufacturer to contract out postmarketing surveillance to distributors. Wholesalers, in case you haven't noticed, are performing vital functions that go beyond hauling drugs from point A to point B. Any more questions?

Koseisho has created a win-win situation for every manufacturer who deserves to be in this business. The expense of collecting bogus case card reports will come to an end. Medical representatives should be proud to collect and disseminate truly useful information. Innovators will have an extended lease on product lives. But most important, the patients this industry serves will be given an extra measure of protection. Every efficacious drug has some risks. Assessing that risk objectively will be a solace to those who don't like to be sick.

Pharma Japan 1339, February 8, 1993

Chapter IV

How Japanese Companies Compete

In a short 10-year span Japanese management methods went from worldwide envy to disinterest. Pharma companies who championed the virtues of diversification and vertical integration lost competitiveness in their core drug business. Characterized by too many products and too many people they faced the real possibility of hostile take overs and unfriendly mergers. For the first time relative company performance diversified. Former stalwarts lagged as they failed to cope with new competitive challenges.

How Japanese Companies Compete

Sumo and the Pharmaceutical Industry

There is nothing more indigenous to the sporting world in Japan than sumo. As a national institution it mirrors the mores of society. I thought it would be fun to compare sumo to the pharmaceutical industry, but this will be a tough read if you don't know anything about sumo. If you know the industry you will recognize the similarities.

A strong family tradition exists in sumo. Take the young man (19 years 5 months) who won the January tournament. I remember watching his father perform in the early 1970s, and his uncle was a former grand champion who coincidentally just retired as head of the sumo association. It was a dramatic moment when this older man awarded his last grand prize to his brother's son.

As in many pharmaceutical companies, we are witnesses to a changing of the guard. Younger people are assuming positions of rank. Their techniques are different, faster, and more agile. Their bodies are more muscular. They attract more media attention from a wider cross section of the public.

The sumo association sets a salary scale for all *rikishi* in every ranking. It is not a free market in which individuals negotiate a salary. Ability, not necessarily size, wins matches, but you would never know it when the winner is interviewed on TV. He shuns praise and attributes his success to fellow stable mates, and his stable master. He does not say, "I did it," but says, "We did it."

An aspiring wrestler joins a certain stable and never, never leaves it. He is a member of the group, the team, and that team is his career. There are no free agents.

Sumo is dominated by Japanese nationals although the sport is open to all comers. During the 1970s and early 1980s only one foreigner rose to the top ranks and actually won a tournament. Now three foreigners are serious contenders, and one is on the verge of becoming a grand champion. If he makes it, it will be the first time in the history of the sport.

Sumo is going abroad. Late last year, there was an exhibition tournament in London, and this spring there will be a tour of Germany and Spain. It may be only a matter of time before branch stables are established in foreign countries.

There is a tight, ritual stability to sumo. Winners do not pump their fists in ecstasy. Losers do not pound their fists on the surface in despair. Rather, each bows to the other gracefully before leaving the ring. There are no comebacks for former champions. Their retirement is signified in a ceremony where their knot of hair is cut off one strand at a time, until at last, the stable master severs the hair from the head. It is a moving ceremony that belies assertions that public displays of emotions are suppressed in this society.

Sumo is a study of determination and will. It is rare for a bout to last more than seconds. There are elements of timing, technique, skill, and good luck. There are no weight classes and fans like nothing better than to see a 225 pound wrestler topple a 400 pound behemoth.

Have I taken the inference that if two things are alike in some respects they must be alike in others? You decide, but as I anticipated at the beginning, it was fun making the comparison.

Pharma Japan 1293, March 2, 1992

A Generation Change

I stood in the long line of mourners who had come to pay their final respects to Mr. Nakagawa, Chairman of Meiji Seika. There were at least 1,000 people. Probably all of them knew this man personally. During moments like this, it is time to pause and to reminisce about the leaders of the Japanese pharmaceutical industry.

After World War II there was a scramble in Japan to import technology from Western companies who were entering a great age of discovery. Merck licensed Meiji to produce streptomycin. Mr. Nakagawa worked as a trainee in their Virginia plant to learn the process. He went on to build world class fermentation facilities in Japan.

Mr. Shiono of Shionogi traveled to Indianapolis and forged a relationship with Eli Lilly. He stayed in the private home of a Lilly International Vice President because hotels were not particularly cordial to former enemies.

Under Mr. Shiono's leadership, Shionogi became a powerhouse with the combination of their strong marketing and Lilly products. He took equity positions in wholesalers to control distribution and built manufacturing facilities that had capacity for growth far into the future. Mr. Miyatake of Dainippon was the joint venture king. Through numerous partnerships he secured a product flow for his expanding sales force. Then he turned his attention to building a research capacity to provide in-house products.

My home in Kobe looked down on the Takeda mansion. For six years I watched Mr. Chobei Takeda tend to his bonsai plants and dream of a global business. His energy transformed Takeda from a wholesaler into a fully integrated pharmaceutical company that continues to lead the industry.

All of these men are gone. Others of their vintage are old men. Funerals are so routine it is time to buy a black suit and tie. It sounds grim, but it isn't. These men touched the lives of many people inside and outside their organizations. They were builders with missions and visions. It was my good fortune to know them.

If they had a common fault, it was the size of their shoes that they left for others to fill. They dominated the top position for so long that successors appear bland. Often, sons and relatives are not as capable.

These men built enterprises which dominate the Japanese market today. The next generation of managers must protect this position and establish a presence in the world. This may be a more difficult task. Yet no one should minimize the achievements of the past.

Funerals are a sad reminder of a generation change sweeping the Japanese pharmaceutical industry. Parties at the Okura to celebrate the changing of the guard are happier occasions. We need more of the latter to prepare companies for the 21st Century.

Pharma Japan 1256, June 3, 1991

Design and Execution—the Twain Must Meet

Once again experience has proven to be the best teacher. It happened in Hawaii where I was brought face to face with the reality of fundamental differences between Japan and the United States. At the bottom line it is this: If you want a creative idea or design, go to the United States, but if you want an idea or design executed to detailed perfection, go to Japan. Here is what occurred.

We decided to completely remodel our condominium kitchen in Honolulu last summer when we contracted for a turnkey job, from design to finished product. For $60,000 I expected superior performance and completion before Christmas.

Upon our return in December we opened the door and stood transfixed at the quality of the design. Removal of a wall gave the kitchen a more open, airy feeling. The new cabinets provided a significant increase in storage space. Creative placement of lights eliminated shadows and dark spots. The color coordination between cabinets, counter tops, and the floor was spectacular. In short, it looked beautiful—until we had a closer look.

The floor was smudged with the paste used to install it. There were scratches and bumps on doors. Corners of drop ceilings were not straight, the counter top leaned, etc., etc. In the end, two single spaced pages of defects were noted.

"Not to worry," we were assured, "everything will be fixed, and there is a one year warranty." So it began. The floor people came with a solvent and cleaned up the floor. Crooked places were made straight. Rough places were made smooth. As of this writing the work continues, and I believe the flaws will be corrected, as many were before we left Hawaii.

But why wasn't it done right the first time? Think of the time and money expended to schedule repair work. Think of the opportunity costs as new jobs could not be started or were delayed.

If this article has a misspelled word, you, the reader, will be put off no matter how brilliant the prose. A new car with a scratch on the exterior will offend you, even though it does not affect the performance of the engine. Yes, the dealer can fix a scratch, but the customer is left with an uneasy feeling there may be other defects he cannot see.

I do not think we could get a better designed kitchen in Japan. On the other hand, I am sure the job could be executed right the first time. Herein lays the essence of quality.

A friend imports audio equipment from the United States because of the creative designs and reproduction of sound demanded by audiophiles in Japan. But each shipment must be double-checked for finishing flaws, and often parts are missing. It is a frustrating task because the manufacturer never apologizes or admits to the deficiencies.

Honda has established a design center for new cars in California. Japanese pharmaceutical companies are investing in U.S. biotechnology companies. My dentist's daughter wants to study jewelry design in the United States. Thousands of Japanese are doing post-graduate work in U.S. universities.

Why? Because the United States is unbeatable when it comes to creativity, i.e., new ideas.

But! If you want an idea developed into a "right the first time" finished product, come to Japan. Manufacturers here concentrate on the details that satisfy customers.

Both sides of the Pacific have their strengths. Those who learn to combine them will have an enormous competitive advantage. When the twains meet there will be a level playing field and customers will be the ultimate beneficiaries.

Pharma Japan 1289, February 3, 1992

Sumimasen—But I Can't Resist

Exiting the Hong Kong airport is not an easy task; it is a very crowded place. Picking my way through the crowd, I noticed a Japanese man barging straight ahead, insensitive to others, pushing them aside. Further observation revealed he was inebriated, probably a result of more than one too many drinks on his flight to Hong Kong.

I set my own course to intercept him. As we passed, a well placed block perfected long ago on the gridiron sent him sprawling over a pile of luggage. As he sat stunned but unhurt, there were smiling glances of approval from those he had abused.

This incident comes to mind every time I hear supercilious statements which imply Japanese superiority over other countries, specifically my own. Here are three recent examples and my verbal, abusive response.

"American businessmen are overpaid, short-term thinkers with no clue how to manufacture a quality product or motivate employees."

This presumptuous statement was made by a Japanese president of a U.S. pharmaceutical company in Japan. He neglected to say that for years he had ripped off his U.S. employers for perks not granted to the president of NTT. Nor did he mention that his own employees were abused, and never, no never, could they threaten his shogun-like rule. Fortunately, finally, he was removed and the company is now prospering.

There are over 20,000 Japanese nationals enrolled in U.S. business schools. Many are sent there by elite companies of Japan's business world. Many pay their own way. Executive programs at the Stanford Graduate School of Business are swamped with Japanese applicants. If what we teach businessmen in the United States is so bad, why are so many trying to get in?

American pharmaceutical companies in Japan employ over 15,000 Japanese, and newly hire about 1,500 per year. Not a bad record for "Short-sighted managers." They must be doing something right.

"The U.S. health care system does not provide basic medical care for a significant percent of its population." This statement was made by a Japanese researcher employed by a pharmaceutical laboratory in a rural area outside Tokyo. His conclusion was derived from a recent two-year stay in New York at a prestigious university medical/research center. Of course, the training he received there was unavailable in Japan.

The Japanese I know are not particularly happy with their medical system that keeps people waiting three hours to see a doctor for three minutes. Practically every distinguished clinician in Japan recalls with fond memories his experiences in the United States, including my own doctor who keeps going back for more.

Are the foreign doctors going through Narita here to study Japanese advances in medicine? Those that do pass through are more likely here to teach rather than to learn. I admit New York has problems, but it also has some of the best medical institutions in the world. When the best exists in Japan, upstarts will have the right to bash the U.S. system. Until then, I hope the researcher in rural Japan does not need emergency medical care. He is unlikely to get it.

"Entrepreneurial drug research is carried out inside Japanese companies. We don't need venture businesses; they already exist within the present structure."

This self-serving statement has been made by people who are at a loss to explain the lack of new companies in Japan. It would be much better if these same people boasted about the real strength of Japan. That is, the ability to take an idea from elsewhere and develop it. Hey, this is a great strength.

But give me a break. Research in Japan is risk-averse. Translation—it follows the leaders.

Sumimasen, but I can't resist pushing back on those who are bashing others. It works both ways. Sooner than later we must learn the fastest way through a crowd is to cooperate with those around us.

Pharma Japan 1295, March 16, 1992

Root Bundling Doesn't Always Work

Next to my home in Tokyo's Minato Ward is a baseball field and tennis courts. Two years ago the green area surrounding both was improved. The work entailed moving trees, old and young, big and small. I watched the process of digging around and bundling the roots prior to moving the trees to their new locations. It gave new meaning to the word *nemawashi*.

An admirable strength of Japanese companies is their capacity for involving everyone in the decision making process. Involvement translates into commitment when decisions are implemented. The quality of decisions is enhanced by inputs from those who are closest to the action.

This process of getting everyone on board is known as *nemawashi*. Some companies formalize the procedure through a "ringi" system whereby each department "signs off" on a proposed decision by stamping their seal of approval. Other companies employ a more informal process of having a "champion" of the decision talk personally with all concerned.

It is immediately evident to outside observers that this process is time-consuming. Visitors complain about the lack of decisions, only talk, particularly if they have imminent plane reservations out of here. A recent visitor told me he was being "ringed" to distraction.

Nevertheless, once a decision is made the implementation is carried out with blinding speed. In the United States we are better at identifying problems, but slower in fixing them. Each system has its merits, but as long as we are here, it is best to play by local rules.

Nemawashi is sometimes confused with consensus. The latter word implies decisions are modified to insure complete agreement. It is wrong to assume every decision made in Japan is universally and positively embraced by every faction. There are dissenters, but fortunately dissent is usually expressed in non-violent terms. The best examples are employee strikes carried out during non-working hours.

Nemawashi is also confused with bottom-up decision making, said to be characteristic of Japanese firms. This implies the president has nothing to do except wait for decisions to reach his desk for final approval. It is a myth to believe there are no top-down decisions. Most presidents hold feudal-like power and demand unwavering loyalty from their subordinates.

In the process of preparing a tree for transplanting, not all the roots are saved. Many are severely cut back, but never too far that they cannot sprout again in new soil. All of the roots are cut back equally and bound tightly into a symmetrical ball. Wild growing upper branches are also trimmed, but again, enough is left to support new growth.

It is a meticulous procedure that is carefully carried out with the precision of a surgical operation. Everything is done to save the tree. Think of the similarities to the decision-making process in a Japanese company. Some people are trimmed, but never killed. Everyone is bundled together tightly to preserve the entity. Potential for new growth is preserved.

In spite of all their careful preparations several trees near my home are standing stark naked in their new locations. They died. The fatalities are not correlated with size, or age, or species. Why did one survive and another perish?

I don't know the answer, but there are several lessons one can learn. *Nemawashi* is not 100 percent effective; it can be a dangerous procedure. I guess some decisions are basically bad. Trimming mavericks and bundling everyone together can kill the spirit of an organization. Open dissent often sows the seeds of creativity and growth into unexpected directions. Not everyone makes meaningful contributions to the decision-making process. There are opportunity-costs associated with the time required for an effective *nemawashi*.

Now I am waiting to see what happens next. Will they plant new trees in place of the dead ones? Or are they bundling up other trees in the countryside to move into Tokyo? I will keep watching as there may be further management insights into how Japan deals with failure. No system is perfect, and an ability to cope with mistakes and failures may be more important than living with success.

Pharma Japan 1260, July 1, 1991

Nemawashi That Didn't Work

In a previous article I described a large scale *nemawashi* operation conducted near my home in Tokyo. Many trees had their roots bundled and were moved to different locations as part of a project to beautify the baseball and tennis grounds.

Nemawashi is an integral part of the decision making process in Japanese companies. The word literally means bundling together the roots. In a corporate setting it implies getting everyone on board to implement a decision. It is generally a very effective process, but it can fail, just as it did when one of the trees died after being transplanted. I wondered what would happen to a *nemawashi* failure. This summer I got my answer.

Everyone knows failure is unavoidable in business and in life. There is no known way to avoid setbacks, mistakes, and poor judgement. Since it is going to happen, the real issue is what to do when it does happen.

Tom Peters, author and management guru in the United States, suggests organizations should celebrate failures as important lessons for future action. If people are afraid of making mistakes they will not act. If everyone plays it safe, risks, often with the greatest potential rewards, are avoided. Risk adverse companies do not do well unless they are in the business of selling insurance.

In Japan, groups (a bundle of roots) take the risks and share in the rewards. This is why individual incentive awards are shunned. Bonuses are given to everyone in the group. This may limit individual initiative but there is great strength in numbers.

The U.S. system values individual initiative and by any measure the results have been outstanding. Yet many U.S. companies are learning the value of team efforts. As we emulate the value of *nemawashi*, the Japanese are trying to emulate the value of individual effort. It would appear that both systems have a lot to learn from each other.

I was interested to know what would happen to the *nemawashi* failure in my "back yard." Would the dead tree be taken out and replaced? In company terms, this means the mistake maker gets fired. This summer the dead tree was not removed, it was carved into a monument. Now it looks like a kind of windmill turning a grinding wheel. Only those who knew it was once a stately tree will recognize the remaining base, about 15 feet high. The bark was shipped and the remaining wood varnished to a bright luster.

Tom Peters would understand. The "mistake" has been transformed into a beautiful sculpture. There was a new kind of life born out of failure.

Pharmaceutical research may be the most failure-prone business. Thousands of potential drugs fail in early tests. No one has yet devised a system to ensure that every idea will translate into a safe and effective drug. Nevertheless, failures are instructive and offer important clues as to what will work.

Somewhere in Tokyo there is a team of tree transplanters who have formed an alliance with a team of sculptors. It could be a good business because *nemawashi* is not a risk-free procedure. Sometimes it fails.

Pharma Japan 1272, September 30, 1991

Product Life Cycles

Generalizations help us get through life without using up precious brain capacity. Like tying our shoes or riding a bicycle, once learned we don't have to think about it anymore. But when I attended the Stanford Graduate School of Business a professor left an indelible impression with this statement, "All generalizations are false, including this one."

All Japanese are short. Have you ever been in a hotel when the Japan girls volleyball team walked through the lobby? There are some tall ladies in this country. All Japanese are thin. Park yourself outside a high school at eight o'clock in the morning-you will see a lot of fat kids.

Product life cycles are short in Japan. I do not know the exact definition of short, or shorter than, but a monthly visit to Akihabara will prove the point as far as audio equipment and electronic gadgets are concerned. On the other hand, our neighborhood *tofu* maker has been going strong for two generations. I wish *natto* would go away, but it has held on to the same amount of shelf space in the local "super" for as long as I remember. Vending machine offerings change frequently, but who would have guessed the staying power of a product with a name like Sweat?

What about drugs? In the August 3 and 10 issue of this paper my eye caught a statement by Mr. Okamitsu, Director-General of Koseisho's Pharmaceutical Affairs Bureau. He was commenting on the problems of generic drug manufacturers: "Under their current marketing system the product life cycle comes to an end in two years. We should therefore consider 'stable supply' as the key to discussions on distribution practices.

I do not believe Mr. Okamitsu will evoke sympathy from the research-based pharmaceutical industry for the plight of generic manufacturers. Nevertheless, a two-year life cycle in this business is really short.

There is anecdotal evidence that drug life cycles are short in Japan. It is a rule of thumb that a product goes up the sales curve for two years, stays flat for two years, and then begins an inexorable decline for about five years. After that, the product is no longer of interest to anyone.

This has enormous implications for the launch strategy of every new drug. A company has a two-year window to drive sales up the curve; there is no second chance. Kicking new life into a three-year old product is rarely worth the time and promotion cost.

Combine declines in volume with no way to raise prices and you have a product portfolio scenario that does not include cash cows. The only way up the price curve is to come out with something new, anything new. This drives innovation, but in small steps, or short-term innovation. It is too risky to bet resources on "breakthrough" therapy alternatives. Safer to stay with improvements of existing therapies.

Downward price revisions influence this pattern. Two factors drive market prices down. One is the demand for discounts by dispensers; the other is a willingness by manufacturers to accede to these demands for the sake of volume. Price instability has not been in the best interest of manufacturers, dispensers, or payers. If Mr. Okamitsu's definition of stable supply includes stable prices, he is on the right track

Short product life cycles provoked by regulated price reductions lead to unstable supply. New is often better, but the old maxim, "Don't fix it if it ain't broke" also has a place in this business. I am happy my doctor does not give me a new blood pressure drug every month. The present drug is effective, so I hope its life cycle is long.

That's Business in Japan

A Japanese company director of marketing and sales invited me to lunch in Tokyo. At one o'clock he rushed off to Yamanashi Prefecture for a late afternoon meeting with an important doctor. The next day, Saturday, he was in Kyoto to attend a medical conference. His presence is requested at important meetings with wholesalers the length and breadth of Japan.

A state of perpetual motion would describe this man's daily schedule. Contact with people—face to face contact—is what oils the business machine in Japan. Think about these examples:

- Desks in offices are set next to each other rather than separated by walls or modern dividers. I know that the price of space dictates cramming as many people into the least possible space. But, when you are elbow to elbow everyone knows what is going on. No need for voice mail here, everyone in the group is instantly available. The department head, sitting with his back to the window, can track every move of his subordinates.
- Medical representatives all have a desk in an office. I know that the average Japanese home would not accommodate a dining-room table, let alone an office. But, when you start and end the day surrounded by your colleagues there is a kindred spirit which is motivating. Not to mention the sharing of information about what works with which doctors. A rep's life can be lonely lined up behind five other reps to see the same doctor.
- Price negotiations and clinical protocol discussions with Koseisho officials are carried out within earshot of five other people. I know that privacy is a rare commodity in Japan. Why else are there so many love hotels? But, when more than one person is "wired in," secret deals are kept to a minimum. It keeps the system honest without the need for a Freedom of Information Act.
- Territories of medical representatives are restricted because doctors are seen so frequently. I know that many of these visits cover subjects totally unrelated to drugs. But, reps get to know their doctors. Boy, do they get to know them, including their sons and daughters, friends and patients. A six-week doctor call schedule is akin to meeting strangers rather than important customers. In the old days I met Shionogi reps who knew a surgeons' operating schedule by the hour, patient, and procedure—every day.
- Meetings always include a room full of people, most of whom never say a word. I know the productivity index is low. But, no one is sitting outside speculating what is going on inside. A group picture in Merck's 1992 annual report

shows 30 "senior executives," all in dark blue suits with red ties or scarfs. The caption says they "coordinate and integrate Company activities." In the first row are seven executives of the Chairman's Staff who "deal with strategic issues." I presume they meet in a small room. In Japan, coordination, implementation and strategy are not so neatly set apart. Planners are implementors.

- I never meet Japanese men who work at home. I know about space limitations, etc. But, business in Japan is not conducted via fax, letters, or phone. Those devices are for sending maps or arranging meetings. Real business is a face to face affair. I know it keeps the Shinkansen cars full, and airplanes fully booked at outrageous prices. But, belly to belly, eye to eye, a deal is not a promise, it is a commitment.

That's business in Japan. Access to and success in this market will never result from setting numerical targets around a negotiating table behind close doors. It results from one-on-one, non-stop, muscle aching, stomach churning, liver abusing discussions. And yet, this country has the longest life expectancy in the world. Amazing. The only explanation must be high per capita drug consumption. I must run and talk face to face with my Koseisho friends about this.

Not My Idea—But Worth Repeating

Summer is a good time to catch up on a reading list, a time to get out of the trees and take a good look at the forest. In early July I retreated to the rolling hills of the Appalachian Mountains in eastern Pennsylvania where we have a small cabin on a lake. There was no newspaper fax, TV, or telephone—just books and periodicals that were put aside in the Tokyo rush and hassle.

An author worth repeating is Jeremiah Sullivan, Associate Professor of International Business at the University of Washington School of Business. I read his analysis of Japanese management philosophies which will be included in his upcoming book, *The Japanese Business Presence in America: Myth and Reality*. He did not study the Japanese pharmaceutical industry, but I saw a lot of stuff that is relevant.

Professor Sullivan is convinced that, ". . . while trust-building and cooperating with public officials play a part, the real essence of Japanese managing is the use of power in service to society." I will elaborate on this later, but just listen to what Sullivan says is the "sheer nuttiness" or myths abut Japanese management.

- A Japanese who prefaces his remarks by saying, "We Japanese . . . " is asking you to accept what he has done or will do as a culture-bound act emerging out of the essence of Japaneseness. To argue against it would be like arguing with the wind or the rain. The Japanese will be delighted if the American falls for this line of reasoning, but he probably does not expect him to."

I laughed when reading this because it brought back memories of a dinner with the number two man of a family-controlled Japanese pharmaceutical company. Every time he said, "We Japanese . . . " I secretly put match stick in my pocket. At the end of our dinner, the entire box of matches was in my pocket.

- The samurai-like loyalty which Japanese employees supposedly exhibit isn't so. In a study of several thousand workers in the United States and Japan, researchers found that Americans exhibited more loyalty to their employers than Japanese did. What looks like loyalty in Japan is often really submission to inevitable and not easily assailed managerial power.
- On average Japanese put in 225 more hours a year in the workplace and are substantially less productive than Americans.

Sullivan cites many examples to prove that managing in Japan "turns out to be the exercise of power to control the workplace so that society's needs can be served. American managers maximize profits, Japanese maximize order."

This conclusion caused me to reminisce about the many visits I have made to Japanese pharmaceutical research laboratories. Everyone wears a uniform, and a rigid daily schedule is followed. More attention is given to maintain order than on fostering or nurturing creativity, i.e., discovering something. There are many petty rules whose real function is to put employees in their place.

Sullivan claims his research shows that both American and Japanese firms tolerated failure for the same amount of time. "An executive will be allowed about four years in which he fails to achieve 25 percent of his goals. After that he is plateaued. He can fail to achieve 50 percent of his goals for three years. With 75 percent failure he will last only two years." However, the Japanese did differ from Americans in their strong efforts to learn from small failures.

When you combine a theory of work as meaningful living which primes employees for group activity, as does the belief that the company has a legitimate social mission, with a regime of powerful managers who demand that employees participate and do not worry about little mistakes, you get team spirit. But this is not something unique to Japan, nor do Japanese abandon their human identity and submerge it in the team.

I was left with the feeling that the reality of Japanese management practices is not strange to most Americans. It is "foreign" if you view work only as something to be done to acquire leisure; or if executives view the company as a wealth-generating machine for its shareholders; or if employees are treated as cogs in a wheel that can be easily hired or fired.

Those of us associated with the pharmaceutical industry need not shrink from a definition of managing as the use of power in service to society. Clever managing is not a unique Japanese phenomenon.

Pharma Japan 1315, August 1992

What Japanese Companies Need

I have a problem finding time to write this piece because my family is busy trying to figure out how to spend ¥60,000 in coupons we received from the government. We were entitled to this amount because we have three children under the age of 15, and each is worth ¥20,000. This is serious work because the government expects us to jump start the economy by shopping.

We pore over a book listing all the shops that will honor our coupons within the boundaries of Minato-ku. The pressure is on to spend before the June deadline. The Hotel Okura is on the list, also my barber shop and National Azabu supermarket. So many choices—so little time.

I mention this because Japanese pharmaceutical companies, like this government, need a reality check. Neither we, nor our coupon recipient friends believe for one minute it will prompt us to spend more. In fact, the administrative costs alone are a waste of money. Likewise, the industry demonstrates a proclivity to spend money on non-productive projects.

For example, the Return on Equity (ROE) of nine major Japanese pharma companies in 1997 was 7.1 percent. For five medium-sized companies the ROE was 8.8 percent. In the same year, the ROE for seven U.S. majors was 36 percent. It may surprise you to know the operating profit margin of the U.S. seven was 25.1 percent while the Japan medium-five was 25 percent, and the Japan major nine was 14.9 percent. So, the ROE gap is not due to differences at the operating profit level.

Rather, the low ROE is due to cash lying around in low-interest-bearing financial assets, a management strategy akin to stashing cash under the mattress.

Another area ripe for a reality check is the astronomically high SG&A expense to sales ratio of Japanese manufacturers. At about 31 percent, SG&A is loaded with vague expenses that could be cut without diminishing core capabilities. They are not cut because management abhors unpopular decisions. Or is it because they do not want to look too profitable?

As you read the financial results for FY1998, note where losses are recorded. You will see securities appraisal losses and losses in affiliates that have nothing to do with the drug business. Who gives these guys a license to invest money, big money, in schemes unrelated to the human health mission they proudly proclaim in glossy annual reports?

There are two needs at stake here. One is corporate governance, the other is focus.

Who Owns This Company?

Too many senior managers in this industry act as if they were running a family business and they owned a majority of the shares. Their Boards are bloated with insiders who pay homage to the feudal chief. Dissent, or even productive debate, is rarely heard. Thus, the best way to get along is to go along. The future is an extension of the past, stifling creativity and rewarding allegiance. For example, Sankyo has 26 directors and their average age is 66. A college graduate joining this company can look forward to 45 years of laboring in the trenches before he is eligible to become a director. Although 29 percent of Sankyo's shares are owned by foreigners, the prospect of a foreign director is nil.

Focus

Scratch the surface of a typical pharmaceutical company, and you will find a whole lot going on besides human drugs. There are agricultural chemicals, foods, diagnostics, nutritional supplements, OTC's, medical devices, cosmetics, vitamins, real estate, golf club memberships, etc., etc., etc. Digging into a financial statement is like peeling an onion: you never get to the core and cry a lot in the process.

How many different drugs are MRs asked to promote? I do not know the answer, but we do know what manufacturers ask wholesalers to push, and it is an incredible array of products that defy reasonable support within the time available. Targeting specific doctors for promotion is not a well developed science.

Managing Change

Change is a constant in the history of this industry and the Japanese have shown a remarkable ability to adapt to new realities, from the jolt of devastation in the 1940s, to liberalization in the 1970s. But the pace of change is accelerating and the Japan market alone will not sustain growth.

So-called globalization is not a process of establishing liaison offices abroad or licensing out products. It is about accessing innovation from venture businesses; it is adopting global standards; it is focusing on core competencies and managing financial resources to achieve adequate returns on capital employed in the business.

Unfortunately, in many companies change is not a threat because they are sitting on a pile of cash. This head in the sand attitude is obvious from a quote by an executive of a large firm, "Of course I am nervous about the future. However, I need to consider things carefully for another five years. I don't think our company should change just because those around us have."

Incredible that anyone is this industry honestly believes they can sit around for five years and think about change rather than acting to implement self-reform. From 1992 to 1997 the average annual growth of the drug market was 1.4 percent. During the same period of five years, the domestic annual sales growth of Japan's top 15 companies averaged 1.4 percent. In other words, they stood still, they stagnated.

The Japanese pharmaceutical industry does not lack quality people in responsible positions. What is lacking is a sense of crisis, or at least a wake up call to realize the market is changing. Growth is not automatic and regulatory protection is gone. Action after the cash box is empty is too late. As the president of Takeda said, "If you leave things to the last minute, blood will be spilt and people will be hurt."

Pharma Japan 1653, June 1999

Vertical Integration—Foresight or Folly?

The in-house newsletter of Merck & Co. described its merger with Merck Containment Services as ". . . a bold strategic move to create America's first co-ordinated pharmaceutical care company." Ads run by Merck in the *Wall Street Journal*, *The New York Times* and other newspapers across the United States proclaimed, "Merck and Medco will provide the most appropriate and cost-effective medicines—whether they are patented, generic or non-prescription—regardless of which company makes them. The result will be improved quality of life, lower drug therapy costs, and real savings for the health care system. That's why we believe Coordinated Pharmaceutical Care is the right medicine for America."

We can expect a certain amount of hype with every acquisition/merger to justify multibuck bets of corporate resources—it's part of the game to create value for the players. Is this reminiscent of another time when pharmaceutical companies were buying into cosmetic companies? The argument then was the application of science to skin care. A coordinated approach to a healthy body—inside and out.

Today, cosmetic labels and package inserts read like a dermatology textbook, but pharmaceutical people are not writing them. The dealmakers who were paid to acquire cosmetic companies were paid to divest them. Then there were forays into environmental health and health foods. For some in this part of the world, herbal medicines looked like a good bet—convert the Chinese art of medicine into a science. Oh yes, I almost forgot medical devices, a natural integration for coordinated pharmaceutical care. Companies who made these acquisitions spend more time fighting law suits than introducing new products.

Integration into the OTC market is touted as an attractive extension of product life cycles, and once again we hear the old refrain of providing "cost effective" medicines. Of course, generics should be mentioned as the ultimate answer for cost-conscious buyers. Sensing the feeding frenzy, Wall Street has bid up stock prices of generic companies to unbelievable highs, while solid research-based stocks languish at 12 month lows.

In Japan's past, vertical integration strategies resulted in equity purchases of wholesalers by manufacturers. As a result, four companies had a lock on distribution through the undivided attention of partner/wholesalers who were assured exclusive marketing in their territories. The result was a powerful competitive advantage, but times change and so do the dynamics of competition. Broad line wholesalers, not dependent on a single manufacturer, are now the winners.

There is talk in Japan about manufacturers selling direct to pharmacies and dispensing doctors, thus bypassing wholesalers. Might the next logical step be direct sales to patients? Why not follow the lead of Merck/Medco or Schering AG's U.S. subsidiary Berlex, who is reportedly planning to sell Betaseron directly to patients through a managed care network administrated by PCS Health Systems? Nothing is impossible.

But wait one minute. Many fine pharmaceutical companies trace their roots to a pharmacy, or as wholesalers before they focused their resources on research to discover rather than distribute new products. They gave up integration because the mentality or culture of a research-driven firm is different than a dispenser of drugs.

Cosmetic companies sell image first, science second. Food salesmen sell nutrition. Chinese medicine makers sell 4,000 years of history. Device companies sell engineering; OTC salesmen sell a quick fix without waiting to see a doctor; generic hucksters sell price period.

Could it be that the emergence of small, research intensive, innovative firms in the U.S. biotechnology industry is a result of the big boys losing their focus on what made them big in the first place? There is a story worth quoting in Merck's history book, "Values and Visions, A Merck Century." In 1897, Merck & Co (at that time a manufacturer of fine chemicals) opened its own stylish pharmacy in downtown Manhattan. George Merck, the founder of Merck & Co in 1891, "found himself at loggerheads with his own best customers, the German druggists of New York and vicinity. It ended two years later when George bowed to the demands of his customers and closed his elegant pharmacy."

Research-based pharmaceutical companies in the United States and Japan might be wise to reread their own history, or as the saying goes—they are doomed to repeat it.

Pharma Japan 1369, September 20, 1993

Restructuring to Do What?

U.S. drug companies are going through a frenzy of restructuring, in my book a euphemism for layoffs. The costs are reported in the Wall Street Journal, that is, the charges against earnings. Who is recording the human costs of broken careers? What do kids tell their friends, "My father was restructured out of a job?" How do you cope with waking up on your 50th birthday and realizing you are now too old?

One leading company labelled their actions as "The New Reality." Others say they are becoming "lean and mean." Management gurus, safely ensconced behind lifetime tenure, advocate "cutting the fat." CEO's, backed by a hand-picked docile board of directors, pompously declare they are restoring competitiveness to the firm. Men with "slash and burn" reputations become corporate heroes. Young men are elevated in rank without ever having had responsibility for anything, but press releases laud their "meteoric" rise in the company. National sales responsibility is given to people who never "carried a bag."

Hey, I try not to be like the kettle who called the pot black. Long ago a wise man gave me a small stone to carry in my pocket to remind me of the bible adage, "Let him without sin cast the first stone."

I own a company in Hawaii called Galaxy Business Products. It sells office supplies to small businesses throughout Oahu. In 1991 we had 36 people, now we have 17. The recession is a factor, but the main reason for the cutback was bad local management. At first I was happy with what I thought were decisive, tough actions to cut expenses, and our expenses are primarily related to people (aren't everybody's?). Then I realized we were laying off people but not questioning our mission.

Just a few years ago drug company executives were adding sales people in quantum leaps. Now we hear talk like, "Ten sales people can cover 60 percent of our sales through centralized buying groups." Corporate planning, business development and licensing departments staffed up. Now they are the first to be tapped on the shoulder and told, "We expect you will find our early retirement program a deal you cannot refuse."

We all read about cutting expenses to be more competitive. It would be nice to read about a change in mission to justify less people. For example:

"Mr. CEO of XYZ pharmaceutical company announced today that 30 people in the corporate planning department were laid off (nicely, of course). Mr. CEO hastened to add that the company would not stop planning, but would allow people who run the business to plan the business. He regrets the decision to hire people to plan the business although they never had any responsibility for running a business."

There seems to be a common thread in many early retirement programs. The company announces the program and expects to reduce personnel by 1,000 people. Surprise, surprise, 2,000 people say thank you—tah, tah. My guess is that the really good people see the writing on the wall and take the money and run.

Reducing head count may be realistic. Youthful enthusiasm and vigor are always welcome. But some hard questions need to be answered about mission before personnel departments are turned loose with their "boy do I have a deal for you" schemes; before "fire them" artists hand out pink slips; before "fortyish" people are given the helm although they have no idea how to build a ship.

Note: The author enjoys business in Japan because at 55 he is considered young. Age, like most things, is relative.

Pharma Japan 1368, September 13, 1993

Don't Write off the Pharmaceutical Industry

Japanese critics of U.S. companies' competitiveness in Japan have deliberately overlooked the performance of U.S. pharmaceutical companies. A few of the standard criticisms can be blasted away by actual facts:

1. "No long term commitment." Most U.S. drug firms have been in Japan for over 20 years and a significant number will celebrate 40 years before the year 2000.
2. "Do not appreciate Japan is 'open.'" Since liberalization in the mid 1970s, U.S. companies have taken decisive but deliberate actions to establish a majority-owned presence in Japan. Joint ventures have been dissolved with ownership shifting to the U.S. side.
3. "Do not make products suitable for the Japanese market." U.S. pharmaceutical research is on the leading edge of medical technology, and clearly dominates the fields of biotechnology. U.S.-origin products are the leaders in many therapeutic categories.
4. "Unacceptable quality." In the pharmaceutical business quality is a matter of life or death. Companies of all nationalities have rigid quality control standards.
5. "Think short term." A new drug requires 10 years to go from discovery to marketing. Long-term thinking is a must.

No doubt we could make a similar case for European companies in Japan. The market share of foreign origin products is on an upward trend. Aggressive move have positioned many foreign companies as major players in the market. They can not be labeled as outsiders as they are more inside than many Japanese companies.

Major Japanese drug companies continue their slow inexorable push into overseas markets. The latest annual reports from Yamanouchi and Daiichi are very slick presentations. I can remember when there were no English annual reports, just a few typed pages on plain paper. But it is the content that is impressive. Page after page highlights their activities in foreign countries.

In the early 1980s there were dire predictions that government mandated price reductions would put the research based pharmaceutical industry of business. Those short-sighted analysts forgot that the Japanese do not kill innovation; they nurture it, improve on it, and reward it.

Now other parts of the world appear to be insane. U.S. government officials bash the industry, stock market valuations tumble, and generics are promoted as the best thing since sliced bread. German authorities cause sales to drop like a punctured balloon. Italian drug executives are incarcerated. India fights for the god-given right to copy discoveries made elsewhere.

Beneath all this smoke burns the hot fire of unfettered research that will cure, not just treat, diseases of our fragile mind and body. It is a good bet that a pharmaceutical company will find a way to arrest the horrible consequences of multiple sclerosis, AIDS, Alzheimer's disease and genetic mistakes that put a newborn baby behind the eight ball before it can enjoy the wonder of life.

My first district manager told me his goal in life was to live until 90, then be shot by a jealous husband. Who doesn't pray for good health? And in this century more people have it because of well-managed industrial enterprises that organize research to wipe out diseases and enhance the quality of life.

I remember my mother when she had a severe case of poison ivy that came from clearing, then burning the overgrowth of it in our back yard. The doctor came to our house with his black bag, and as best as I remember he gave her a shot of morphine for the pain. There was no relief for the swelling and oozing of the vesicles that covered her body. So my father said it was time to go and see a woman in the valley who did "pow-wow." Mind you this was in Pennsylvania, not Africa.

No one will ever take the art out of the science of medicine. Compassion has amazing restoration powers. Faith can heal a broken mind. But put your money on the brains and talent that exist in Japanese, U.S. and European drug companies. They don't do pow-wow. The know how to make a zillion tablets with the right amount of stuff each time, every time. They know how to communicate benefits and risks to their customers.

Don't write off the research-based drug industry. It has never, and I mean never had so many opportunities to succeed, and never have there been so many good people translating theory into reality

Pharma Japan 1367, September 1993

Future Scenarios for Japan's Pharmaceutical Industry

No person knows for certain what the Japanese Pharmaceutical industry mission and structure will be in the future. However, as one who lives and works in Japan, I believe there is a reasonable consensus within the ranks of Japanese executives on what must happen in some respects to ensure the continued vitality and competitiveness of their companies.

Discovery Research

Japanese research management must accomplish two missions. First, it must shift discovery research from minor modifications of established drugs, or Improved Chemical Entities (ICEs), to the discovery of entirely new molecules, Unique Chemical Entities (UCEs), that cure diseases rather than alleviate symptoms of disease. Also, given the rapid aging of Japanese society, the focus will be on the leading causes of death, i.e., malignant neoplasms, heart disease, cardiovascular disease, and diabetes. As the top categories of prescription drugs no longer include antibiotics, a therapeutic class that spawned innumerable ICEs, it suggests the change of focus is well underway.

The second mission is to enter a new world of drug discovery based upon what we have come to label as biotechnology. The old techniques of screening substances derived from synthetic chemistry or natural sources is rapidly being supplanted by rational drug design and molecular modeling based upon the isolation of specific receptors on or inside the living cell.

These new techniques of drug discovery appear to be best understood by young new companies and by young researchers. Big pharma in Europe and the United States is trying to catch up with these developments by forming alliances with small, venture type companies, generally centered in the United States. It is surprising how quickly a significant proportion of their research budgets were allocated to "outside" research versus "in-house" research. Japanese deals, while highly publicized in the trade press, are not a significant percent of the total at the present time.

This restructuring that must occur in Japan will not be easy. A Japanese friend who heads the research laboratories of a major company provided a comparative analysis of biotechnology enterprises and attitudes between the United States and Japan which succinctly suggest why. See Table 1.

The point emphasized was that young researchers in Japan are not empowered to create and innovate. Rather, they are required to carry the bags of their superiors throughout their most creative years. That is, they must fit into bureaucratic groups instead of demonstrating individualistic achievements.

Development

Product development, both preclinical and clinical, must now be conducted to satisfy regulatory requirements on a global basis. The challenge is therefore, to staff regulatory affairs departments with people who are as familiar with foreign regulatory agencies as they are with those of the Ministry of Health and Welfare in Japan. Furthermore, issues beyond demonstrating safety and efficiency must be integrated into the development process. These include product liability, informed consent, quality of life, and pharmacoeconomics. Clinical studies in Japan have been focused on gathering proof for high reimbursement prices, and premarketing in as many medical facilities as possible, both of which often compromised the quality of data.

Marketing

The marketing mission must be reengineered away from "human wave" tactics and a total reliance on personal relationships to strategies that selectively target specific doctors to transmit value added information. The focus was on quantity, i.e., the number of medical representatives, the number of calls; it must shift to quality, i.e., the quality of the representative and the quality of information.

The medical representative is no longer a purveyor of price information and wholesalers are more independent than in the past. Coverage of doctors, particularly in the launch phase of a new drug, will require flexible allocation of costly in-house marketing resources, consolidation of distribution channels, and utilization of newly emerging contract promotion services

Internationalization

A competitive international presence is now a strategic necessity. Japanese executives do not believe the current wave of mergers abroad will diminish their opportunities for international expansion. Nor do they appear interested in playing an acquisition game to acquire presence. Rather, they have faith in their ability to discover UCEs that will offer windows of opportunity to penetrate foreign markets.

Corporate Culture

The pharmaceutical executives I talk with believe they will experience fundamental changes in business practices. The shocks of 1995 in Japan, both natural and man made have already sensitized the participants to expect change. They know that corporate cultures wedded to the past will not be a competitive threat.

As this analysis implies, Japanese business practices such as lifetime employment, seniority based promotion, and allocating all work to full time employees are being replaced by more flexible policies designed to enhance productivity and creativity in the work place. These changes will make the Japanese industry more competitive at home and abroad. But they also enhance the opportunities for foreign firms who wish to expand their presence in Japan.

Table 1   Comparative Analysis of Biotechnology Enterprises and Attitudes between the United States and Japan

	United States	Japan
Academia		
National and private	Both strong	Only national is strong
Government control	Weak	Strong
Scientist mobility		
Between universities	High	Low
Between univ. & co.	High	Low
Scientific entrepreneurship	Positive	Not allowed
Industry		
Scientist mobility	High	Very low
Scientist advancement	Not age related	Age related
Society		
Venture capital	Available	Unavailable
People	Appreciate small companies	Suspect small companies

Market Letter, June 1995

Chapter V

The Modified Role of Sales and Marketing

Medical representatives (MRs) employed by drug companies communicate the benefits and risks of their products more effectively than any other known method. Their role changed during the 1990s as doctors stopped dispensing drugs and began to demand useful information to go with a smiling face. Training programs were enhanced and alternative organizational structures were introduced. It was not enough to have more MRs calling on more doctors. As drug margins narrowed, productivity became an issue.

Marketing vs. Sales—the Unending Story

I was transferred to Japan in 1970 with the illustrious title, Director of Marketing. Although destined to live and work in Kobe, I spent the first month in Tokyo attending a Berlitz Total Immersion program in Japanese. After progressing beyond "Kore wa pen desu," I was eager to learn how to introduce my title to Japanese businessmen.

The word "director" was a challenge—it could be *bu-cho*, *honbucho*, *jomu*, or *senmu*, depending on my position in the company hierarchy. This was understandable, but I was not prepared for the shock of no Japanese translation for the word "marketing." My teacher sadly informed me that the concept of marketing did not exist in Japan.

In a country where the name card is a passport for one's identity, one's status in society—I was to be a nonentity, Director of Nothing. No power, no prestige, no mandate to operate. Prior to leaving the United States, my company believed exactly the opposite.

The above flashback occurred to me recently as I sat at a conference room table in the offices of a foreign pharmaceutical company in Osaka. In front of me were the name cards of three bright young men who were on the other side of the table. Each was a product manager in the marketing department. I apologized for not being able to read the Japanese on the reverse side of the card after 25 years in this country, an inexcusable lapse of adaptation due to intellectual laziness. I asked what Japanese word was used for marketing. The prompt reply was "marketing," written in katakana, the phonetic approach to foreign words that have no Japanese equivalent, like my name, Maurer.

I suggested to them that in 25 years nothing had changed. Marketing is here (using my left hand extended far to the left), and sales are there (using my right hand extended to the right), both are disconnected inside and outside the corporation. Their embarrassed laughter confirmed my assumption.

Ask a sales manager the function of the marketing department and he is likely to reply, "They prepare reports for the home office and make presentations to visitors." Ask about marketing people and the reply is, "They like to crunch numbers and study English." An interview quote defines the issue succinctly: "I don't think that there is anyone in the company who can clearly define the function and role of strategic marketing or understand its importance."

My interest in this subject goes beyond gathering information to write an article for this paper. Answers could determine the fate of our new business venture, Nippon Pharma Promotion (NPP). For those who haven't heard, we are offering a service of contract promotion directed to doctors practicing in small hospitals and clinics. In essence, we leverage the access of our wholesaler/shareholders' Marketing Specialists (MS)—who visit 90 percent of these doctors every other day. Doctors not visited by your (MRs)—to promote and sell the clients' pharmaceutical products.

Our success to date has come from linking initiatives considered "marketing activities" directly to the activities of MS. This relationship is woefully lacking in most pharmaceutical companies who are married to the concept of human relationship selling and maintaining large numbers of MRs.

Marketing departments, in most cases, simply act as a supportive arm of the sales division. Marketing people tend not to be involved in true "marketing tasks."

Consider two examples:

Selecting Target Customers

Ask the question, "What does a doctor prescribe/dispense?" or "How much does a doctor prescribe/dispense?" and you will get an answer to within three decimal points. This is a "hardware" type question Japanese excel in answering, and you can measure usage more accurately in Japan than in any other country. Data is readily available, and computers facilitate the process of presenting it in unlimited formats in living color.

But ask the "software" question, "Why does a doctor prescribe/dispense a particular drug?" and the typical answer is a shrug—"Every doctor has his or her own reason."

Thus, marketing departments produce data with little or no interpretation. They engage in hardware activities like preparing product catalogues, distributing clinical information, and planning advertisements brochures that the average doctor does not have time to read.

The answers to "why" type questions facilitate targeting of the message and the doctor. In NPP programs we ask manufacturers to train MS on a single three-minute message, which will be delivered to a pre-selected audience of target doctors. What drug benefit is important to a doctor? In our experience it is one tenth the information clients believe doctors need to know.

Sales managers tend to be internally focused, with only 5–10 percent of their time spent in the field meeting and talking with doctors. Most of their time is spent in the office coping with administrative tasks, keeping morale up and providing "human leadership." "Managing" is defined as "monitoring," usually the number of calls made by MRs under their control. A Japanese sales executive told me proudly his company MRs call on 20 doctors per day. Hardware success comes via the number of calls. The quality (software) of a call is not important, measured, or rewarded.

Incentives/Rebates (to wholesalers)

Marketing should, but rarely does, have any influence on incentive programs for wholesalers. As a result, human relationships between sales managers and wholesalers dictate the outcome. The end result is no correlation between sales and incentives. Sales increase to achieve a target number, then a correction occurs during ensuing months, only to be repeated during the next campaign.

Foreign companies succumb to this routine on a quarterly basis with particular emphasis on the fourth quarter. Japanese companies are inclined to play the same game at the end of their fiscal year, but are particularly enamored with the process when launching a new drug.

In NPP we measure success by adoption of a product for particular indications or patients. Once adopted, usage is expanded step by step over time, varying the message to encompass patients actually seen by a particular doctor. Information on usage is both quantitative and qualitative.

Possibly the word "marketing" will be incorporated into the Japanese language. Changes are unfolding in Japan that were considered impossible in the past. Foreign firms should take advantage of these changes to enhance their presence and clout in the market.

One key area is marketing, a Western concept that improves sales efficiency. Unfortunately, many foreign firms underutilize their marketing departments because they are bullied into adopting traditional Japanese sales practices as a localization strategy. They would be better off sticking with their global marketing strengths.

Pharma Japan 1478, December 1995

Restructuring Pharma Marketing In Japan

Japanese pharmaceutical marketing executives and their multitude of medical representatives (MRs) have been successful by many measures. Note these facts:

- In 1993 Japan represented 22 percent of the world pharmaceutical market, about equal to the entire market outside Japan, the United States and Europe, and second only to the United States, with half the number of people;
- Ethical pharmaceutical market growth averaged 6.1 percent per year in value in 1984–93. Volume growth averaged 10.5 percent;
- Annual per-capita spending on drugs is $254 in Japan and $179 in the United States;
- In 1993, 16 of the top 20 drug companies in Japan were Japanese, two European (Bayer and Sandoz), and one and a half U.S. (Banyu [half Merck] and Pfizer);
- Only two of the ten leading products in 1993 were marketed by foreign companies—Adalat (nifedipine) by Bayer, and Iopamiron (iopamirol) by Schering AG, both with negative growth rates;
- Only three of the ten fastest-growing products in 1993 were marketed by foreign companies;
- Products lunched since 1984 accounted for 57.8 percent of the 1993 ethical market.

Unfortunately, the combined effect of regulatory changes and economic conditions has changed the key factors for future success. The past is neither prologue nor model for the future.

In the traditional environment of Japan's unique market, large sales forces and distribution coverage were key factors for success. Consequently the industry now employs 50,000 MRs, a ratio of four doctors per MR vs. the U.S. ratio of 14 per MR. Major manufacturers managed distribution through a relationship (*keiretsu*) network of wholesalers, controlled by equity and "back margins" to guarantee profitability for "friendly" wholesalers. Therefore, the industry grew but remained fragmented, is stable but enjoys only modest returns, and is strong at home but weak abroad.

In the past three years structural reform of the industry has accelerated. Consequently:

- Wholesalers are consolidating into regional but not yet national players. "Mom and pop"-sized wholesalers are no longer viable;
- *Keiretsu* relationships are breaking down. Successful wholesalers are not tied to one manufacturer, but carry a full line of drugs from many manufacturers;

- The traditional monolithic sales strategy must be modified to a targeted approach to doctors. There will be a need for value-added services rather than a total reliance on personal relationships;
- The fully-allocated cost of one MR has increased to $150,000 per year, prompting executives to talk more about reducing MRs than adding MRs;
- Pricing responsibility was transferred from manufacturers to wholesalers, causing MRs to assume a different role in which new knowledge of markets and products is required;
- Independent pharmacies are emerging and patients are demanding more information on drugs. This will require a direct marketing and merchandising capability;
- Wholesaler account management expertise must be developed to leverage influence over fewer wholesalers who have direct access to buying groups and pharmacies;
- Co-promotion with wholesalers is more economical than increasing the number of MRs to cover small hospital and clinics.

A large sales force (over 900 MRs) is more a bane than a blessing; the expense is only one aspect of the problem. Drugs without incremental benefits over existing drugs cannot be "pushed" through the system by offering financial support or services to doctors. Back margins used to secure wholesaler support are now illegal. "Product pull" strategies are required, and redeployment and retraining of existing MRs is more sensible than adding MRs.

Restructuring of marketing must begin by forging strong bonds with research. Minor modifications or "me-too" drugs will not receive premium reimbursement prices and the fat margins which facilitated the "human wall" selling approach are disappearing. Conversely, innovative drugs and unique product forms will receive higher prices. If promoted by a smaller but properly trained and deployed sales force using sophisticated targeting models, they will yield greater returns.

There must be a change in the mentality of sales managers who are firmly locked into the status quo. Such thinking perpetuates old-fashioned ideas, thus:

- More MRs are better than fewer MRs;
- more calls on doctors are better than the right calls on the right doctors at the right time;
- cash incentives to doctors are more effective than delivering useful information; and
- using more wholesalers is better than making choices to select "winners:"

Surveys show MR visits to doctors have declined as a result of recent changes, but no one doubts the effectiveness of a well-trained, skillful MR. Restructuring the mission of MRs is a major headache for many traditional companies, but will yield a plethora of opportunities few companies willing to innovate. Such actions include:

- Employment of women MRs;
- utilizing new technology to deliver product information and increase responsiveness to doctor needs;
- providing pharmacoeconomic data to show the benefits of drug therapy; and
- developing a capability for direct access to patients and pharmacists.

The type of innovation may be less important than taking action, any action, that responds to changes occurring in the external environment. A mandate for change must be instilled in the culture of the firm. For this there is no secret recipe or list of do's and don'ts.

A surprise-free conclusion is that restructuring of the Japanese industry will open up opportunities for foreign companies. The new keys for success in Japan are not unfamiliar to marketing executives in other countries. Applying this knowledge to a more open Japan will create favorable odds for success. Japan is not a mystery or an enigma; a challenge yes, but a promise of higher returns than in most other developed markets for the winners.

Market Letter, May 2, 1994

Medical Representatives in Japan

About 45,000 medical representatives (MRs) are employed by the pharmaceutical industry in Japan to call on a doctor population of 210,000. However, 70 percent to 80 percent of MRs are assigned to 130,000 doctors practicing in the hospital market, or medical institutions with 99 beds or more.

In the past, Japanese "experts" claimed foreign companies could not recruit and retain qualified MRs for the following reasons:

1. No opportunity for advancement, except for foreign language speakers.
2. Instability of employment because of arbitrary home office decisions.
3. No commitment to seriously compete in Japan on a long-term basis.

4. Professors and family members do not recommend foreign companies.

These arguments are old-fashioned and do not reflect the reality of today's labor market. Indeed, there are criticisms that foreign companies have become too Japanese. That is, their salary structure and opportunities for promotion are based on seniority rather than ability.

Foreign versus Japanese classifications are not useful. MRs may be badly managed in a Japanese or foreign company. The entire pharmaceutical industry must compete with other industries for the brightest and best graduates. Efforts to enhance career opportunities for MRs will benefit everyone.

Until recently, it was the objective of every pharmaceutical company to recruit as many MRs as possible. The rationale was quite simple—sales correlate to the number of MRs. No other single factor gives a nice straight line on a sales chart. More calls on doctors directly yields higher sales.

In the latter half of the 1980s, sales executives discovered that female MRs could do as well or better than male MRs. This opened up a new pool of recruits to increase the total number of MRs. Executives confidently predicted they could control a sales force in excess of 2,000 people.

Since 1990, the economic reality of costs associated with MRs forced reevaluation of the "human wall" approach to promotion. The average all inclusive annual cost of one MRs reached ¥15 million ($140,000), or about ¥12,000 ($112) per doctor call. Sales managers could not automatically add people without a complete analysis of the cost/benefit equation. At the same time, territory allocation of doctors was questioned. Should we call more intensely on hospital doctors and reduce the coverage of "GP" doctors? What kind of territory is best suited to older MRs? Should MRs be specialized by products and/or type of doctors called on?

Economic considerations alone forced customer targeting rather than blanket coverage of all doctors. Rather than thinking about the maximum number of MRs, companies began to think about the optimal number of MRs. Quality versus quantity became the new guideline.

In 1992, the role of the MR was forever changed by the new Antimonopoly Law and FTC guidelines. MRs could no longer negotiate price, this became the sole responsibility of wholesaler salesmen, or MSs (marketing specialists). There were predictions of mass confusion, of wholesalers cutting prices to gain market share, or MSs not capable or qualified to negotiate price.

The doom scenario did not occur. Invoice prices went up, discounts came down, and wholesalers assumed their new responsibilities without hesitation. MRs who were only qualified to discuss price became redundant, or in need of retraining and reallocation. Restructuring strategies came into vogue and sometimes-painful adjustments were made in many companies, particularly the large Japanese companies.

Where do we go from here? There are several unmistakable trends:

1. MRs incapable of transferring valuable information to doctors will not be welcomed. The MR job was never easy—now it is becoming more difficult. Yet, the pharmaceutical industry has not found a better way to sell than face-to-face contact between and MR and a doctor. Nothing on the horizon will substitute for a good MR.
2. Companies with more than 800 MRs must restructure. New recruits will not decrease, but older MRs will be asked to retire early. Thus, the average age of the sales force will decline.
3. Companies with less than 600 MRs will increase their number. On balance, the total number of MRs will level off.
4. Coverage of GP doctors by MRs will decrease, leaving the field open to wholesaler salesmen, who will level up their capabilities to promote, rather than acting as order takers.
5. Marketing departments will be challenged to support MRs with more than computer point-outs of sales data, or computer disks of product information. Seeing the right doctors at the right time will be more important than seeing 10 doctors in 8 hours, or 50 doctors in a seminar.
6. MRs must be equally adept at talking about both benefits and risks of drug therapy. Recent drug "accidents" have alerted the public to risks buried in the product literature.

Changes occurring in Japan will enhance the prestige of MRs. Useful information is welcomed by doctors to minimize risk and optimize benefits for the patient. Good MRs are not an expense, they are a valuable resource that must be nurtured to full potential. The number of MRs employed by a company is no longer the key issue for success in Japan. A large sales force may be a competitive disadvantage— a remarkable change in a short time.

Pharma Japan 1391, February 1994

Quantity Is Out, Quality Is In

The first pharmaceutical company employee extracted or synthesized a drug that alleviated human suffering. The second employee was a person who could sell the discovery to a customer.

Modern day pharmaceutical companies employ thousands of people, but discovery research and sales remain the keys to a successful business. All other operations support these two. Production, finance, personnel, licensing, legal, and public relations are important ancillary services, but they are not critical to a viable pharmaceutical business. People employed in these functions disagree, but they are the first to go in merged or downsized firms.

A "virtual corporation" in its extreme form, employs one person with access to substantial financial resources. Discovery research is conducted by academic institutions and venture capital firms, contract research organizations develop products, manufacturing facilities are leased, co-marketing agreements take care of promotion and distribution. This may be a theoretical possibility, but I doubt its practicability in the real world.

The challenge for most pharmaceutical companies is the reengineering of their core functions of discovering unique new chemical entities, and communicating the risks and benefits of their products to doctors through medical representatives (MRs). This article will discuss the future role of MRs.

The pharmaceutical industry has not found a better way to communicate with doctors than through face to face discussions with medical representatives. Alternative methods have been tested and failed, or were found to be useful tools to complement the MR, but not replace the MR. They include direct mail and journal advertising, satellite symposia, lunch or dinner meetings, displays at medical conventions, telemarketing, video tapes, interactive computer systems clinical workgroup, etc., etc., etc. Not one has replaced the need for personal contacts by MRs with doctors.

In Japan there is a direct relationship between the number of MRs employed by a company and its sales. On a graph this relationship appears as a straight line, that is, more MRs equals more sales. No other factor has a direct relationship to sales.

This undeniable correlation motivated every pharmaceutical executive to recruit and employ as many MRs as possible. As the pool of available male candidates diminished, females were recruited and often outperformed their male colleagues. The boom of co-marketing and co-promotion agreements was driven by the need to increase the number of MRs promoting a specific product. More doctor calls equals more sales.

Until recently it was assumed this relationship had no limit. Everyone talked about more MRs. Since 1992 the pattern changed. Why?

There are many factors. Hospitals restricted MR visits. FTC and anti-monopoly rulings prevented MRs from discussing the purchase price of drugs. Restrictions on samples and entertainment expenses reduced the rationale for frequent doctor visits.

The most important factor is the cost of maintaining an MR in the field. The fully allocated cost of one MR now exceeds 15 million yen per year. This translates into a per doctor call cost of 12,000 yen. Thus, there are financial constraints to increasing the number of MRs beyond a certain level. What is this level? Much depends on the product portfolio of a company. New products demand more calls. Products prescribed by a limited number of doctors, e.g., anti-cancer agents, can be promoted by fewer MRs. Assuming a balanced line of products, the critical mass of MRs is 600 to 800 people. Companies with less than 600 MRs are at a competitive disadvantage to companies with 800 MRs. Companies with more than 800 MRs have productivity problems.

On an industry-wide basis, sales per MR in Japan are signifcantly less than in the United States.

Responses to Japan's sales productivity problem vary by company, but most executives talk about limiting or "freezing" the number of MRs. Koseisho officials suggest more research, less promotion; and the public media is critical of the industry's human wave selling methods.

This is good news. The emphasis was on quantity, i.e., number of MRs, now the focus is on quality. But I am not only talking about the education level, or product knowledge of individual MRs. Quality relates to allocation of MRs, territory management, and segmentation of target doctors, in other words, the productivity of MRs.

Promotional time, and therefore money (12,000 yen per call, is spread evenly over all doctors, rarely is it focused on the "right" doctor. Sales managers reward MRs by the number of calls, and allocation decisions are based on relationships rather than the needs of doctors. What do doctors want from MRs? To my knowledge, the answer to this question may be known to good MRs, but the information is not organized for the benefit of all MRs.

Let me use a non-pharmaceutical product as an example. The company will launch a new disposable lighter and you want to target doctors who use some kind of lighting device, gold-plated lighters. In the hospital market, MRs identify these doctors. You pay wholesalers to conduct surveys of the GP market.

MRs are instructed to call on doctors who use lighting devices. Do you allocate their time to concentrate on the doctors who use disposable lighters? Do you ask MS to call on specific doctors? Or, do you give wholesalers promotion money and have no idea who they call on?

My guess is most sales managers do not help MRs to answer the key question, i.e., Why does a doctor use a specifc lighting device and how will our product satisfy his or her needs better than that product?

Under the old price reimbursement system, the answer was a high reimbursement and a large discount. MRs learned to concentrate on patient inputs, i.e., price and product features. Under the new system, patient outputs are more important. Someone must effectively communicate patient benefits and the risks of therapy. That person will be an MR.

MRs are here to stay, they will not be replaced by computers or drugs that sell themselves. The first employee of a pharmaceutical company did not want to hire an MR, he presumed customers would demand his unique discovery. Some researchers have the same attitude today. Research and promotion are inexorably linked—you can't have one without the other.

Doctors have access to more than 14,000 drugs in the reimbursement tariff, they need a fraction of these to treat their patients and in many cases do not need a drug at all. How many patients with borderline high cholesterol would benefit from more exercise and less weight?

Nothing happens until a sale is made. This is true in business and personal relationships. MRs need the guidance and assistance of a good marketing team. Together, they can make something happen. The future of MRs is as bright as it always was. There are never enough good MRs. Quantity is out, quality is in.

Pharma Japan 1431, December 1994

More Reasons Why Contract MRs Will Fail

In a previous article I suggested there were three reasons why a Western contract MR system will fail in Japan. Briefly, the reasons were:

1. Space. MRs will not work out of their homes because of space limitations and the negative image of a home address on a business card. What would the neighbors think?

2. Self image. Psychological support and economic incentives are provided through association in a group. A lone entrepreneur may be admired in the fashion or media business, but not in a pharmaceutical company sales organization.

3. Cost. Outsourcing works if it enhances productivity, and/or lowers costs for the client. Public announcements by Innovex and CMIC suggest contract MR costs will be higher than company employed MRs. It remains to be seen if they can achieve a higher level of productivity to offset the increased costs.

Before discussing more reasons why the Western contract MR model will fail, let us review some factors that will not inhibit the development of a contract MR system:

1. Availability of qualified MR candidates. There are more qualified people applying for MR positions than the industry can employ. Talented people are available.

2. Certification. Talented people will have no problem passing the basic tests for certification.

3. Outsourcing. As various legal restrictions are removed, there will be no barrier to outsourcing MRs to a third party.

4. Women MRs. In the West, contract MR organizations recruit a large number of women who want to work part time. Women in Japan are proving to be effective MRs.

Other Reasons for Failure:

1. Accountability for Result

Both Innovex and CMIC are contract research organizations. The value of outsourced development work can be measured by a number of parameters, including the timing of an NDA submission. Time is money in development. Delays, which incur huge opportunity costs, are minimized by an effective CRO.

At the present time, the value of an individual MR defies exact quantitative analysis. MR promotion is designed to create demand, a "pull-through" function that is supplemented by media advertising, scientific publications, and medical conferences.

About 85 percent of all MR details are given to doctors in large hospitals. While data exists to track purchases by hospitals, it is difficult to track the influence of specific doctors for these purchases. Therefore, assigning sales results to specific MRs is not an exact science. Companies will find it difficult to measure the cost of a contract MR against well defined, quantifiable sales data.

2. Lack of Data to Select Target Doctors

The lack of doctor data makes it difficult to organize an MR territory. Of course, it all depends on the product. Target doctors for a sophisticated cancer drug are relatively easy to target. A cardiovascular drug is much more difficult. Will the contract MR company make rational territory assignments when established manufacturers fight this problem every day?

3. Wet versus Dry Relationships

Seller/buyer relationships in Japan tend to be "wet." That is, the frequency of contact is extraordinarily high. Contacts are often made to offer services or simply to say, "Please use my product." Doctor visits in the West are less frequent, and the detail itself is structured to cover three products, primary, follow up, and a brief reminder. Hence, the Western relationship is "dry," that is, product oriented, businesslike, and often by appointment.

In the West an MR can represent company A one month and company B the next month without any problem if he provides useful information to the doctor. Job hopping is a badge of honor. Moving up by pursuing one's self interest is respected. In Japan such behavior is considered a serious character flaw.

4. The Passion Factor

MRs expect to remain in one company until they retire, and they have ambitions for promotions to positions with broader responsibilities. Beyond acquiring product knowledge, they study the company's history, research achievements and vision. If asked what they do, their response is not, "I am an MR." It is, "I work for Company A." A person's self worth is not derived from a particular skill, but from the relationship with a company. It influences ones business and personal life in so many ways.

Will the contract MR tell his customers, friends and relatives he or she is a professional MR available to any company willing to pay the fee? Will he or she be able to communicate with passion the merits of the company's products?

Conclusion

Japan is changing. Past business practices are no longer effective. The health care reform big bang will not be kind to those who hang on to tradition.

Yes, Japan is changing, but it is a mistake to assume change will make Japan more like the United States or Britain. The MR role in Japan is different from the role in the West. This role must change, but not necessarily in the direction of global harmonization. There are many possible outcomes, but the contract MR model as practiced in the West is not of one of them.

Iyaku Keizai, November 1998

Generics—Talk Cheap

Strategy debates continue inside companies as they evaluate the pros and cons of entering the generic business. News from abroad suggests generics are taking a larger share of new prescriptions. Governments mandate generic substitution. Patients welcome lower out-of-pocket expenses. Japan must follow the trend—it is inevitable, therefore, get in now and ride the upward sales curve.

I am not convinced. During the past three years I have objectively and patiently listened to the pro generic arguments by those who are in the business, by those who want to get in, and by those who make money by recommending others to get in. At the risk of oversimplification, their arguments are summarized below.

- There will be a widespread adoption of the flat sum reimbursement system. Compared to the fee for service system, drugs will become an expense rather than a source of income for clinics and hospitals. Therefore, doctors and purchasing agents will be motivated to select the least expensive rather than the most expensive drug.
- Government, primarily the Finance Ministry, wants to reduce the drug bill and price reductions based on the reasonable zone will not do it fast enough or in amounts that are significant. Thus, low price drugs are an attractive option.
- The low quality image of generics will be reversed if a major pharmaceutical company (Japanese of course) introduces a line of generic products. Eisai is often cited as the trend leader.
- The Japan Medical Association will accept low price generic prescribing if the "savings" are used to increase medical fees.

- Higher patient co-payments will create discriminatory consumers who demand lower price drugs.
- Manufacturers with too many MRs and too few new products will launch generics to maintain sales growth and avoid the painful effects of downsizing.
- Listing by generic name rather than by brand name, the spread of "bungyo," chain store pharmacies, and group buying practices are presumed to favor the spread of generics.

My problem with these arguments is they sound too Western, and do not recognize the historical, cultural, and economic drivers of the health care system in Japan. Many are tempted to believe Japan changes in the direction of Western thought and policy.

Their rationale is neatly linear. If U.S. and European governments support generics, indeed, make them mandatory in certain instances, surely the Japanese government will do likewise. If pharmacy benefit management is a big business in the United States, it will be a big business in Japan. If Merck goes into the generic business, Takeda will follow. Fortunately or unfortunately, the Japanese rarely clone Western practices. Baseball is a good example. The rulebooks for the game read the same in the United States and Japan, but the game is played very differently in Japan.

Drug usage in flat sum reimbursement institutions is no longer a matter of speculation. Experience indicates the quantity of drugs does not increase. The drugs eliminated do not compromise patient benefits, and the drugs retained are essential. I presume the essential drugs do not have generic equivalents, and if they do, the price differential is not significant.

Here in lies the fundamental difference between the West and Japan until after 10 years of marketing the original drug. During this period, the price is systematically reduced in Japan. The end result is the absence of a price umbrella at the end of market exclusivity. The Japanese government has been effective in progressively lowering drug prices over time, thus eliminating the economic rationale for low priced generic equivalents.

The government and insurance societies have learned that reducing the supply price, or reimbursement price does not lower the total drug bill. In fact, one can argue it increased demand. Thus, actions like the flat sum reimbursement scheme are primarily designed to reduce demand, not, I repeat not, to increase the use of generic drugs.

In fact, I cannot think of a single policy initiative by Koseisho that is specifically designed to increase the use of generics. On the other hand, there have been many initiatives to promote new chemical entities.

Mr. Yasuta Araga, director-general of the Pharmaceutical Affairs Bureau, is the latest in a long list of Koseisho officials who encourage technological leadership and strong R&D efforts by the Japanese industry. This objective is not achieved by promoting generics. MITI, the Finance Ministry, or any other Ministry has never been known to promote old technology.

The idea of patients demanding generic drugs is unlikely given the patient/doctor relationship. It could change, but there is no compelling motivation for it to happen. Out-of-pocket costs for drugs are low, why ask questions? The key consumer issue is rational use of drug therapy—a demand side measure to reduce consumption.

Pharmacists, 65 percent of whom are women, do not have the political power of will to interfere with doctors' prescribing orders. There are laws against substitution. The pharmacist association is primarily interested in promoting "bungyo," a system that rewards pharmacists for filling prescriptions—period.

Who will legitimize the market for generics? Is quality the real issue? Talk is cheap, the real issue is how to make money selling a product that has been on the market for more than 10 years.

Three years ago I talked with the president of a Japanese company who believed he had the answer. His generics company was growing rapidly. He was hiring retired MRs from major pharmaceutical companies, and his market focus was on institutions operating under the flat sum reimbursement system. He was optimistic and bullish.

A few months ago I talked with the same man. He was discouraged, growth had slowed, problems, problems, and problems. Direct sellers were cutting prices, and his MRs were tired of talking about the same old drugs. His solution was to develop something new—a super generic, about funding development would be expensive. He asked, "Do you know a foreign company interested in buying this business?" I promised to keep my ears open, maybe a high flying U.S. generic company who thinks Japan is Westernized will be interested.

Chapter **VI**

Wholesalers Consolidate to Survive

One half of the drug wholesalers that existed in 1985 were gone by 1999 through mergers and acquisitions. Their business model changed from control by major manufacturers to independence, from local to regional presence, from 20-percent to 10-percent gross margins, and distribution as a value added function was seriously questioned. They began the learning process of leveraging information which could be transmitted to medical institutions and sold to pharma companies. Will they succeed?

Will Wholesalers Be Kings or Paupers?

Ryukinkyo, *Bungyo*, *Chuikyo*, and now *Dokkinho*. The first three words are a part of our English vocabulary. The fourth is becoming a symbol for dramatic changes in pharmaceutical distribution practices. They refer to the Anti-Monopoly Act.

Wholesalers must cope with the implications of these words. Do they bode disaster? Are they a boon? Before giving an answer, let's take a brief look at the historical record and current status of wholesalers in Japan.

When I came to Japan in 1970, there were over 1,200 wholesalers. In 1990 there were 379. The Federation of Japan Pharmaceutical Wholesalers Associations expects the number to decrease by 18.5 annually. At this pace there will be 190 wholesalers in the year 2000.

U.S. companies who distribute their drugs in Japan cover the entire market by using 80 wholesalers. Thus, there is a clear trend toward consolidation. For the survivors, this implies strength versus the weakness inherent in too many players chasing a finite number of customers.

Undoubtedly the survivors must trim personnel costs which account for 64 percent of total expenses. It is difficult to imagine a scenario whereby gross margins increase. They currently average 13 percent. After expenses there is less than 2 percent net profit margin pre tax. Given these slim margins, a forecast of doom is a reasonable assumption.

But there is another side to the story. When I meet wholesalers who are confident of surviving, they exude optimism. Is this like the group of ants who are merrily enjoying their life on a log, unknown to them, floating down a river about to plunge over a waterfall?

Consider these facts. Wholesalers physically distribute 99.9 percent of all drugs in Japan. Manufacturers are not eager to sell direct. Wholesalers are rapidly automating many of their labor intensive operations. Although wages annually increase at a 5 percent rate, merged wholesalers have reduced their total labor force. Three wholesalers have gone international by establishing offices in the United States.

So, as Yogi Berra once said, "It's not over till it's over." I expect several wholesalers will establish a national distribution network. *Dokkinho* will give wholesalers responsibility for pricing decisions to customers. This can be a powerful weapon, particularly when combined with customer contacted throughout Japan.

Today the outcome is anyone's guess. But I would not bet against the resourceful, practical men I know in the business. There may be problems, but as a character in a Woody Allen movie said, "It's nice to be king." The meek may inherit the earth, but until they do, the wholesalers who survive will enjoy the benefits that accrue to kings, not to meek paupers.

Pharma Japan 1247, March 25, 1991

The Wholesaler Evolution

The old rule of thumb for manufacturers was to assign distribution rights by prefecture, typically two wholesalers in each of Japan's 46 prefectures. Throw in a few more because of special relationships and it was normal to do business with at least 100 wholesalers.

Since there were hundreds of wholesalers, they had to compete with each other for these coveted sales rights. Manufacturers basked in the attention they received, and if the bows were not low enough, they could easily sign on another wholesaler who showed proper respect.

In short, wholesalers competed for suppliers, not for customers. The biggest prizes were those with lots of MRs and a steady flow of new products. MRs created demand and negotiated prices with dispensing doctors and hospital pharmacists. Wholesalers competed with each other to supply demand. Manufacturers encouraged this competition with a compensation package that was heavily weighted toward rebates, campaigns, account opening bonuses, and a basket of incentive payment terms. The system, ingeniously devised, was so opaque as to completely obscure the net purchase price for a given drug.

Transparency was not encouraged because it would mean erosion of control. When the FTC stopped the practice of MR price fixing, there were so many MRs sitting in coffee shops contemplating what to say to doctors that a new disease was identified as "coffee shop syndrome."

Manufacturers grudgingly moved to a single invoice price system but rebates and short term incentives die hard in the mindset of sales managers. They believe demand for a drug is directly linked to its margin vis a vis the reimbursement price and/or the wholesaler's net selling price versus its purchase price. In other words, price margins rather than drug benefits create demand.

Wholesalers Merged and Changed Their Focus

Wholesalers merged to establish a regional presence beyond their local origins. The surviving entities were no longer confined to prefectural boundaries, and they secured the distribution rights from more manufacturers. Figure 1 portrays this change.

Figure 1

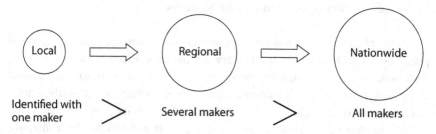

Full line wholesalers need not compete for manufacturers' sales rights unless the manufacturer elects to sell direct to pharmacies. This situation exists in the OTC market but prescription drugs are almost exclusively distributed through wholesalers. Thus, a maker's influence in a nationwide wholesaler is not derived from the allocation of its sales right, rather, influence is directly related to sales presence, that is, sales as a percent of the wholesaler's total revenue base.

One obvious way to increase sales presence is to use fewer wholesalers. Rather than using 100 or more wholesalers, most manufacturers have cut back to 50 or less. In fact, 50 of the largest wholesalers out of the 240 that exist today account for 80 percent of the pharmaceutical market.

Because full line wholesalers are not controlled by manufacturers, they focus on competing for customers. These changes are depicted in Figure 2.

Figure 2

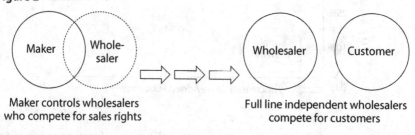

As wholesalers move away from maker control, they react to customer needs, a more "normal" marketing orientation than satisfying suppliers' needs. When the shift occurs, wholesalers realize their customers want more than prescription drugs.

Hence, they diversify to sell medical devices, hospital supplies, diagnostics, management services, and medical related services and products for home care. Give the customer what he wants rather than what the producer thinks he needs.

Value Added Functions Yield Higher Margins

Under the old paradigm, wholesalers were expected to supply demand created and priced by MRs. Order taking and delivery are low value added services that can be preformed by anyone with a warehouse and a fleet of trucks. It was only natural that as Koseisho slashed reimbursement prices, manufacturers squeezed the wholesaler margins down to a level commensurate with the service provided.

Wholesalers can respond in four ways to protect and increase their margins, i.e.:

1. Downsize and automate their order taking, warehousing, and delivery functions.
2. Create demand by promoting products to customers not seen by MRs.
3. Shift demand from one product to another product through awareness of customer needs.
4. Leverage knowledge of customer needs to sell information to manufacturers.

Figure 3 indicates the range of margins available for these value added services.

Figure 3

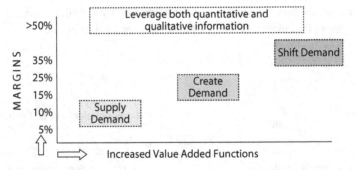

Wholesalers on a going out of business curve believe their function in life is to supply demand. They lobby insurers for a fixed distribution fee as they slowly die on the vine. Wholesalers who create and shift demand, and stop giving away information for a pittance of its value will prosper. The new paradigm is all about using information to create value versus physically moving products from a warehouse to a pharmacy.

Pharma Japan 1627, December 1998

Wholesaler MS: Burden or Opportunity?

Wholesalers face a triple threat to their viability—indeed to their survival as independent business entities.

The first is negative growth since 1996. At best, the market in calendar year 1997 will be flat, fiscal year 1998 negative, and the prospect for growth during calendar 1998 is dim. The shrinking pie environment prompts marginal, local wholesalers to "buy" sales at prices that do not pay operating expenses. Preservation of market share is a powerful motive when regional competitors encroach on their territory.

About 160 of the 260 wholesalers in Japan fight for a mere 5 percent of the market. Further consolidation through mergers is a foregone conclusion. Meanwhile, erosion of profit margins for all is accelerated by those who cannot increase their revenue within a limited customer base. They are a menace to themselves and to the manufacturers who elect to distribute through them.

The second threat is the severity of looming reimbursement price reductions, not just in 1998, but through the year 2000. Whatever the percentage reduction rates, manufacturers will not adjust their invoice prices in proportion. If the average reduction rate is 10 percent in 1998, expect manufacturers to lower invoice prices by no more than 2 percent. That leaves eight percentage points for hospitals and wholesalers to digest. Since hospitals deal with multiple suppliers, they have more negotiating power. As a result, double digit gross margins enjoyed by wholesalers in the past are history.

Very few wholesalers have operating profit margins above 2 percent. The average in well run wholesalers is 1.5 percent, with many others below 1 percent. When volume growth does not provide relief in absolute money terms, the need to reduce expenses is acute.

A third threat is the perception that wholesalers do not add value. The key issue is whether or not wholesaler MSs create demand versus supplying demand created by manufacturers' promotional activities. One example is the payment of fees to wholesalers for newly opened accounts. The going rate is ¥3,000 per account. This is money well spent if the initial purchase to open the account proves to be the first of routine orders. It is a waste of money if the first order is the last order.

Purchasing agents must distinguish between wholesalers who rely on long standing personal relationships rather than value added services. Relationships are fine, but business is business and administrators of medical facilities are too busy trying to stop the flow of red ink on their own accounting statements to worry about wholesalers who are part of the problem instead of the solution.

In this context, it is appropriate to consider the contribution of wholesaler MSs. To get a handle on the numbers, I took a sample of nationwide wholesalers and analyzed their financial performance based on FY1997 results. A summary of the data is shown below:

Average annual sales (¥Bil): *Range ¥19 to ¥276*	¥119.4
Average Annual Operating Profits (OP) (¥Bil): *Range ¥0.3 to ¥5*	¥1.8
Average OP as a percent of sales:	1.5%
Average No. of MS:	536
Average sales per MS (¥Mil): *Range ¥171 to ¥330*	¥223
Average OP per MS (¥Mil): *Range ¥1.6 to ¥6.3*	¥3.4
Average MS cost as a percent of sales: *Range 3% to 6%*	4.5%

Within this sample of wholesalers you can plot a straight line between their total sales and number of MSs. That is, sales correlate directly to MS headcount. Operating profits follow a similar pattern. However, both sales and operating profits per MS show widely scattered points on the graph, implying large gaps between the productivity of an individual MS.

The above analysis suggests that a 20 percent decrease in the number of MSs could be achieved by a relatively modest overall increase in sales per MS. It would also decrease the MS cost as a percent of sales by one percentage point, or from 4.5 percent of sales to 3.5 percent, thus enhancing profits. However, the take home message is not about reducing headcount, rather, it is the challenge of increasing MS productivity.

As an aside, in a sample of 38 pharmaceutical manufacturers, the MRs cost as a percent of sales averaged 8.4 percent, with a range of 3.8 percent to 25.3 percent.

The MS cost average of 4.5 percent of sales is not the burden some manufacturers assume it to be.

MSs represent an opportunity not only because they account for a small proportion of the wholesaler cost structure, but they are the only people in the customers' face asking for an order. They are an irreplaceable resource to supplement promotion by MRs. Good promotion is only talk unless you get the business.

MSs often represent the only sales contact with a doctor, nurse or pharmacist, particularly in small hospitals and the large majority of clinics not called on by MRs. Wholesalers who demonstrate the capability to create demand or to shift demand from one product to another will justify the indispensable value of their MSs to manufacturers. In fact, they can make a strong case for exclusive representation in a particular geographic region. Those manufacturers who do not respond favorably could be excluded.

The idea of wholesalers excluding manufacturers is completely at odds with the current practice of manufacturers excluding wholesalers or assigning wholesalers to overlapping territories. Nevertheless, wholesalers have the power of information concerning customer transactions. When MSs use this information to influence demand, they will more than justify their existence.

Pharma Japan 1585, February 1998

Suzuken + Akiyama = A Major Discontinuity

Gradual consolidation in the distribution sector went according to plan for 25 years. Since the early 1970s, over 700 wholesalers vanished through mergers and acquisitions. Only two wholesalers went bankrupt, a tribute to Japan's bailout procedures that save the losers' face.

Each new merger received its day of infamy in the trade press. Reporters dutifully noted the merged companies received the blessing of their major suppliers. Manufacturers made the necessary incremental adjustments in their supply chain management strategies. Reliance on gradual change was sufficient for survival.

Then Suzuken and Akiyama announced a merger that changed the pace of evolution. Newspapers ran special editions on the significance of the merger and interviewed every pharmaceutical executive who was not escaping the summer heat at a villa in Karuizawa. Why the fuss? Isn't this just an extension of the familiar consolidation process?

As one who studied biology before Watson and Crick elucidated the structure of DNA, it is tempting to relate recent events to evolutionary biology. In nature, adaptation to change occurs gradually over long time periods, even in microorganisms that multiply rapidly. The process, as Darwin pointed out, is one of selection and adaptation to external changes in the environment.

Then, the fossil record of dinosaurs led to proof that cataclysmic events can interfere with gradual selective processes. Sudden changes in temperature or the availability of food sources caused discontinuities—what is now called punctuated equilibrium. Under severe stress, reliance on gradual change was a one-way ticket to obliteration, or in business terms, liquidation. Survival went to those species, in the dinosaur example our mammalian ancestors, who were endowed with characteristics needed to exploit the new environment.

In a new book, *Winning Through Innovation: A Practical Guide to Leading Organizational Change and Renewal*, the authors say, "Organizations most able to adapt to a given market will survive—until there is a major discontinuity, at which point managers are faced with the challenge of reconstituting their organizations to adjust to the new environment. Those who respond with incremental change alone are unlikely to succeed." In other words, companies can become complacent in the false security of short-term success built on gradual change, then get blindsided by unconventional competitors, new technology, or distributors who no longer act like obedient serfs to their pharmaceutical manufacturer masters.

Sales managers and reporters take considerable comfort in the labeling of a given wholesaler as a clone of Takeda, Shionogi, Sankyo, or Tanabe. Although mergers often blurred this distinction, the roots of their existence remained intact.

How do we classify the new Suzuken/Akiyama entity? Shionogi's business position is number one on the list of manufacturers in the newly merged company, but the new Suzuken sales are greater than those of Takeda. It has achieved a position of strength, diversity, and geographical influence able to withstand the pressure of a single manufacturer. Suzuken has achieved independence, a reality that will be the norm of all surviving wholesalers.

To think of the new reality, picture manufacturers at one end of a horizontal plane with customers, i.e., hospitals and doctors, at the other end. Wholesalers were next to, or under manufacturers, but are now moving inexorably toward the position occupied by customers. Suzuken and Akiyama punctuated the equilibrium of the status quo. Get a new life, the old one has changed.

Dinosaur sales managers will resist trashing the strategies that made them successful in the old environment: strategies that were premised on wholesalers as underlings or second class citizens. You know their controlling strategies:

- Give cash rebates for account openings.
- Offer sweet margins tied to arbitrary, short term sales goals.
- Push sales to maintain shelf space.
- Transfer employees into wholesalers to maintain control.

Pharmaceutical company managers who want to reconstruct their companies must destroy what has been created through gradual change.

Wholesaler executives will shift their focus from top line revenue growth to bottom line income. One obvious answer is to focus on unit margins over the long term rather than on one-time payoffs. Another is to eliminate excess personnel in the physical movement of goods and in the processing of orders. Most important will be to add value to the proprietary knowledge wholesalers have of customers' needs.

The consolidation of wholesalers will continue until another 180 entities are merged out of existence. Yet the emphasis has already shifted from merging to achieve economies of scale over a wider geographical area, to reducing operating inefficiencies, and diversifying their service options for customers.

Manufacturers do not have the luxury of gradually reducing the number of wholesalers to whom they devote time and resources. Gone are the days of setting up two wholesalers in every prefecture and playing one off another. Territorial allocation is passé. Partnering is in as both manufacturers and wholesalers must work together to satisfy customers—one by one because they are all different.

The executives of Akiyama and Suzuken have done the industry a favor by executing a major discontinuity. It is a good time to root out dinosaur—like sales managers who are preoccupied with internal procedures and old relationships rather than understanding the changing market.

Why Japanese Pharmaceutical Wholesalers Merge

Since the early 1970s, over 700 pharmaceutical wholesalers in Japan ceased to exist as independent businesses. Bankruptcy occurred in only a handful of cases, mergers accounted for the rest. What were the driving forces behind this consolidation? How do the survivors relate to their suppliers and their customers?

Local to Regional, Not Yet Nationwide

Historically, wholesalers serviced accounts within a limited geographic area, and competed with each other for sales rights granted by manufacturers. Manufacturers typically sold through 150 wholesalers to achieve nationwide distribution. Independent pharmacies were not a significant factor in the drug supply chain, and only a few manufacturers sold direct to hospitals and clinics.

Merged wholesalers restructured their operations to accomplish three objectives:

1. Efficiently utilize their infrastructure to service more customers.
2. Access a wider range of products from more manufacturers.
3. As full-line wholesalers, become less dependent on any single manufacturer and focus on the needs of customers.

The process of regionalization was most pronounced in the urban corridor extending from Tokyo to Osaka, an area which accounts for 70 percent of the drug market in Japan. Wholesalers in more remote areas also consolidated to protect themselves from regional competitors.

As a result, today 50 leading wholesalers account for 80 percent of the market, the top 100 have a 92 percent share, leaving a mere eight percent for the remaining 230 wholesalers. Given these numbers, consolidation is certain to continue. Nevertheless, it will be some time before a true nationwide wholesaler emerges.

Impact on Manufacturers

Regional, independent, full-tine wholesalers wield more negotiating power vis-à-vis manufacturers in matters of pricing than they ever could as local players. But other changes have altered the relationship:

1. Equity ownership of wholesalers by major Japanese manufacturers has declined.

2. Wholesalers are utilizing their army of salesmen (approximately 30,000) to perform functions beyond order taking. They are learning to create demand rather than simply supplying demand.
3. Wholesalers are paying attention to pharmacists who operate independently. At the end of 1998 almost 30 percent of all prescriptions were filled outside hospitals and clinics.

Manufacturers responded to the changes by cutting the number of wholesalers they sell to. While 150 accounts were common in the early 1980s, the typical number is now under 50 and declining. Although this is a much higher number than in the U.S. and European markets, it is a drastic drop from the past.

The most positive impact will be on foreign manufacturers who shied away from distribution because of its complexity. No foreign company with a presence in Japan needs to forfeit distribution to a Japanese company, a sea change from past assumptions of doing business in Japan.

The Future of Wholesalers

Wholesalers will continue to merge at an accelerating rate during the next several years. Declining margins are the economic drivers as localized wholesalers cannot achieve economies of scale to lower their operating costs.

The survivors will be independent from control by any single manufacturer, thus changing their focus to providing the best service to their customers. The process of supplying demand will be automated to reduce personnel expenses.

Sales promotion resources will be redirected to three value added functions.

1. Creation of demand in medical facilities not called on by manufacturers' representatives.
2. Establishing relationships with physicians and pharmacists to shift demand from one drug to another.
3. Leveraging both quantitative and qualitative information on drug usage obtained through a sales presence in medical facilities and independent pharmacies.

These higher value added functions will enhance profitability and allow wholesalers to further expand their services to customers. An example is to broaden their product line to include non-drug products like medical devices currently distributed by more than 3,000 dealers.

Finally, a strong wholesaler network with fewer participants will provide more transparent access to the market. Companies who defined distribution in Japan as a black hole need to take another look. There is light at the end of the tunnel.

Chapter VII

Drug Company Image

No one knows the number of lives saved because of the availability of effective medicines. No one can quantify the economic value that drugs create by extending productive lives. The benefits are incalculable. And yet, everyone loves to hate the drug industry. Company images are tarnished by bad news while good news goes unreported. This seems like a perfect scenario for a good public relations program. Then why does the industry shoot itself in the foot?

Pharma Delegates—Its Meaning Is in the Experience

I write this on the Shinkansen, a Hikari super express train whooshing its way at 200 kph from Nagoya to Tokyo past flooded paddy fields, Mt. Fuji, and cherry trees shedding their blossoms. It is a time of renewal in Japan, desperately needed in this year of shocks inflicted by nature and deranged people. My mood is pensive, a condition enhanced by a cup of sake and the events of the past 24 hours.

Nagoya was the site of the 13th Pharma Delegates Healthcare Seminar attended by 120 members and guests—an all time record. The speakers were stimulating and provocative—their subject matter was germane and practical. Anyone who considered going to Nagoya but did not because of the need to shuffle papers in an office missed a unique learning experience.

But this is just one facet of an organization that has grown from a few people sitting around one table to a dynamic, effective presence in the lives of men and women who share an interest in the delivery of healthcare. I began to analyze why Pharma Delegates is a success—not only in terms of membership, but in the intangible, unquantifiable needs it satisfies. Before the train arrived in Tokyo, I concluded there were three reasons, i.e., people, mission, and character.

People

The basis of success in any organization is people. A unique product or idea cannot be converted into a commercial reality by unimaginative, dreary people. Pharma Delegates has been managed by men (no women yet, but they will be there in the future) who are willing to devote countless hours to the mundane tasks of organizing meetings. Some have done it for a long time without any reward except the dubious distinction of occupying the head table at luncheons. They pay their dues just like everyone else.

Behind each man is a secretary. OK—she gets paid, but what company ever included this work in a job description? Think of the myriad of details and the hassle factor that must be dealt with on a daily basis. Yet they do it with aplomb, making all feel welcome.

Most important are the members who show up, volunteer, contribute to discussions, serve on committees, and make each other feel good about the simple pleasure of coming together to talk common interests. They are in it for friendship, a precious commodity in this busy world.

Mission

Pharma Delegates is a success because it adheres to a simple, well understood mission: an organization made up of members who work in or serve the healthcare industry and desire to network with each other. It is not an organization designed to lobby for policies that will benefit the industry. It does not offer a venue for the commercialization of specific services. It does not promote or advertise a product. All of these objectives are the domain of trade associations, chambers of business, and trade negotiations.

Nor is Pharma Delegates designed to bring foreigners together with Japanese, or newcomers with old timers, or government officials with executives. There are no membership quotas. If you pay the dues, you are welcome. That's it, no special recognition for the privilege of your presence. What a relief it is to meet new people and exchange name cards without the customary apologies and deep bows. Every speaker is extended the same courtesies and receives the same modest honorarium concealed in a paper bag.

Another mission is to keep the price of entry within the means of people not on a generous expense account—then provide enough food and spirits to more than satisfy the most ravenous appetite.

In short—no hidden agenda, no cliques or dynasties, just good cheer, friendship without pretensions, and fellowship at a bargain price. Throw in knowledgeable speakers and anyone not brain dead will come away from a meeting with at least one new contact, one new idea, a full stomach, a worm glow, and recharged batteries. It is not surprising so many enter a meeting with a frown and leave with a smile.

Character

The culture or character of an organization is not easy to define, and Pharma Delegates is no exception. Character is the outcome of people and mission as described above, but there is more:

- No one comes to a meeting expecting an embarrassing confrontation. Guest speakers do not expect a bashing, and every member is given an opportunity to offer opinions.
- The venue may be the American Club, but the atmosphere is nationality neutral. The conversation noise level is created by a babble of languages.

Chairmen throughout the years have had to apologize for cutting into the free discussion to introduce speakers.

- The chair regularly changes, although there are no term limits. This creates an atmosphere in which change is acceptable. Each new executive committee has fresh ideas for speakers and the format of seminars. Yet there is continuity and stability enhanced by the service of volunteers with long memories.
- The nonpolitical, non-confrontational mission of Pharma Delegates makes it a marvelous place for newcomers to enter Japan. This is not an exclusive, secret society of insiders.

It is naïve to believe Pharma Delegates will or should change the world. Its chairmen are not called into the Prime Minister's office to advise on multilateral trade negotiations. The mass media does not report its proceedings. Every speaker does not hold the audience in rapt attention. The number of members may not set a new record every year. The success and vitality of Pharma Delegates is based upon an opportunity to sit around a table and talk. There are more tables today, but the concept is the same.

The train arrived in Tokyo and passengers exited the station into a rainy, cold, spring evening. My taxi driver asked where I came from, I said Nagoya. He said, "Business trip?" Actually it was not a question, rather a statement. I almost responded with the usual, "Hai," but remained silent. There was business, but also pleasure, study, and reunions in what I had done since leaving Tokyo the day before. How do you describe Pharma Delegates? You don't describe this organization—you experience it. I rode home with a contented smile on my face.

Pharma Japan 1449, May 1995

It's Worth Doing

Her face is only a vague memory and there is no way I can recall her name. She lived across the street as an only child to parents who were friendly with my parents, but not close, if you know what I mean. She and her father were often seen together riding bicycles. Hers was shiny black with bright silver sprockets, never tarnished by grease.

In a small town, on a small street you see people—you know when they are around. We somehow knew she was sick, then heard she was taken to a hospital.

There were gruesome reports about the gallons of pus they were draining from her body. It seemed to go on for a long time—then she died and we went to see her frail, lifeless body at the wake. After that her father always rode alone, using her bike—not talking.

I learned—about appendicitis. Years later, when I was teaching human anatomy at Woman's Medical College in Philadelphia, I made sure the medical students looked carefully at the appendix in their cadaver. A minor appendage to a mass of intestine that killed a young girl.

Actually it was a bug that caused the pus, then septicemia, finally toxemia and death Appendicitis is not considered a life threatening disease these days, antibiotics took care of that. Too bad the girl with a name I cannot remember had a ruptured appendix before the pharmaceutical industry discovered so many antibiotics.

Everyone has their own story why they are in this business, and don't want to leave it. They indoctrinate newcomers with their passion for the benefits that go beyond career objectives and financial needs. Sales reps may be the first to know it's worth doing.

In my case the memories are still vivid. A patient who most certainly was going to have a leg amputated except for the effectiveness of a new antibiotic called Keflin, introduced in 1964. There was so much demand we went on allocation after five days. Reps were asked to stop promoting the drug. My district manager said, "Keep talking, the production guys will do their job." We did, and when supplies became available we sold every vial that was shipped.

A mental hospital was using Brevital, a short-acting anesthetic to put patients asleep before they were given electroshock therapy. Following administration, patients complained of pain in their arms. I was asked to check the procedure and immediately noticed the Brevital was brought out of the refrigerator straight to the therapy room. It was like injecting ice water into the vein. A slight change in the procedure allowing the drug to warm up to room temperature solved the problem.

I wish a good sales rep had convinced my mother's doctor there was a better drug than reserpine to treat her hypertension. She knew the side effects and did not take her medicine as prescribed. Much later, in a hospital for an operation, she was put on Aldomet. However, the years of uncontrolled blood pressure took their toll, and she died of a cerebral hemorrhage after a stroke.

Critics argue that sales reps are a lousy way to communicate product information to doctors. In some new age of medicine that may be true, but we don't have a more effective mode at the present time. It has been said that doctors who have been out of medical school for five years are out of date, unless they continue to study. They learn from their peers and their patients how to diagnose. Treatment is largely a function of drug therapy, and an awesome number of new drugs debut annually. Tried and true in this business has a short half life.

Recently I was in a hospital out-patient waiting room at the end of doctor visiting hours. No less than 12 medical representatives waited their turns to see the doctors. Each was given time, quality time to relate his products to the everyday needs of the doctor. I felt envious of their task. At the end of the day they can go to sleep and know it's worth getting up for tomorrow.

Pharma Japan 1275, October 21, 1991

Passion and Profits

Bar none, the pharmaceutical industry is the best place to work on the face of this earth. And if that wasn't enough, it keeps getting better every year. Those of you in the business count your blessings; those of you who are not—try to get in.

Before this industry existed, doctors put leeches on patients to bleed them free of noxious elements in the blood presumed to cause disease. Hospitals existed primarily as a place to die, not to live. Pharmacists compounded foul smelling liquids from substances meant for a witches brew. Dentists pulled teeth after giving their patients a stiff drink. Surgeons operated, then watched their patients die of infections. Women gave birth in excruciating pain, but lost half their babies before the age of 10.

Brilliant doctors and academic researchers labored in dingy laboratories to unlock the mysteries of plagues that routinely wiped out entire communities. Nurses wiped the brows of their patients while they slowly slipped away. Home remedies and snake oil were promoted to people with unbearable afflictions. Mentally ill patients were put in chains. People died in the prime of their lives from unknown causes.

One of my vivid childhood memories is of a young girl who lived across the street. Every night she and her father rode their bicycles around the neighborhood much to the envy of all the other kids. She was an only child who one day got sick. We didn't know the problem, but she was in the hospital and reports filtered back through the grapevine that doctors were draining quarts of pus from her body. She died. We went into the house to view her fail body and came out wondering why God took her away. They told us she had appendicitis, an almost incurable disease.

It was the pharmaceutical industry that took chance discoveries out of isolated laboratories and organized their development into useful medicines. It put teams of people together to devise manufacturing methods that increased the yield of biological substances and insured consistency in the final product. Fleming's penicillin mold in a petri dish was nothing until the antibiotic was mass produced—unfortunately the girl across the street was born too soon.

It was the pharmaceutical industry that organized teams of researchers to isolate antibiotics from soil samples gathered at sites around the world. Its chemists went beyond reserpine to provide drugs that lowered high blood pressure with minimum side effects. Organic chemists went beyond ether to provide anesthetic agents that permitted surgeons and dentists to ply their skills without pain.

It was the pharmaceutical industry that established distribution networks to supply drugs everywhere, whenever they were needed. It trained people to communicate the benefits and risks of drugs to doctors before they tried them on patients. Its advertising gave consumers confidence in the quality and safety of drugs, a far cry from the claims of medicine men operating out of the back end of covered wagons.

Thirty three years ago I was sitting in a sales training room in Indianapolis while a doctor stood before cameras to talk about a new antibiotic. The film would be shown to salesmen as part of their education program. As is the case with making a film, numerous "takes" were required to get a final version. The doctor was describing a patient with an infected leg. None of the available antibiotics stopped the infection. Amputation of the leg was the only alternative until our new antibiotic was flown in on a trial basis. The leg was saved.

While relating the story, the doctor broke down in tears. The dramatic efficacy of the antibiotic was a medical miracle. These were not tears for the camera, they were heartfelt emotions. The story that went out to the salesforce was filled with unadulterated passion. One week after the drug was launched, we ran out of stock. We sold every vial that could be produced for months. The company made a lot of money—but first came passion.

Unlike many other industries, no single company dominates the pharmaceutical industry. Drug discoveries are not the automatic end result of more money or more people. Innovation is not confined by national boundaries or necessarily restricted to multimillion dollar research complexes. Economics of scale work in reverse. Entrepreneurship is alive and well as the industry constantly reinvents itself.

The people in this industry reflect the values of their customers and the critical nature of their products. It is a dynamic mixture of extreme caution and the need for calculated risk; of almost overbearing regulation and intense competition; of stability and rapid change. The workforce is highly educated, but the diplomas on the walls are not restricted to elite schools.

The industry has its share of critics who are all too often answered by apologists with weak arguments cloaked in a veil of the necessity to do expensive research. People who need the industry's products would rather not take them. Not infrequently they are told to take a drug even though there is no perceivable problem. Critics appeal to a captive audience of consumers who have no choice in what they must buy at a time when they feel lousy. This is an industry you can easily love to hate.

And yet—the industry prospers. Predictions of impending doom as blockbuster drugs go off patent do not become a reality. Investors enjoy above average returns. Mega-mergers attract headlines in the business press alongside initial public offerings by startup companies. Drug company CEOs are rarely cited as captains of industry or get listed as the richest men in the world, but they quietly go about the business of running successful enterprises. Many companies have an admirable history of survival and growth.

Why? Not because the industry attracts the top financial MBA graduates. Not because it attracts deal makers or hot shot promoters, savvy lawyers, or public relation whiz kids. Most of its leaders grow up in the business; promotion from within is the norm not an exception.

Why? I suggest it is because the people in the pharmaceutical industry exhibit an undisguised passion for the inherent value in products that will cure a disease, offer a longer, more fulfilling life, and change the course of medical practice. They know these things are possible, they did it before.

Those without this kind of passion gravitate to other lines of work. Those with it stay and make a difference—and the profits that follow are a natural consequence of their passion.

Pharma Japan 1571, October 1997

Do You Make Medicine?

Conversation around our dinner table is not intended to be heavy, hopefully a review of the day's activities and a chance to share life's small victories. My daughters are seven and 10 years old so I do not expect to discuss deep philosophical questions about the misery of life. Alas, the nightly routine changed because of two questions and a forthcoming event, each relevant to the business of healthcare.

The pharmaceutical industry is beginning to understand the growing influence of patients on the selection of drug therapy. Patients want to know what they are taking and why. Is it cost effective? Is it available in generic form or over the counter? Patient representatives who lobby government officials and attempt to restrict the choices of therapy available to doctors do so under the banner of cutting healthcare costs.

Books about drugs are best sellers in Japan. Product recalls are big news in the media. Local medical society meetings host programs entitled, "How to talk with (not to) patients." Doctors who only say, "Take this and come back in two weeks," are losing patients. This is serious because more doctors are chasing fewer patients, particularly in urban areas with a surplus of doctors. Patients are better educated, and I learned one reason why from my fourth grade daughter at the dinner table.

My question was innocuous, "What interesting subject did you study today?" The answer was short, "Our bodies," she replied. I imagined a lesson on physical fitness of on the virtues of eating a balanced diet instead of demanding pizza and fast food. How out of date I am became apparent listening to her explanation on the ill effects of drugs and what to expect when the monthly period begins.

I listened intently but gratefully the conversation turned to other subjects. If this is what is taught in fourth grade, can you imagine what will be imparted during eight more years? She will know more about the body than the first year medical students I was teaching human anatomy to in 1962. She already knows more about genetics than I learned in high school.

The second shock came from my seven-year old. One evening she asked, "Do you make medicine?" I have been in the pharmaceutical business since joining Eli Lilly in 1964 and truthfully, not once did I make medicine. Nor have I ever worked at a lab bench to discover medicine. As an MR, the most enjoyable job I ever had, I sold medicine, but that ended in 1967 when Lilly moved me into a corporate position.

I searched for an answer. A baker makes bread, a carpenter makes things, an engineer designs things, a doctor treats patients, a nurse gives TLC. What did I "make" as Vice President of Merck? As Japan Representative of PMA? As a writer and speaker about the pharmaceutical industry? As a founder of a company to promote medicine? Damn tough question to answer in practical terms demanded by a child.

I responded that most things get made by groups of people working together like a team. I said I help people to work together. Someday she may be impressed with this answer, but for the moment she was nonplused.

As children are prone to do, she asked another question on an entirely different subject. "If you didn't marry Mama, who would you marry?" I responded without hesitation, "If I did not marry your Mother, you would not be here and that would make me so sad I could not think of marrying someone else."

The third change in table conversation is due to our expecting a baby late September. You can imagine this has provoked many questions, and I can assure you the old story of the stork delivering babies is not operable. The story of Santa Claus is OK, a tooth fairy yes, but stork delivering babies—no way.

Our obstetrician and hospital is laterally next door, physically attached to our apartment building. The nurses live on the second floor. We are a three-minute elevator ride from the delivery room.

For others, the trek to the hospital is not as convenient, and until recently expectant mothers would arrive for regular checkups and await their turn to see a doctor, typically a three-hour ordeal. It finally dawned on someone that appointments should be patient friendly, after prospective customers took their business elsewhere. Japanese patients may not complain verbally, but they will register displeasure by voting with their feet.

Pregnancy is a special case, as it is not considered a disease, thus not reimbursed by most insurance plans. High out-of-pocket costs encourage patients to be more assertive and demanding of quality care. Is this a model for reforming other aspects of health care services in Japan?

We have gone through a procedure unknown to my parents. It is called amniocentesis, whereby a small amount of fluid is taken from the sac surrounding the fetus with a needle inserted through the womb. Cells belonging to the baby are analyzed to give a chromosome karyotype, that is, a vivid picture of each chromosome—46 is considered a normal complement, 46 XX is female, 46 XY is male.

Some people go through this procedure because they want to know the sex of their unborn child, other to detect certain well-defined abnormalities like Down's syndrome. Our motive was not for the purpose of intervention, as we are determined to accept whatever we get in this miraculous process of conception, development, and birth.

Our baby's karyotype is a mystery; it is 47 XY, an extra chromosome. The best cytogeneticists in Japan and the United States assure us the odds for a normal baby are high. What we have leaned through this multinational medical consultation process is sobering. The more we know about cells in our bodies the less we know. The discovery of one missing link between two points creates two new missing links. We can "see" chromosomes but want to know the functions of their component, i.e., the genes.

This unraveling of nature is not depressing, indeed the medicine makers should be ecstatic. Prospects for future discoveries, for new therapies are practically limitless. In this context, deliberations to restrict access to health care, to capitate what may be spent on health care, or to discourage innovation in any of its insidious forms in undesirable, to put it mildly.

Perhaps educated consumers of health care will join the medicine makers and both will encourage medical science to uncover more missing links, and we will profit form the discoveries. I could start by asking a few anti-innovation people to come to my house for dinner.

Pharma Japan 1460, July 1995

PR Is Self-Defeating

This is a tough subject. Think about it for a few minutes, honestly. Does the public like what we sell? There are a few hypochondriacs out there who love us, but most people believe healthy is better than sick. Many people equate drugs with illness not with wellness. At cocktail parties people will wax eloquent about their RX-7 or notebook computer. No one is interested in the wondrous properties of a calcium channel blocker in reducing elevated diastolic blood pressure.

Our basic PR manuals, which I started reading 27 years ago, continue to say we must make a profit to fund research. NEC does not justify prices by telling customers they need a profit to develop their next generation of computers. Toyota does not justify its profits by publicizing the research costs for a new engine. The R&D "story" is time worn.

We literally cry to our regulators for price increases, and then brag to security analysts about rosy profit projections. Public representatives notice these contradictions and become more determined to regulate prices (read regulate as reduce).

Possibly bad press goes with the territory and our PR mission is damage control. Unlike most industries, we do not sell our products to the consumer. Our customer is the prescriber. Perhaps this explains the current interest in OTCs and direct consumer advertising—eliminate the middle man, he is the problem.

It is sad to think we must remain on the defensive. The PR is familiar. No, the Japanese do not take too many drugs. No, the industry does not make excessive profits. No, research is not focused on minor modifications. No, drugs do not provide doctors' income. No-No-No.

We should say YES and take the offensive. A nice hospital or good doctor cannot cure AIDS. A cure, when it comes, will be a drug or a vaccine, probably from a pharmaceutical company. Government ministries or social agencies cannot cure Alzheimer's disease. A drug will eventually relieve the debilitating symptoms. These are offensive weapons and should be used aggressively.

Like it or not we are a regulated industry, from product approval to price reimbursement. Stop thinking of the government as an adversary, since we do not operate with the same kind of freedom enjoyed by those in other high-tech industries.

People don't want to be sick. The government exists to promote the welfare of people. We have the answers, or the potential to provide answers. Government laboratories do not discover many drugs. Industry and government need each other and should help each other to accomplish mutual objectives. An offensive strategy can nurture this partnership.

In Japan there are over 40,000 medical representatives calling on 200,000 doctors. Very few people call on Koseisho (MHW) or politicians. This allocation of PR resources deserves some serious rethinking.

Pharma Japan 1254, May 20, 1991

Communicating the Industry Message

Writing in this paper about the value of an innovative, profitable pharmaceutical industry is like a minister preaching to the choir. But you read many self-serving messages in the trade press that never appear in front of audiences that really count. It does not take a rocket scientist to conclude this industry needs something done about its public image.

No one ever said it would be easy. A woman willingly shells out ¥10,000 for a skin moisturizer but balks at paying ¥1,000 for hormone replacement therapy. Has any activist ever claimed the cosmetic companies were making too much money?

For many years the U.S. industry has shot itself in the foot. On one hand a company will bemoan the high R&D cost per approved new chemical entity, then proudly announce to the investment community a zillion dollar stock buyback program. The layman must conclude that investing in stock is a better bet than investing in research. Japanese companies cannot buy their own stock, but the public questions the zillions of yen spent on entertaining doctors.

In the United States, industry proudly claims pharmaceutical costs have not risen as a percent of the Gross National Product. How many people can relate their out-of-pocket costs for a prescription to the GNP? In Japan, out-of-pocket costs are a pittance, but the public questions why they are given so many different drugs.

The point is that audiences are different, therefore the message must be tailored accordingly. In Japan, the consumer is indifferent to drug prices. In the United States, where drug costs represent 30 percent of the total out-of-pocket costs for health care, the consumer is acutely aware of prescription prices.

In Tokyo this week is the CEO of the Syntex Corporation and current chairman of the U.S. PMA Board of Directors. Mr. Paul Freiman says it is time to strengthen the industry's communication program. In his message to the industry he made some very specific suggestions:

"We need to define our audience . . . patients are our most natural allies. We will cure or alleviate their diseases. They need to understand this natural linkage."

"The quality of life for the elderly can really be influenced by our discoveries. We have not done enough in working efficiently with the elderly."

". . . We need to pay more attention to experts in health policy and economics. A great deal of what we see in terms of health legislation is shaped at universities and 'think tanks' around the world."

Mr. Freiman went on to eloquently define the message. It could be quoted here, but I want to switch to a message delivered to the shareholders of Forest Laboratories by its president, Mr. Howard Solomon. Forest is not a PMA company, but it does know something about communicating effectively with its audience.

Mr. Solomon speaks with a clarity others may emulate. He said in relation to critics of drug pricing:

"It is obviously easier to bear down on the drug pricing than face the difficult moral and political questions posed by attempts to limit the availability of expensive procedures and care. This is not to say that there have not been cases of exploitive drug pricing which have been properly criticized. I do feel, however, that critics of drug pricing tend to disregard, or are not aware, that drug companies in general are the most speculative and at the same time often the best managed companies in our country."

Mr. Solomon then went on to define speculative in real life terms for all his small company. An incontinence drug they were developing in the United States appeared to be a good bet. The drug produced excellent clinical results, had been previously approved in 20 counties and administered to about two million patients. Then a group of cases of a rare arrhythmia turned up in Britain. The drug was withdrawn from the markets in which it had been launched and Forest had to abort its programs.

This kind of risk, Mr. Solomon modestly concludes, "perhaps deserves a greater reward than a simpler, safer business." Well said, and I bet the average guy in the street would agree. This is not the business of selling cleansers and moisturizers. It is about the lives of people.

Pharma Japan 1320, September 21, 1992

More Adverse Reports Equal Safety

With regularity (on slow news days), the public media picks up an adverse drug reaction report and gives the story two inch headlines. The average Suzuki-san is led to believe drug companies poison the human race on the altar of profits. Favorable images are forgotten, lives saved are not recognized, and government officials become risk adverse, delaying approvals of new drugs. The public demands zero defects and "Don't give me that line about all the profit you need to conduct research."

Face reality, we are not selling placebos in this business, although a Japanese company president once told me the ideal drug was a placebo with a high NHI price (sadly, he wasn't joking). There is risk associated with every drug or internal diagnostic procedure. The key is to tilt the benefit/risk ratio in favor of the patient, thus the need for more information. Which brings me to the subject of this article, more adverse reaction reports equate to a higher level of confidence and hence a greater safety margin for patients (this is not a joke).

The number of adverse drug reaction reports in Japan is low by any international standard. Only someone with half a brain would conclude that drugs are safer in Japan or that Japanese doctors prescribe fewer drugs, or prescribe them more carefully than elsewhere. There are three reasons for the low numbers:

1. An effective monitoring system does not exist. Koseisho is well aware of this problem and expects to correct it with the implementation of GPMSP, an acronym for Good Postmarketing Surveillance Practices, beginning April 1994. The voluntary system did not work (do they ever work?).

2. On an unlevel playing field, the company that strives to collect adverse reaction reports loses if his competitor is less diligent. The true incidence of side

effects may be similar, but the drug with more reports is considered less safe. I am not implying a deliberate attempt to cover up adverse reactions since I honestly believe the risks of doing so are too great. However, under the new guidelines, GPMSP monitors must be independent from sales management, a step forward in objective reporting.

3. The absence of informed consent and the doctor/patient relationship in Japan is not conducive to creating an educated patient. Patients may not be aware of adverse reactions because they were not told what to expect. They "grin and bear it," or quietly stop taking their medication. Complaining to a doctor is not polite behavior.

If Japan is lax in this area, I submit the pendulum has gone too far in the other direction in the United States. This past summer I had a camera inserted into my stomach and another so far up the other direction I swear they must have met somewhere in between. Prior to the procedures, a nurse and doctor reviewed with me a written statement that covered all the possible risks, then I was asked to sign copies in triplicate.

Below is one of the eleven foreboding paragraphs quoted from the consent form:

"I have been informed that there are many significant risks, such as severe loss of blood, infection, cardiac arrest and other consequences that can lead to death or permanent or partial disability, which can result from any procedure. No promise or guarantee has been made to me as to result or cure."

In other words, you may die Maurer and we made no promises you wouldn't. I had a similar procedure done in Japan a few years ago, and as best as I remember the doctor's instructions were limited to "drink this," and "lay down here."

Good medical practice must lie somewhere between these two extremes. A patient has a right to quality information, but it is ludicrous to convert doctors into lawyers.

Balanced, objective information will increase the public's confidence level in drug therapy. Defensive, legalistic documents create, rather than allay, suspicion. Pharmaceutical companies should embrace the new GPMSP guidelines or the media will create fear and a Japanese version of ambulance chasers eager to prove what went wrong rather than what went right. Life itself is a risk. As a risque bumper sticker proclaimed, "Shit happens."

Fortunately, in the overwhelming majority of cases, drugs minimize risk and increase the odds of a beneficial result, if not a cure. This is the message Suzuki-san should hear, not "We need more money to do research," etc. ad nauseam.

Pharma Japan, October 1993

Internal Focus Saps Productivity

Very good data suggests sales managers spend less than 10 percent of their time in the field, i.e., away from their office duties to meet people who prescribe or use their products. Anecdotal data suggests foreign companies spend more time talking about what to do in Japan versus doing it. Japanese executives are consumed with studying internationalization rather than implementing actions that take their companies abroad.

Their focus is internal. Time devoted to meetings between employees far exceeds the time employees devote to customers. Internalization is the bane of most organizations, sapping efficiency and negating productivity increases. Like many diseases, the symptoms are obvious but cures are elusive or difficult to apply. Consider the following two examples where names are fictitious but the situations are real.

The Frequent Traveler

John was sent to Japan to assume overall responsibility for one of his company's major divisions. The products were relatively new but market shares in Japan were below other markets. The company imported raw material to manufacture finished products, distributed them directly to wholesalers, and employed 500 MRs to promote their benefits to doctors.

The position John assumed was highly visible in the corporation, in fact, sales were second only to those in the United States. Lots of people recognized Japan as a key growth opportunity.

John was "connected" to all the modern technology for communication. His PC could be plugged into a hotel phone line to receive E-mail messages. The company had a videoconference facility, his car had a telephone, and he carried a portable phone. His home computer was linked with the home office. In short, he could receive and send messages anytime, anywhere.

Electronics did not diminish the apparent need for face-to-face meetings. Visits to the home office were scheduled every other month. Regional meetings were held every six months, and "emergency" meetings outside Japan cropped up two or three times a year. In addition there were constant meetings in Japan with visitors from the home office who also expected to be entertained at night.

It did not take a time management guru to tell John he was more often out rather than in Japan, both mentally and physically. His cure, albeit with the help of a supportive boss, was to restrict international travel to one trip per quarter, and home offce staff were put through a rigid justifcation process for every proposed visit. At least two field visits in Japan were scheduled each month.

John believes he is now getting into Japan but sees the need for more therapy. He wants to study Japanese so he is not totally dependent on others for every action outside the office. He needs more time with his peers in Japanese industry, and with key customers. He is on track but fears he will be transferred before taking the complete cure.

The Meeting Addict

Suzuki-san is responsible for developing a presence for his company in the United States. He is well suited for the task. His company sent him to a 12 month executive program at a prominent West Coast business school. He worked for five years in his company's liaison office in New York. Suzuki-san knows the United States better than I do.

The company licensed-out its products in the past but now insists on conducting its own development. Marketing agreements are non-exclusive. The goal of building a fully integrated company in the United States is eloquently articulated in the annual report.

Suzuki-san believes the U.S. operations must be given as much autonomy as possible under the leadership of a U.S. executive. He wants the company to establish an R&D center in the Northeast or California, forge alliances with research intensive biotechnology companies, and initiate co-marketing agreements with larger pharmaceutical companies.

Every director in the home office has some idea how to do business in the United States although none have ever lived there. Suzuki's boss is a team player, thrives on consensus, and made his career through the domestic sales force. The international division does not have a clear mandate to execute actions which will achieve the company goal. Every issue is discussed by a committee. It takes two weeks to schedule a meeting, a month to get everyone to sign off, and then it goes to the Board.

Suzuki-san gets to the office at 8:30 a.m. after a 90 minute commute. At 9:00 a.m. he starts his round of meetings which go on until 5:00 p.m. At least three nights a week he has evening meetings, and drags home after 11:00 p.m. A year ago he was "temporarily" asked to plan a strategy for China, and there is no end in sight. Meanwhile, a promising U.S. executive left the company because of constant demands for nit-picking information on the fax every morning from Japan. Two biotechnology "deals" went elsewhere because they were tired of waiting for a decision.

The cure in this case is pending, but Suzuki-san has taken the gamble of directly appealing to the President to restructure international operations. He proposed a clear separation from the domestic business and recruitment of foreign nationals to work in the home office. These are not drastic actions, but Suzuki-san cannot appear to be ambitious at the expense of his domestic colleagues. At 43 years of age he is no match for older men in the company. He has been advised to be patient.

The Ultimate Cure

In my own case, I realized the only way to achieve almost 100 percent external focus was to form a virtual corporation. Nippon Pharma Promotion (NPP) was established in 1994 to provide a variety of services to the healthcare industry. We have one full time employee. The real business is conducted by our shareholders who include 11 top-ranked, independent pharmaceutical wholesalers who employ more than 6,000 salesmen calling on 72,559 doctors, 25,889 pharmacies, and virtually every hospital in Japan.

We have one "internal" meeting per week. Every other meeting or communication is with customers. Our objective this year is to link NPP with its shareholders through an intranet system, thereby reducing or eliminating mail and fax communication. We force ourselves to push everything out to people who interface with customers.

John, Suzuki-san, and others like them are making "wake-up" calls in their companies. The changes they initiate will put pressure on those who crawl into the corporate womb and believe a good day is a full calendar of internal meetings.

Chapter **VIII**

Managing People for Success

If new products are the fuel that propel growth in the drug industry, people are key to ensuring the engine runs smoothly. During the 1990s the search for good people in Japan became easier than it ever was. Once in the firm, managing people within the context of local cultural practices remained a challenge. Language barriers prevent understanding, but corporate strategies and the chain of command often undermine the good intentions of the best people.

The People Chase

Once upon a time, every year in Japan when the rice fields turned to gold and the maple trees burst into their fall colors, company personnel executives opened their doors to applicants waiting in line. It was an annual rite of passage. Young men donned their newly purchased blue suits, white shirts, and black shoes for interviews. Anyone who knew someone even remotely related to the personal director was pressed into service as a go-between. I remember in the late seventies, when we were adding medical representatives to the Merck Banyu sales force at a rate of 80 to 100 per year, we had 5 to 10 applicants for each job.

Amazing how much can change in 10 years. Recruiting efforts now start with the rainy season. Does anyone really abide by the gentlemen's agreement to wait until September? Recent articles in *The Japan Times* have exposed some ingenious methods for recruiting and signing up the star players. The breath of innovation in this field must be admired.

For those of us in the pharmaceutical industry the trends are not encouraging. There are about 45 million "employees" in Japan, and only 146,000, or 0.3 percent, work in companies who are members of the Japan Pharmaceutical Manufacturers Association. The old fashioned question as to whether foreign affiliated firms could recruit good employees versus their Japanese competitors is no longer the issue.

The real issue is whether the "industry" can attract talent in competition with those who employ 99.7 percent of the work force. We are in danger of not being heard above the noise level. We need to take an industry approach to carrying our message to the students in order to increase the potential pool of applicants for everyone.

Secondly, many people are going to require brain transplants to change their attitudes toward women employees. How much talent is going to waste because of outdated notions concerning women in real jobs, and serving tea does not fit this definition. Attitudes toward foreign employees may be due for a transformation. Who will place a long term positive bet on a company or industry with a "one race, one sex" employment profile?

In my early days in Japan, executives complained that the pool of junior high school graduates who elected not to finish high school was drying up. Later they rued the fact that the pool of high school graduates was diminishing because of a desire by so many to enter college. Now the fundamental demographics are changing. There are fewer births and a declining population of men and women in the 20 to 24 year age group.

Although many are adept at innovative recruiting efforts, the real winners will be those who can think differently about who they want and, more importantly, what will be done with new employees after entering the firm. Chasing good people is a highly developed exercise and the pharmaceutical industry must do a better job. But, what to do after catching them is the real challenge.

Pharma Japan 1168, August 21, 1989

Making Room at the Top

Think of the shape of a pyramid. One upon a time this shape was descriptive of the age structure of a Japanese company—lots of young people and a few old timers. Also recall that salary scales are primarily related to seniority, so older employees always make more than their younger colleagues. Firms with many younger employees are more competitive than firms with relatively more older employees because their personnel costs are lower. Firms that grow rapidly recruit more new employees, which means their wage structure is lower than firms that are not growing and not recruiting young people. Growth fuels growth.

Think of the shape of a column. This is the present age structure of Japanese society. It is a consequence of two factors, people living longer, and declining birth rates. Fewer young people will be entering the labor force, causing firms to recruit intensely for available talent.

Think of the shape of an inverted pyramid. This is a future picture of the age structure in Japan. Very few young people relative to the total population. Entry level workers will be at a premium, but those between 40 and 60 years old will be in surplus. Remember that promotions are also driven by seniority. In the old days there was room at the top, now it is crowded. As a person gets older it is more difficult to receive a promotion because there are so many people waiting in line.

All of this is not just interesting demographic theory. A recent report about Yamaha, a diversified producer of musical instruments and sporting goods, indicated the company has been hit by the double punch of an aging work force and lower sales because of the declining birth rate. For example, pianos are generally purchased for young people, and since the target audience is shrinking, the market is saturated with pianos.

Yamaha launched a voluntary resignation program with a name you would only find in Japan. It is called "Job Switch Life Plan Assistance." Translated it means that the company will assist employees switching jobs in their life plan. In 1991 the plan targeted employees over the age of 40 with a combination of their normal retirement benefits and "gift" money which ranged from 64,000 dollars to 112,000 dollars. A fairly reasonable incentive to make room at the top by enticing people to leave.

Remember that this is the land of "lifetime employment," so encouraging people to leave after the age of 40 is big news. Yamaha's union was not particularly happy. Also remember that this is supposed to be the land of employee loyalty and dedication. Yamaha expected a reasonable thinning of the older ranks. What they got was a major surprise.

When the dust settled, 722 employees applied for job switch life plan assistance. Some changed their minds, and finally 710, or 5.5 percent of the work force, are saying sayonara to Yamaha. More surprising was that 100, or 7.7 percent, of the managers elected to take their money and run. This number was higher than expected, and a Yamaha spokesperson said, "It helped us to make a generation change, but so many retirements are a problem. Next year we will make changes in the practice."

Now think of the curves of a classic pin-up girl. This shape characterizes the age structure of many foreign pharmaceutical companies in Japan. They have successfully recruited people at the top and bottom of the age structure, but lack good people in middle management. The Yamaha case may indicate good people are willing to walk away from slow growing companies to be part of an organization with a dynamic future. The rapidly changing demographics of Japan are creating opportunities not imagined in the past. Making room at the top is a problem for some—an opportunity for others.

Pharma Japan 1279, November 18, 1991

Good People Are (Not) Hard to Find

A distinct advantage of socializing within the ex-pat business community is the absence of conversation about the "good old days" in Japan. One reason is few executives are posted here longer than five years and most rotate out after three years—hardly long enough to qualify as experts on the "old" days. A better reason is that the old days were not good—they were bad, particularly if you drop references to the yen-dollar exchange rates. Operating conditions are now easier, a lot easier in terms of hiring good people.

In retrospect it is remarkable how fast attitudes have changed. I was fond of telling people that a personnel search is like a pregnancy—it takes nine months and the outcome is not guaranteed. Anyone remotely interested in joining a foreign firm was held suspect by family, professors, and peers. To overcome the cultural obstacles, economic perks and status symbols were lavishly bestowed as part of the employment package.

Some foreign managers, ignorant of the game, did not know the Japanese title on one side of the name card was two ranks higher than the English title on the reverse side. Those who recognized the need for status, created a two-tie system, i.e., business titles and social titles. The latter were used with family and neighborhood acquaintances.

Recruiting barriers were formidable if not impossible to overcome. The attraction of a joint venture was in part due to an offer by the Japanese parent to staff the venture. Only much later did it become clear that the JV was a dumping ground for people who were substandard performers. Was there ever a Japanese president of a JV pharmaceutical company that was respected as a leader in the industry?

It pains me to reminisce about the amount of time and effort devoted to recruiting and retaining mediocre people. More time was devoted to internal personnel affairs than to any other phase of the business. How many times was it necessary to feign sincere interest in lecturers on the wisdom and benefits of life-long, seniority-based employment and wage systems? The most vocal supporters were those least capable of marketing their personal qualifications to another company.

It was a pleasure to read about a government survey conducted by the Management and Coordination Agency in October 1995. One conclusion of the report: "There is a growing awareness that life-long employment and the seniority principle, two typical features of the Japanese corporate system, should be revised," was a classic Japanese understatement considering 77.4 percent of those in their 30s said they would consider changing jobs. Furthermore, 27 percent of all respondents, up from 16 percent in 1987, dismissed the practice of basing pay raises and promotion on seniority rather than ability, calling it "a bad system for both employees and management."

This is not news for companies who are inundated with employment applications, or for those who initiate a manager search and fill the position in three months. I get many more phone calls from people looking for a job than from companies looking for people, and I am not in the personnel placement business.

But the good news for a foreign executive new to Japan is:

- You need not sit through more than one lecture on the benefits of life-long employment.
- You need not reward mediocre performers with the same bonus as outstanding performers.
- You need not hire people with minimum acceptable qualifications.
- You need not pay premium salaries or assign infated titles.

But the best news is you can politely say *sayonara* to the guy who always tells you what cannot be done in Japan. Or find a closet for the guy whose English vocabulary is limited to three words "Japan is different." Or dismiss the guy who entertains on the Ginza then pays for everyone to take separate taxis home to Yokohama. Or do not hire the girl who speaks English but cannot type a decent letter in less than one hour. Or find warehouse job for the sales manager who likes to sit in an office but hates to call on doctors. Or say no thank you to the Japanese partner who graciously offers to appoint a very nice person as your personnel director.

God, it makes me feel good to write about the present. Yes, good people are hard to find in any country, but no longer in Japan do you need to employ poor people because they are the only applicants.

Pharma Japan 1491, March 1996

Hunters and Farmers

Company loyalty isn't what it used to be. Have you noticed the number of men opting out of the corporate hierarchy to establish their own businesses? If these entrepreneurial pioneers succeed, others are sure to follow.

Because, many Japanese firms stifle creativity; many fail to reward talent as they fear the disruption of old-fashioned, out-of-date, seniority-based salary scales; many are in organizational gridlock as controlling family members attempt to transfer power to their younger, often less capable relatives; many have not recognized that the world and Japan have changed.

Yet, leaving the corporate womb is not an easy decision. Within is security, a name card that people can identify with, a group within which one can relate to. Corporations can make mistakes and abuse people, but momentum carries dead weight a long way. Start-up companies burn cash surprisingly fast. Former "friends" are not eager to convert their encouraging words into material support.

The men I meet are enthusiastic in the face of these difficulties. They are knowledgeable and have the capacity to provide invaluable information based upon years of experience. Their problem is to find customers willing to pay for information, a product you cannot measure with traditional business tools.

Japanese companies are particularly adverse to buying information from outside, independent operators. To receive useful information they must expose themselves, reveal their objectives and strategies. But information is meaningless unless it relates to a specific plan. A few good men have been successful with general newsletters, or monthly seminars on what happened. It is more difficult to sell what might happen, and how the firm can martial its resources to cope with the future.

I attributed the sparse use of consultants by Japanese firms to group mentality. Those outside the group are not to be trusted with inside information. Recently, a friend who has established his own information business politely suggested I was wrong.

His explanation was that the Japanese have an agricultural or farmer mentality, while Westerners think like hunters. Farmers need to work hard at tilling the soil, planting and harvesting. Good seeds and hard work yield fruit. The weather will be beneficial or harmful; it comes no matter how much is known about the process. Information is in the memory of the participants, derived from experience.

Hunters, on the other hand, need information inputs from many sources. Their targets are elusive, always on the move. It is not enough to work hard, hunters must be smart. Scouts and guides save time by giving directional signals. Information often comes from outside, but implementation is internal.

Hence hunters are more prone to value outside advice prior to and during the implementation of strategy. Farmers are suspicious of outsiders because they know the land and what it can yield with hard work and a bit of luck.

What did happen is important to a farmer because he will plow the same field next year. What will happen is important to a hunter because his quarry is a moving target.

Hunters in Japanese pharmaceutical companies are eager to move on. Foreign companies can take advantage of their information to build competitive advantage at a relatively low cost. Never before have there been so many scouts eager to lead the uninitiated through the wildness of the Japanese market. Get them on your side before the farmers realize there is more to business than harmony and hard work.

Pharma Japan 1328, November 16, 1992

Throw the Bum Out

We all met one, or know one, or have the misfortune of coping with one in our organization. It is a distressing, frustrating, time consuming experience that can sour the most optimistic foreign executives' view of the entire Japanese race.

Let me profile this person.

Nationality: Japanese

Sex: Male

Age: Over 45

Language: English and Japanese, fluent in both.

Position: Senior executive

Education: College degree in Japan, some form of postgraduate education in a U.S. business school.

Experience: Two companies before joining yours. Paper credentials are impeccable.

Hobbies: Golf, karaoke, and fine (expensive) food.

So far, so good. And that is exactly why this person was hired in the first place. He was the perfect person to bridge the cultural and language gaps that existed between the home office and Japan. Everyone he interviewed was impressed because they finally found a Japanese they could relate to in straight business English. When senior executives visited Japan, he made certain they were well cared for, thus enhancing his reputation and status in the organization. He was someone they could trust. His presentations were masterful, the envy of a Harvard B-school professor. He cited well known Japanese government officials as close personal friends. The guy was a dream come true.

Let's go on with the profile, but with information not included in the personnel file.

Attitude toward subordinates:

No one is allowed to question his absolute authority or to raise objections. Tokugawa himself could not exercise more complete control in feudal Japan. His style resembles the player of a popular Japanese arcade game. You stand with an oversized hammer in front of a flat panel with holes. On a random basis, small rodents pop out of the holes. The player scores points by knocking the animals down. As the game proceeds, they pop up faster and faster. Our man wins every game because he visualizes subordinates as rodents in holes.

Communication with others:
Controls all communication in English that comes into or goes out of the company. No one gets an E-mail address except himself. He translates for all home office visitors and they never talk alone with his subordinates. He gets daily reports from the secretary of his gaijin boss. Coincidentally, he hired and recommended this particular secretary.

Presentation skills:
Professional, positive, we can do anything style. But, the presentation is the objective. Not much is done to implement actions that will accomplish the plan objectives.

Motivation:
Money, perks and status utterly impossible to achieve if he was in a Japanese company. He makes constant demands for more, and threatens to resign if his wishes are not granted.

Use of company money:
Extravagant entertaining of Japanese doctors, friends, and assorted cronies who presumably will help the company. Most expenses are billed directly to the company, thereby not appearing on his own expense account. Outright theft is rare, but his lifestyle is akin to a gross misuse of funds.

Status in the industry:
A virtual unknown in industry associations. Exposure to his Japanese peers is uncomfortable because they recognize his faults immediately.

Devotion:
To himself and to his position which must be protected at all costs. Succession planning is a joke.

Is this someone you know in your organization? If so, you are not alone, these guys exist with appalling frequency in foreign firms. To an outsider, they get results and hide their destructiveness. High staff turnover rates are rationalized, and those who leave are not brave enough to blow the whistle. Autocracy works, particularly in this confrontation avoidance society.

But sooner of later a boss comes along who recognizes the problem. Unfortunately, the foreigner is often outwitted or outflanked by this man's well honed political tactics. Or, his delaying moves prolong the decision. No one likes to make a scene, particularly a foreigner who cannot read signals coming from within the organization.

These subtle signals or clues are difficult to evaluate given the obvious language barriers. We are duped into believing that this man's actions are the Japanese way to maintain harmony and to secure the good will of customers. We forget that good common sense is universal. Well run Japanese organizations would not condone this behavior for more than a day.

Advice? Solutions are not painless. For support, talk to senior Japanese executives in affiliated or allied organizations. You may get lucky, as I did years ago when I described my own problem to a distinguished Japanese advisor and friend. He said, "Throw the bum out."

PostScript: We did, and the organization flourished.

Pharma Japan 1512, August 1996

Building a Career in Japan (But What about the Business?)

Build a solid foundation for our company's business in Japan, recruit good people, train them well, imbue them with passion for our products, and establish long term goals.

Is this good advice? If followed, will it advance the career of a foreign executive assigned to Japan? Ideally yes. In reality, no.

The idealists are accused of eating too much rice and failing to recognize who pays their salary, let alone the costs of housing, schools and clubs. Their stellar reputations fade as fast as they learn to bow and avoid confrontations in staff meetings.

The realists write memos and preach about methods used successfully in the country where they came from. Their reputations soar as the home office believes it finally found someone who knows how to make a business work in Japan.

Guess who gets a promotion?

The men assigned to run foreign owned operations in Japan are an elite class of highly qualified, experienced executives. They were selected because of their success in the past and their potential for broader responsibility in the future. An assignment in Tokyo or Osaka for a three year term provides a level of visibility unmatched by any single country market except the United States.

Companies need not be reminded of the importance of this market. They are also aware of their relatively poor performance vis-à-vis Japanese competitors. The old excuses of a closed market do not cut it anymore.

Not too long ago people had to be convinced it was important to succeed in Japan, that the doors were open, that a foreign company could recruit and hire good people. Now they know they must improve their performance, the question is how.

A good place to start is to figure out what is expected from the man at the top. Hard to imagine he comes here with the idea of staying forever, at least initially. It happens. Japan can be like an *onsen*. The water is so hot you can't enter without some degree of pain. But once submerged, it is difficult to leave.

But, the Japan experience is most often like an airline mileage program. Accumulate a sufficient number of paid miles and you are entitled to an upgrade.

A man's success prior to Japan may have been due to an ability to organize a harvest. The plants were growing but weeds and poor field management threatened superior yields. The short term objectives were clear: Cut the weeds and slow growing plants; fertilize those with potential; organize an efficient harvest; prime the distribution channels to receive the fruit; launch an aggressive marketing program to create demand; report the results and move on to another farm.

The Japan job may be more akin to clearing the land of rocks and debris. A man must cut through red tape to receive permission to plow the land from local authorities who prefer the status quo; then plant seeds that may or may not be fertile.

Long before seeds sprout above ground they grow a root system that nobody can see. Impatient bosses see brown dirt when they expected to see green fields. The farmer is asked to leave.

The question of how to succeed is often answered by a reorganization. In a recent Dilbert comic strip the first frame says, "Our executives have started their annual strategic planning sessions." The second says, "This involves sitting in a room with inadequate data until an illusion of knowledge is attained." And finally, "Then we'll reorganize, because that's all we know how to do."

Many men were promoted to Japan while others were moved out because their bosses knew nothing about how to succeed in Japan except to reorganize. Japanese staff in these companies become very good at internal politics. They know more about fighting colleagues than how to beat competitors.

Building a career and building a business is not necessarily a mutually exclusive objective. Change at the top can be refreshing. We all know Japanese companies that would benefit from a change. There are foreign companies run by Japanese presidents who do a better job at protecting their own positions than building dynamic organizations.

Net/net companies get out what they put in. If a man is assigned to Japan to enhance his career, he knows success is measured by short term results. Seed planting is definitely out, reorganization is in.

If a man is expected to accumulate mileage points, he will maintain the status quo until it is time to move on.

In short, men sent to Japan are smart enough to sense what they are expected to do, and do it very well. Once in awhile a guy gets lucky with a boss who says:

"Move to Tokyo and do what you have to do for six months to learn about our operations and people. I will not tell you what should be done or how to change what we have. Then come back and let's discuss what you expect to do, why you want to do it, and what you believe you can accomplish."

I had the good fortune of this conversation in 1976 when I joined Merck in Tokyo. We did some harvesting, some pruning, but mostly plowed new ground. For those of us involved, it was an exhilarating personal and business experience.

Pharma Japan 1639, March 1999

Talkers Talk But Don't Do

Two Stanford professors writing in the May-June, 1999 issue of the Harvard Business Review described a phenomenon applicable to the performance of pharma companies in Japan. They call it the "Smart-talk Trap."

Citing their own research and that of others, they describe the "blabbermouth" theory of leadership. The authors say, "People who want to get ahead in organizations learn that talking a lot helps them to reach their goal more reliably than taking action or inspiring others to act does." The message is: Don't worry about your accomplishments, just make sure you sound good.

Other evidence is presented to show that being critical of one's peers makes a person appear smarter. In other words, pessimism sounds profound, optimism sounds superficial. The authors conclude, "If those with the courage to propose something concrete have been devastated in the process, they'll either leave or learn to be smart-talkers themselves. As a result, a company will end up being filled with clever put-down artists."

We all know this is so true, either because we suffered the barbs of criticism for an idea, or we smart-talked our way into a promotion.

Consider the many Japanese employed by foreign firms because they sounded good in an interview, that is, they could speak English. Subsequently they were promoted far beyond their level of competence on the basis of what they said rather than what they actually accomplished. Some use their language ability to filter all communication with the home office, thereby controlling the information flow.

During the six years I represented the U.S. pharmaceutical industry trade association in Japan, it was most instructive to watch the formulation of initiatives that were to be negotiated with the Ministry of Health and Welfare (Koseisho). Executives who smart-talked and/or criticized Koseisho's policies were successful in leading the discussions, although they did not have constructive ideas of their own. Furthermore, their knowledge of Japan was superficial.

How many guys responsible for operations in Japan fly to the home office with concrete ideas for improving performance only to be shot down by staff people who specialize in the put-down game? After a few of these experiences, good people look for a company that values action rather than talk.

Unfortunately many executives are promoted to senior positions in Japan because they were smart-talkers. These are the some people we hear criticizing the way things are done in Japan. Since they based their career on intelligent sounding critical analyses of other people's ideas, they find Japan a gold mine in which to ply their trade.

Some years ago, a man became president of a U.S. firm only to be ceremoniously dumped in a boardroom coup. There were many theories as to why this occurred as the man had many supporters in the organization. I asked the opinion of a Japanese company president. He said, "During the years this man moved up the ladder, he never had to prove he could do something."

Of course, Japanese companies are not immune from this disease. Take a Board with 30 directors, all insiders, and all beholden to the CEO for their jobs and the timing of their retirements. With few exceptions, they are masters at sensing what the boss wants to hear rather than what he should hear. They do not rock the boat because they know they would be the first to end up in the water.

Over the years I had the pleasure of knowing some exceptions. Two come to mind. Mr. Honda of the car company that bears his name could not be smart-talked by an engineer or production manager because he knew how to get his hands dirty on the shop floor. Mr. Morita, founder of Sony, knew what it was like to market a product in the United States because he lived there and was the company's sole salesman. Both gentlemen built organizations that rewarded innovation and entrepeneurship. Interesting that both companies had their greatest success outside Japan.

Since I attended the Stanford Business School 31 years ago, I receive their various publications. One annual report lists the salaries and jobs taken by new

MBA graduates. A person can go into industry, become a plant manager, and make between $80,000 and $100,000 a year. Or a person can earn double these figures by joining a consultancy where the job is to give advice to plant managers.

This is not to say that companies do not need good advice, particularly if it is objective and untainted by internal politics. The inherent problem is the message in the pay scale gap. In essence, it is more rewarding to talk than to do.

One subject that engenders more talk than action is acquisition. Building a presence in Japan through an acquisition is not the only way to get the job done, but it is a viable option, more so today than at any time in the past. Many companies publicly say they are interested in making an acquisition should the right opportunity come along. The words suggest commitment, but the reality is something else. Give these people a target company and they will find innumerable reasons why it is not the right opportunity. Again, the real issue is that people score points by pointing to problems not opportunities. They specialize in why an acquisition should not be made rather than on how to make it.

I am amused by how frequently the Merck purchase of Banyu in 1983 is referred to as a brilliant strategy. Since I played a key role in that transaction, the praise is gratifying. Little do they know how many people in Merck considered it a dumb move at the time. If these smart-talkers were a part of the decision process, the deal would never have happened.

People who want to act face an uphill battle in Japan. In Japanese companies the notion is to stand in rather than to be outstanding. In foreign companies it is OK to be outstanding if you articulate why something will not work. Be pessimistic, it signifies deep thought and profound intelligence. Optimists are accused of eating too much rice.

Pharma Japan 1661, August 1999

Beware of the Corporate Immune System

Enough evidence exists to convince die-hard champions of the status quo that the Japanese pharmaceutical market is undergoing massive change. Those who don't know the facts are either dead or living in a dream world created by chemical substance abuse.

However, a high degree of uncertainty exists as to the proper response to change. I see three general reactions:

1. "We are doing all right in this little part of the world and making good money. Why should we change?" Even those who recognize the need to change and hire high priced consultants do not know what to change into. They conclude, "Thank you very much, we will not trade a certain present (still profitable) for an uncertain future."

2. An attitude of this too will pass. A common comment is, "We will survive by reengineering and restructuring our operations. We will seriously reevaluate 'how' to do business; make ourselves leaner and meaner; cut costs and become more efficient in our existing competencies." They use business school buzz words, but fail to ponder "who" will be their customer, and "what" products or services should be offered to their chosen customers.

3. A realization, often grudgingly, that no one knows the ultimate outcome of change; what core competency will be needed in the future; or what ideas will succeed. Nevertheless, they are willing to experiment with new ideas.

Companies in the first two categories are depressing. They have well established corporate immune systems that kill off intruding initiatives for fear they might infect the rest of the organism. The immune system protects the status quo. It feeds on complacency, internal politics and fear. Its spokesmen give you a zillion reasons why Japan is different, why it is better to stand in rather than stand out, why they cannot divert resources from established programs.

Take a simple example of change in the distribution sector. As clear as Mt. Fuji on a crisp autumn day, we see fewer doctors dispensing drugs. Prescriptions filled at independent pharmacies are growing rapidly as economic incentives for doctors to dispense are eliminated.

Wholesalers with a regional presence (10 or less) will dominate the Tokyo, Nagoya, Osaka areas where half of Japan's population resides. In less than five years, 50 wholesalers will distribute 95 percent of all drugs throughout Japan, down from 100 in 1997.

It does not take the brain of Stephen Hawking to understand companies must change their supply chain management policies. New strategic ideas are easy to formulate.

One of the most obvious is to focus on fewer wholesalers. But the immune system responds by saying, "One hundred wholesaler customers are too many, but how do we tell 75 they will be cut off?" Their solution is to put 25 on an "A" list and move from the old to the new slowly: let 100 coexist, but over time devote resources to 25 and gradually neglect the rest.

While this strategy minimizes the conflict and trauma of change, it allows the immune system to sabotage the transition. In essence, no one lacks tactics to innovate or change, but most lack the will to put tactics into practice.

The immune system cannot be eliminated. Waging war against it would try the patience of a saint. In fact, kept in check it provides a necessary degree of stability in times of turbulence. After all, a company cannot place bets on every new idea dropped in a suggestion box. A more productive alternative is to create an atmosphere where innovations are not killed by the immune system.

Experimenters or innovators exhibit the following characteristics:

1. They ask questions about "who" is going to be their customer. Is it only the doctor? Not likely when pharmacists, administrators and patients participate in therapeutic choices.
2. They ask questions about "what" services should be provided to their chosen customers. Is it a rebate or discount on the purchase price versus the reimbursement price? Not likely as reimbursement policies change.
3. They are not consumed by "how" to do business. After all the downsizing and rightsizing it is unrealistic to assume the company will reach a state of blissful success. They periodically question the status quo to destabilize the immune system.
4. They find champions for new ideas and protect them from the immune system.

Because every innovation is different from the status quo, it needs support from the top. The worse companies have presidents who defend the status quo. Innovative ideas from below are stifled, employees with passion and self-confidence leave, and the immune system destroys its host. Innovative firms encourage dissatisfaction with the status quo. All new ideas are not good, but a company without a new idea is bad.

Pharma Japan 1611, August 1998

Is Learning Japanese Worth the Effort?

If you read the sports pages, you know Japan recently qualified for the 1999 Rugby World Cup finals by winning the Asian final qualifying round in Singapore. Rather remarkable that Japan keeps coming back for more. In 1994 they were trashed 145 to 17 by New Zealand's All Blacks. A real tribute to the old adage, "Hope springs eternal."

More remarkable is the national side is captained by a New Zealander, Andrew McCormick, who came to Japan in 1992 to play for Toshiba Fuchu. This is the first time a foreigner has been selected as captain. But Andrew doesn't think of himself as a foreign player. He speaks good Japanese and considers it natural that the team is made up of the best players in Japan. In other words, not just the best from certain schools or clubs, or those with a certain level of seniority or racial purity—just simply, the best.

I don't know 31-year-old Andrew but I had the good fortune of playing U.S. style football in college and rugby at the University of Otago in Dunedin, N.Z. A biased view perhaps, but participation in these sports is a great way to learn about people.

Therefore, it is worth listening to a person who walks the talk. His words were reported by *The Japan Times*:

"In Japanese institutions it's hard to do things individually, so they don't get a chance to make individual decisions. When it comes to rugby, you have to make decisions. But lots of guys panic because they haven't been put in that situation before.

They are good players but some of them lack confidence. They are scared of making mistakes instead of having confidence in their own ability. You know, no one is perfect. We do make mistakes. But we've got to go out and do it."

Well said Andrew. I suspect his insights are the result of a commitment to learn Japanese and the fortitude to go out and do it. Which leads me to the title of this piece.

Every executive sent to Japan to run a pharmaceutical business is prone to schizophrenia, that is, a fight between the reality of demands by the home office and the reality of executing them. Or the reverse. Knowing what it takes to succeed in Japan and the reality of corporate indifference or outright rejection.

Schizophrenia sets in when there is a flight from reality. Perhaps some examples will illustrate the disease.

It did not take Henri long after his arrival in Tokyo to recognize his company did not have a qualified senior Japanese executive to execute plans with and through their licensees, let alone build a stand alone business. Henri's limited Japanese helped him understand what had to be done, but would not get it done. He needed an effective right hand man.

A candidate appeared with everything Henri was looking for. Solid industry experience, bilingual skills, and a desire to accept the challenge. Unfortunately the home office took a dim view of the additional expense and killed the deal. If only they understood the investment would have generated dividends for years.

John was selected as president of his company's Japan operations when he was 33 years old, replacing a much older man. John's boss, the president of the International Division, took him aside and urged him to do whatever it took to learn Japanese since no previous foreigner sent from the home office had bothered.

John followed this advice and after five years earned the respect of his older Japanese colleagues. In the meantime the International Division was "globalized" out of existence and John had a new boss and a steady stream of corporate staff visitors. His knowledge of Japanese seemed to intimidate the visitors. They felt John was more like one of them rather than one of us. In short, they believed John had eaten too much rice. With the writing on the wall, John moved before he was asked to leave. He made an immense contribution in another company that appreciated his knowledge of the language.

Hans came to Japan without the slightest interest in learning Japanese. His objective was to faithfully carry out directives formulated by the home office. Based on his experience in other markets, he believed the Japanese staff were asleep and needed a wake-up call. This view was endorsed by his boss and corporate staff.

Hans cut a swath through the Japanese operations. He reorganized, restructured, and replaced. Salary schedules were revised, distributor contracts were renegotiated, and sales territories were realigned. No one could predict what would happen next.

The staff went into a survival mode which meant they stayed out of the way and provided as little information as possible. They learned fast that the messenger with bad news was killed. After three years Hans was rewarded with a nice promotion out of Japan and was last heard bragging about how to do business in Japan.

Recent research on the characteristics of global leaders suggest that a person's ability to bridge cultural, language, and social borders is dependent on two sets of characteristics. About two-thirds of the characteristics apply generically to effective people. They include character, savvy, and inquisitiveness. Andrew, the rugby player, did not become captain of the Japanese national side because he could speak Japanese. He most certainly has leadership skills understood in any language.

About one-third of the characteristics are context—specific abilities. For example, knowledge of the culture, language, and industry dynamics in a specific country. Japanese models of leadership were the hot subject of business seminars until people realized they worked in Japan because Japanese leaders largely interacted with other Japanese. Many of these same skills were useless in Ohio.

No amount of Japanese language skills will compensate for poor leadership qualities. But a good pharma exec will not be an effective captain of the team if he remains ignorant of the Japanese language. Of course he can always run for president of the American Club.

Pharma Japan 1625, November 1998

Break With Tradition

Foreign executives who work in Japan rarely live in Japan. Their temporary quarters in no way resemble typical Japanese homes. Their children walk or ride a bus to an international, English speaking school. Their associations, clubs and social life revolve around western institutions. Their wives plan trips outside Japan to coincide with school breaks, which occur frequently. Their home offices schedule meetings that require more transpacific flights than a United Airlines flight attendant.

It is not surprising they fall into the trap of adhering to business traditions that worked for them elsewhere, or worse, believing the adage, "When in Japan do as the Japanese do."

Tradition, as defined by my pocket electronic dictionary, is "any time-honored set of practices or beliefs." It is good advice to follow tradition if you came to Japan to study flower arranging, be a sumo wrestler or a sake brewer. If you came here to build a software business or a world class pharmaceutical company, time honored beliefs are definitely not the way to do it.

Study traditions as a hobby, but never use them as a guide to good business. By doing so you will not take traditions seriously but impress everyone by your interest in the culture. Second, you will understand what not to do in your regular job; and third, you will appreciate how much Japan has changed and is changing.

There must be a compartment in the western brain that is wired with neurons during gestation whose sole purpose is to process Japanese data inputs into a file marked "The Mysterious East." This prohibits rational analysis and converts otherwise smart guys into advocates of the status quo, uttering phrases that end with the solemn need to "save face."

Why else do so many get sucked into following tradition or listening to traditionalists who have no other motive than protecting their own turf and the perks that go with it? Unfortunately, creative rebels are not allowed to speak. It is tough to stand out when so many believe you win by standing in.

Listen to tradition as articulated by sales executives:
"Women will not make good MRs."
"We need sales offices everywhere."
"We need 100 wholesalers so those guys will compete for our business."
"MRs should see 15 doctors a day."
"Give me a fat rebate to convince wholesalers to push our products."

And the clinical development coordinators:
"Just get the case cards at the end of the trial."
"Informed consent will never work in Japan."
"We can't help it if drugs prohibited by the protocol are administered."
"The sales director wants clinical trials run in every hospital we visit."
"If we put every possible side effect in the protocol, patient enrollment will take forever."

And the personnel directors:
"Seniority should determine 100 percent of the wage scale."
"Individual rewards will damage the harmony of the group."
"Reducing the bonus is impossible."
"Lifetime employment is the fundamental pillar of successful labor relations."

And production managers:
"I don't understand a 'make or buy' analysis."
"Products made outside Japan cannot meet our quality standards."
"We need two more distribution centers."

And finally, the business strategists:
"You cannot buy a Japanese company."
"The only way to do business in Japan is to form a joint venture."
"By licensing out products we minimize expenses and optimize income."

This is a great time to live in Japan because many of the diehard traditionalists are running for cover. Every day we are treated to examples of tradition meltdown in the face of refreshing reality. Do not believe Japan is becoming more western, it is an egotistical view of change in Japan that will never happen. But do believe Japan is changing in ways previously considered impossible.

The best response is to discard tradition. Japan is not going down the tubes, nor is it going to take over the world. Both views have been widely disseminated by the media. More realistic is the middle ground where good common sense prevails. There are well managed, competitive companies as well as badly managed, traditionally arrogant companies on a going out of business curve. It doesn't take much wisdom to know the difference.

Pharma Japan 1589, March 1998

Chapter IX

Mergers, Acquisitions and Alliances

For a long time outside observers predicted consolidation of the Japanese drug industry, but people
inside the industry refused to cooperate. No one
could justify a merger and acquisitions were akin to
rape. Acquisitive minded foreign companies generally lacked the commitment and patience to proceed.
Alliances could not be defined in practical terms. Few
deals were done, but the underlying rational persist-
ed. Is it only a matter of time before the inevitable will
finally occur?

M&A in Japan—A Personal Perspective

Mergers and acquisitions in Japan is a wide subject that could be treated in a variety of ways. An investment banker might trace the number and type of acquisitions in Japan and wax eloquently on the need for consolidation in certain industries. A lawyer might review laws which govern shareholder rights. A tax accountant might discuss pooling of interests and good will. And a sociologist would write about corporate cultures.

My own perspective does not come from any of these specialized areas, nor does it encompass industries outside that of pharmaceuticals. It is a result of being inside the process, of having lived through the excitement and despair of doing it.

In August 1983, I assisted Merck & Co to acquire two Japanese companies for approximately $400 million. One of the acquisitions was the first, and still is the only, majority acquisition of a company listed on the first section of the Tokyo Stock Exchange. The second acquisition was a company protected by major Japanese shareholders. Everyone said it couldn't be done—but it was done, and done well:

Through this experience here is a message which can be summarized in three statements.

- It is a myth to believe acquisitions are not a viable strategy for entry and growth in Japan. The fact that more are not done relates to a lack of commitment rather than culture.
- An acquisition strategy can be justified for only two reasons, that is to save time and to build critical mass;
- A "deal" is only the beginning in building a viable presence which requires a level of passion beyond the capability of most organizations. Stay away from people who like to do deals but have no experience of building a business.

Prior to joining Merck in 1976, I directed the Eli Lilly operations in Japan—which consisted of a long-standing, profitable relationship with Shionogi. Lilly products were imported, promoted and distributed by Shionogi's powerful sales organization.

Although Lilly product sales in Japan were the largest of any foreign pharmaceutical company, and the Lilly name was on every package, Lilly did not have a presence. Why worry about a presence when your products dominate their therapeutic classes?

A key to long-term success in Japan is presence. Presence means knowing your customers—you cannot do that by selling through a distributor. You do not satisfy customers by having a liaison office. And Japan is too important to remain on the sidelines calling in plays to a team that has its own coach. But it did not make sense for Lilly to establish a presence independent of the Shionogi relationship. So we set out to structure a partnership through which our future would be intertwined and mutually profitable. Today, the proper word would be an alliance.

Alliances are difficult to structure anywhere in the world for one fundamental reason. Executives do not know how to manage "Shared control." It is not a part of their training, experience or education. Control has been the operative word since humans stopped being hunters and gatherers, and started to manage systems.

The lessons leaned from the Lilly experience proved invaluable, and included:

- An acquisition strategy must be built on a firm base of commitment. It is not another option to be cast out lightly as though you were fishing;
- The long-term objectives of each party must be fully explored prior to any mention of the word acquire. The word has serious connotations;
- An acquisition strategy must be implemented locally, it cannot be managed from afar;
- Outsiders cannot initiate acquisitions. They help to close or structure financing, but the beginnings are between insiders.

Merck had been inside Japan since the early 1950s, primarily through a joint venture with Banyu called Nihon Merck Banyu. NMB had a development laboratory, a respectable manufacturing facility to finish raw material supplied by Merck, and a 300-man sales force that promoted but could not sell products to doctors. Banyu was responsible for distribution, which in Japan means selling.

As time moved on, the Merck strategy in Japan was driven by new products in the research pipeline. They were coming, but because NMB had been sleeping we needed to build critical mass quickly. We were soon hiring 50 to 100 new medical representatives every year, but our major Japanese competitors already had 1,500. Even with hiring 100 a year, we would need 12 years to catch up.

Furthermore, Banyu was responsible for distribution, which means selling. Therefore there were two options. The first was to take control of NMB and build a distribution capability. In the pharmaceutical industry, the classic joint venture model is dead because of the need to have fully-integrated operations-from research to distribution.

So the first option to buy out the partner was discarded in favor of buying the partner itself. Our first move was to agree on a symbolic, but meaningful 5 percent share of Banyu, to be purchased on the open market. This had to be done in absolute secrecy so as to not drive up the market price, or to arouse any suspicion or idle speculation of our motives.

Purchases were made by a broker in London who dealt with many brokers in Japan on behalf of a company Merck established in Panama. Small purchases were made daily, and the results were reported to only four people in Merck under the guise of a manufacturing operation. It was a beautiful operation, proving that you can keep a secret in Japan—up to a point. All shares bought in Japan go through a central clearing house, and an inquisitive clerk eventually noticed the buying pattern. Having noticed, he had classic inside information, and for the first time we noticed unusual activity in the purchase pattern of Banyu stock. At this point we held 4.5 percent, just a half percent from our goal. We closed quickly with a little help from our friends, who provided a block of shares that put us over the top.

But we never stopped talking about acquiring 50 percent plus of Banyu shares. An outside investment banker was brought in to help with the delicate and difficult structuring of the financial deal. There was much careful hand holding and commitments to respect Banyu management. The process moved inexorably forward for several reasons:

- Merck was committed to achieving critical mass and focussing its Japanese operations in the shortest possible time. In that sense it needed Banyu;
- Banyu did not have new products of its own. It needed Merck or face a very uncertain future;
- coincidentally, Merck had another option of purchasing a majority interest in the Torii company, an alternative that did not go unnoticed by Banyu executives; and
- our efforts to unleash NMB were paying off. The child company was outgrowing its Japanese parent.

The message here is that acquisitions do not happen without pressure, both internally and externally. Public relations aside, one management group is rarely willing to say to another management group, "please acquire us."

Merck, through its acquisitions, achieved a position in Japan beyond any other foreign company. New products were marketed successfully and the company was inside Japan with fully integrated operations. After the announcement of our purchase, the employees said OK—now what? It was like at the end of World War II when, despite U.S. expectations of a long drawn out battle to clear pockets of resistance in every mountain in Japan, the Emperor said the war was over, and instead everyone got on with building a peaceful dynamic economy.

No government ministry delayed or tried to stop our moves. The press said we had bridged the moat of the castle, but not a single shareholder of Banyu objected to the decision to be acquired. Merck proved acquisitions are a viable strategy in Japan. However, it is only one way to succeed. Anything is possible, but there is no quick fix. What works is a passion to succeed, and a total commitment to do whatever it takes to be inside the market.

Market Letter, February 3, 1992

Too Many Pharmaceutical Companies?

According to the gospels of Goldman, Lehman, and Morgan, there are too many pharmaceutical companies in Japan. Their elaborate, computer-driven scenarios predict the consolidation of the industry on a major scale. This is the time to buy in, and when there are acquisitions, there are fees.

Since most readers are familiar with their presentations, I need only summarize the arguments. Over 450 companies have drugs with National Health Insurance Price listing. Approximately 200,000 people are employed by the industry (a number roughly equal to U.S. employment), but 60 percent of the manufacturers employ 50 employees or less.

Relative to other industries in Japan, the pharmaceutical industry is under-capitalized. Markets are fragmented, and the top 10 companies account for less than 40 percent of the market, a number which has remained relatively constant for 20 years. In 1971 it was 41.5 percent.

Relative to the U.S. pharmaceutical industry, Japanese majors report about one-half the net margins, and one-third the return on both equity and total assets. Furthermore, the amount of money spent on research is much lower. To top it off, foreign companies are competing more aggressively in Japan, putting pressure on the viability of Japanese companies who do not have a full product pipeline.

With a drum roll the presentations end, and the "obvious" conclusion is given— the Japanese pharmaceutical industry must and will consolidate.

Audiences nod with bemused understanding and rush off to set up their own computerized data bank on the 1,300+ companies in Japan. Their strategic plans are revised to include an acquisition objective. The ideal target profile is defined, as if they expect to shop in a supermarket where abundant choices are available. Investment bankers are retained.

And then? Nothing happens.

I have heard the same story off and on for 21 years. Yet there are more pharmaceutical companies in Japan today than when I first arrived in Japan. At some time the forecasts may come true. Then we will hear a loud chorus of "I told you."

It might be more practical to assume niche players in this industry will not be driven out. That large companies become so bureaucratic they cease to innovate, that all the diseases of our marvelously complex bodies will not succumb to one magic cure, and that no company will have a monopoly on brains or a lock on all customers.

Just maybe—think about it—there are not enough companies. Not enough centers of creative people searching for cures for common ailments. Maybe small is really beautiful in this business. Next time the pin-striped crowd comes calling, tell them you are too busy looking for a pill to cure a hangover from too many M&A presentations.

Pharma Japan, 1250, April 25, 1991

What Is an Alliance?

Taiwan Aerospace and McDonnel Douglas were negotiating a US$2 billion deal in May for the production of a new MD-12 jetliner that will carry 450 to 600 people. A senior Taiwan Aerospace executive was quoted as saying; we must work as human beings to work out a *strategic alliance* that will last into the 21st century.

Bethlehem Steel and National Steel agreed to form a 50:50 joint venture in May to build a US$100 million steelcoating plant in Jackson, Mississippi. National Steel is 70 percent owned by Japan's NKK Corp., which prompted the Wall Street Journal to report this news as a *venture* between American steelmakers and Japanese *partners*.

Venture, joint venture, partner, strategic alliance—what do these words mean? Are they buzz words for the M&A community, or do they have real meaning for executives responsible for running global business?

In Japan, in the pharmaceutical sector, a joint venture was the only entry model permitted by the government until restrictions were removed in 1973. The structure is familiar, and was cloned by many foreign drug firms for 20 years. It was characterized by shared control—everything was 50:50.

During the last 10 years, divorce rates of joint venture partners far exceeded those in the general society. A few were amicable separations, most were messy, long, drawn-out negotiations over property rights and future payments akin to alimony settlements. The most delicate and distressing discussions concerned disposition of the children, the employees of the joint venture. Maybe this is why prenuptial agreements have come into vogue, that is, predetermined conditions whereby the venture is spun off as a separate whole.

It is not surprising that the word "joint venture" carries a lot of unpleasant baggage. I negotiated the termination of three joint ventures and now cringe at the very mention of the word. Thus, the word venture is more appropriate; partnering may be better.

Ventures can also be international, or at least, transnational. Two parties, each of different nationality, say something like this: "We need help here, you need help there, let's form a venture in both countries, each to our own advantage." This is a creative way to avoid the pitfalls of shared control, but only time will tell if two partners can work out the complexities inherent in cross national arrangements. Venturing in one country is difficult enough.

The word "strategic" has a military ring to it, implying power, clear-cut plans, and effective execution. It fits neatly into the specialized vocabulary of corporations who are accustomed to developing strategic plans. This comfortable word is often used as a modifier to partner or venture, as in "strategic partner."

An alliance model is more than hype, more than a new lease on life for consultants. In my view, the word alliance is applied to an interrelationship that redefines the business for two or more parents. The new whole goes beyond what they might achieve alone, or through a merger or joint venture.

Will more than a few pharmaceutical companies become truly global? Merck is now the largest, yet it has a paltry 4.1 percent share of the world market. No single company dominates research in every therapeutic class.

The interdependence of partners in an alliance optimizes their individual research, production and development strength. Each partner utilized its strong, local, independent marketing force. Time is not wasted creating new entities, or negotiating shared control. Time is saved by expediting global development of new chemical entities. Basic research resources are focused rather than diffused. No part has viability except in an intrinsic relation to every other part in the new whole.

Other models stress the importance of parts. The joint venture model particularly, stressed independent advantage, often unrelated to the purpose of the parents. Alliances imply dependence, while taking advantage of independent local capabilities.

Giant companies in the pharmaceutical industry recognized they cannot go it alone, but megamergers are disruptive. One-off licensing deals and limited ventures are stop-gap measures. Alliances will redefine the business, and they are coming sooner than you think.

Pharma Japan 1310, July 6, 1992

What the Hell Is an Alliance?

Because couples, as well as groups of people legally organized in corporations forged new ways to work together, we lack a proper vocabulary to describe these relationships. It was easy when you only needed three words to describe a women's relationship with a man, i.e., friend, date or wife.

Not too long ago you could describe the relationship between a foreign company and a Japanese company in two ways, i.e., joint venture or licensor/licensee. In the 1980s four new "co" words became popular, i.e., co-development, co-marketing, co-promotion, and co-distribution. Some companies now prefer to use the prefix "joint," or attach an explanation if the same chemical entity is sold fewer than two different brand names.

On March 2, PHARMA JAPAN listed what were called "Major M&As and Tie-ups in 1997." Similar lists by investment bankers are called "transactions" or "deals." The PHARMA JAPAN list had 98 entries. Analyzed closely, many different words were used to describe business relationships:

- marketing agreement
- acquired exclusive rights of a co-developed drug
- agreed to establish a joint venture
- license agreement for exclusive marketing rights
- agreed to co-market
- a development and marketing agreement
- exclusive license contract
- a contract for R&D cooperation
- joint business agreement
- will merge
- contract for the introduction of technology
- conduct joint research, development, and marketing
- licensed out

- began co-promoting
- terminated a business alliance
- made a strategic alliance
- transferred its business
- collaborative research agreement
- reached a technical agreement
- signed an equity participation agreement
- concluded a sole agent contract
- acquired management rights

This is equivalent to the biblical expression of people talking in "tongues," no one understands what is being said, but it must have something to do with business. Are we trying to prove that English can be as imprecise as Japanese in describing a business relationship? But this too is a fallacy. Any language is precise when used properly. People who use the language are the problem.

The phrase "joint venture" is archaic for good reasons—it carries the baggage of undesirable operating constraints imposed by government restrictions or opposing interests by the parent companies. Joint ventures were either destined to be bought out by one of the parents or abandoned by both.

A good example is the recent quote by a Takeda spokesman who said, "Takeda is seeking to take over all of its 50:50 joint venture with Gruenthal which has been in operation since 1991. Negotiations are underway but if these fail, Takeda will expand its own independent drug distribution in Germany." If the Japanese can be so precise about their intentions in a foreign country, why do foreigners feel the need to save face with imprecise language in Japan? (Note: The Takeda spokesman subsequently claimed he was misquoted, and added, "The company does not plan to act independently.") Let's wait and see.

As if the current babble was insufficient to describe business relationships, the word alliance, or strategic alliance is becoming popular. The airline industry uses it frequently to describe code sharing arrangements that facilitate the flow of passengers to destinations not directly serviced by one carrier. Is it a useful word for the pharmaceutical industry?

A foreign drug company with a strong position in Europe sent a senior executive to visit a Japanese company with the following proposal: "We are strong in Europe but weak in Japan. You are strong in Japan but weak in Europe. Let's form an alliance whereby you help us in Japan and we will help you in Europe. What do you think?"

The Japanese response to a concept is invariably favorable because there is nothing concrete on which to offer an objection. The foreigner departed thinking he reached an agreement, and the Japanese waited for a specific proposal. After innumerable letters back and forth, the idea faded into oblivion.

The word alliance can be refreshing because it permits both parties to try something new. It implies a willingness to search for win-win solutions. On the other hand, the word itself is vague and has no meaning unless it serves as a framework upon which specific responsibilities are defined.

Licensing in or out and joint business agreements are usually one off deals confined to a single product in a specific territory. An alliance may include licensing agreements, but specifies broader cooperative efforts to exploit a market previously unserved by either party acting alone.

In the previous Europe/Japan example, the foreign executive was really proposing a cross licensing arrangement, i.e., "We will license our products to you for Japan if you will license your products to us for Europe." That's fine, but save the word alliance to initiate a new business. For example, both parties could form an alliance to make investments in emerging biotechnology ventures in the United States. The technology and products that flow from these investments would be commercialized by each party in their respective markets, i.e. Europe and Japan.

Some foreign companies are marginal players in Japan. Some Japanese companies do not have a prayer of competing effectively in either the United States or Europe. Both need new business strategies that go beyond traditional licensing, joint ventures, or acquisitions they cannot afford or manage. Alliances offer win-win solutions, but the concept alone will die if not defined in operational terms fully understood by both sides.

Pharma Japan 1603, June 1998

Should You Buy a Company?

To buy or not to buy, that is the question. Companies asking the old question, "Can I buy a company?" are out of touch with present realities. Why?

One reason is they still listen to people who only talk about what cannot be done in Japan. Every sentence begins with three words, "Japan is different." Clarifying differences is a productive exercise if the end result is resolution of how to achieve defined objectives in the shortest time. Unfortunately, differences are often cited to block actions that deviate from the old ways of doing business.

Another reason is their past experience with investment bankers who received handsome fees to conduct paper exercises on possible target acquisitions. They typically concluded there was nothing worth buying at the price/earnings multiples common in Japan.

A third reason is the lack of commitment to an acquisition strategy. Management takes the position of wait and see. "If something comes along, we will give it serious consideration." The assumption that opportunities will mysteriously appear is ludicrous, if not an arrogant attitude of "they need us more than we need them" way of thinking.

The first step in reaching a decision to buy or not to buy has nothing to do with the external environment. Rather it is an internal process of evaluating the company's strengths and weaknesses; its product pipeline and capacity to optimize growth; and a realistic assessment of achieving corporate sales targets solely by organic growth. Three brief cases illustrate different answers to the buy decision.

Company ABC built a development team capable of bringing its new products through the entire registration process, but has no marketing force. Products now in development are innovative and will be prescribed by a limited number of specialists practicing in large medical institutions. Japanese companies are lined up outside ABC's door to request marketing rights, promising nationwide promotion and distribution if their cost of product sold is at 30 percent or less of the net selling price.

ABC decided to build its own MR force and wholesaler network, thus directly participating in the value added chain.

Company XYZ is developing and promoting its products, but only recently established its own distribution network. It has 400 MRs concentrated in large hospitals. New products in the pipeline will require more promotion support in smaller hospitals without detracting from the promotion of current products. It has received numerous co marketing proposals from Japanese and foreign companies.

XYZ decided to co market its new products with a Japanese company that employs 300 MRs, in return for an initial equity participation of 5 percent. A written agreement will specify future increases in ownership based on the sales of XYZ's products.

Company A to Z has a fully integrated presence in Japan from research through distribution. It employs 700 MRs. Results to date are OK but unsatisfactory when compared to market penetration in the United States and Europe. New products in the pipeline will appeal to a variety of audiences, but none are in the blockbuster category. In fact, if any falter in the approval process, A to Z will face severe cost cutting measures.

A to Z decided to seriously pursue an acquisition strategy focused on companies in the ¥40 billion to ¥60 billion sales range. It wants an initial controlling equity position of 30 percent through which it can execute immediate cost saving measures and solidify its market position with current products.

XYZ and A to Z decided to pursue acquisition strategies, albeit for very different reasons. Now they must define the attributes of a suitable partner in a flexible manner—recognizing there is no such thing as a perfect wife. While the external environment is favorable for successful acquisitions, it is naive to believe there are an unlimited number of possibilities. Flexibility in the process is essential.

The old question, "Can I buy a company," is passé. The answer is a resounding YES. Why?

The first reason relates to the rapidly changing health care system. In the past there was enough money in the system to keep everyone afloat. The insurers are now running such huge deficits they will fight back with a vengeance, extracting cost reductions from both the providers and suppliers of healthcare. Those who cannot justify their presence in the food chain will be eliminated.

Second, rewards will flow to those who innovate rather than simply adapt. Many participants in the industry survived because they could adapt to price changes and other minor changes in the reimbursement structure. They believe serious problems will somehow go away. But their viability is seriously threatened, and can only be assured by innovating—a skill they sorely lack.

Third, some companies on a firm foundation are going through a generation change of management. The successors, while nice people and well meaning, are not up to the task of running a thriving enterprise. It would be a blessing for them and their employees if they left wealthy and graciously.

This was a buy and hold society. No more. Practical business wisdom dictates that hard choices must be made to preserve the future of the institution. Japan is different, and one difference is a deep appreciation for the benefits of pragmatism, of reality versus theory. The question "To be or not to be?" was never understood in Japan. "To be," is the only relevant issue. A decision to discuss the possibility of being acquired has a direct impact on the "To be" element of the equation.

Acquisition Failure? Don't Blame the Culture

For the past 23 years the only investment barrier in Japan for Western pharmaceutical companies has been their inability to make attractive acquisitions. I say their inability because there is no law, stock market regulation, or company rule that prevents foreign companies from buying Japanese companies.

The fact that acquisitions have been done, albeit only 10 during the past 16 years as shown in Table 1, is proof they can be done. This article will explore why more are not done and suggest the reasons lie inside foreign companies rather than outside.

Table 1   The Number of Out/In Deals Is Limited

1983	Merck buys Torii
	Merck buys Banyu
1986	Merrel Dow buys Funai
	Boehringer Ingelheim buys San-a & Yamaguchi
1989	Boehringer Mannheim buys Toho
1992	Solvay buys Kowa Yakuhin
1994	MMD buys Kodama
1996	BASF/Knoll buys Hokuriku Seiyaku
	Boehringer Ingelheim buys 9% of SS Pharma
1997	Amersham buys Roche stake in Nihon Mediphysics
1998	None to date

Notes: 1. Excludes investments to buy out equity held by Japanese partners in joint ventures.
2. Merck's controlling interest in Torii was sold to Asahi Beer in 1988. Recently Torii was sold to Japan Tobacco.
3. MMD and Boehringer Mannheim were acquired by Hoechst and Roche respectively.

The Environment

Table 2 is one of many ways to demonstrate the fragmented nature of the Japanese pharma industry. The 10 largest companies actually lost market share from 1990 to 1995. Recent data indicates the top 10 regained a 34 percent share; comforting, but hardly a dominant position, particularly since Merck, HMR, and Novartis knocked Yoshitomi, Chugai, and Tanabe out of the overall top 10 list.

Note that 16 percent of the market is occupied by companies ranked below 100th, whereas worldwide companies in this class represent only 3 percent of the market.

The 30 largest companies in Japan represent 56 percent of the market, while worldwide they occupy a 71 percent share. The data strongly suggests major restructuring in Japan is inevitable. When it will occur is debatable.

Table 2   Fragmented Industry

			(% Market Share)
Year	Japan		Worldwide
	1990	1995	1995
1–10th largest	34	31	35
11–30	25	25	36
31–50	13	14	15
51–100	13	14	11
Other	15	16	3

The primary reason for fragmentation is the drug reimbursement system. Historically it provided high prices for every new drug, most of which were minor modifications of first generation drugs and marketed only in Japan. Second, the system provided economic incentives to doctors if they prescribed and dispensed more drugs rather than fewer drugs. In other words, risk free research was rewarded with enough money to ensure survival of all companies. No one went bankrupt.

Health care reform measures are changing this paradigm. Demand is dropping, me-too drugs are less viable, and the prescribing/dispensing functions are being separated. There will not be enough money to feed everyone, particularly those without a productive discovery research effort, a common characteristic of companies who are not in the top 100.

To Acquire or Not to Acquire

—That Is the Question

Prior to 1975 foreign entry into Japan was restricted to joint ventures in which the non-Japanese equity position was capped at 50 percent. After these restrictions were removed, foreign companies gradually bought out their Japanese partners' or increased their own equity positions to get control. For many this was a painful process which continues to unwind at a snails pace.

The experience of buying control of a company partially owned and known intimately does not bode well for making the more dramatic move of buying an unrelated company. The slow progress toward control was justified as a conservative strategy to build a competitive presence through internal growth. This is Japan—don't rock the boat.

A build from within strategy is more viable today than it was in the past. People and products, the key assets, are accessible. Foreign companies once had no choice but to hire any warm body that dared to apply. Today there are more applicants than time for interviews, let alone employment offers.

Therefore, a build versus buy strategy is commendable if executed with a greater sense of urgency and consistency than demonstrated during the past 20 years.

Internal Barriers to Acquisition

I wonder how many strategic plan presentations on Japan include the phrase, "We will consider acquisition opportunities to expedite our growth potential in Japan, the second largest pharmaceutical market in the world." Implicit is the assumption that 'opportunities' will somehow appear from thin air over drinks at a Ginza club.

If the desire to acquire is more than words, be aware of a few barriers. First, there are no "For Sale" signs on the doors of Japanese companies.

Second, investment bankers in Japan, both foreign and Japanese, cannot find the key to open the lock on the door. It might be said they can't find the door. They specialize in listing houses like a Honolulu realtor.

Third, the senior managers of foreign companies in Japan are primarily measured against short term operating objectives, utilizing the resources they have now, not those that might be acquired in some uncertain future. Furthermore, corporate staff resources that evaluate acquisitions are far away physically and in outer space mentally.

Which leads to the fourth barrier of valuation methods. Spread sheets, discounted cash flows, product portfolio reviews, and ROI analyses most often come up short in justifying the investment. Keep the bean counters out of the process as they fail to appreciate the value of presence in this market.

The relatively low market shares of foreign companies in Japan cannot be attributable to the lack of new products or the unavailability of good people. Rather, they reflect a lack of presence, clout and critical mass compared to their Japanese competitors.

There will be an increase in acquisition activity in Japan. But it will not be a vehicle for substantial investment by foreigners who wait, endlessly study their options, or fail to find the key to open the door.

Will Merger Mania Hit Japan?

Investment bankers in Tokyo claim the Japanese pharmaceutical industry is on the verge of consolidation. Their rational is logical and compelling. The only problem—it's an old story and reality belies the logic. Makes you wonder if the economic arguments for consolidation are contrived to earn fees for the bankers.

But hope springs eternal as recent events added fuel to the fire. Asahi Beer, flush with the amazing success of knocking its archival Kirin out of the number one position in the traditional beer market, decided to exit the drug business by selling its majority stake in Torii to Japan Tobacco.

Asahi was never emotionally committed to the pharmaceutical industry. Rather, it acted as a benign safe keeper of a Torii equity stake unwanted by Merck's CEO Dr. Roy Vagelos. Since the Sumitomo group delivered Torii to Merck in the first place, it was returned at a significant premium over the purchase price. Meanwhile, Torii prospered and earned Asahi a nice return on its investment, but never had the clout of an adequately funded research effort behind its efficient sales organization.

Japan Tobacco not only has piles of money (they built their new building in Toranomon with petty cash), they have a respectable product portfolio in need of a dedicated sales force. Happily, Torii found a home where it is respected.

Another event that received an enormous amount of publicity in the media was the announced merger of Tokyo Tanabe with the pharmaceutical business of Mitsubishi Chemical (MCI). Tokyo Tanabe was partially owned by MCI and depended on it for new drugs, not having much of a discovery research base of its own.

On the other hand, MCI concentrated on building a research base but did not own a sales force. Its R&D people were overshadowed by the chemical business. A neat solution, long overdue, was to combine the pharma units of both companies into a fully integrated entity with a new name and independent identity.

The publicity surrounding this "natural" merger was surprising, but indicates the high level of interest in pharmaceutical restructuring moves. Companies that diversified into drugs are asking basic questions about their core strengths. This kind of analysis prompted Asahi Chemical to exit the food business and rumors persist that their pharma business will be the next to go.

Kanebo made a similar move by divesting its prescription drug business to Organon which was struck in an old fashioned joint venture with Sankyo. Organon will follow up its Kanebo purchase by buying out Sankyo from its JV and focus on a 100 percent owned integrated drug business from R&D through distribution.

Organon's move is respectable compared to the slow, painful separations other foreign companies have endured. If a divorce is inevitable, get on with a new life. Take Abbott which is gradually buying out the Dainippon stake in their JV Dainabot. The lingering uncertainty of a minority partner stifles innovation, but more importantly, blurs the lines of control. It is like divorced parents arguing about visiting rights for their child who is old enough to live a life of its own.

These moves, and undoubtedly others in the process of due diligence, will prompt observers to suggest merger mania will sweep the Japanese pharmaceutical industry. There are several reasons why this is only an investment bankers dream. The cases cited above are the result of restructuring.

Companies will exit businesses they should not have entered in the first place. Foreign companies need to take control of joint ventures that outlived their usefulness. Pharma companies will shed allied businesses that sap value from the core ethical drug business. A prime example is the OTC business in most drug companies. Thus, internal restructuring is an essential first step before external M&A can be considered. Best to get your own house in order before a sale or a move into larger quarters.

The reimbursement system cushions the impact of market forces on the drug industry in Japan. There is enough money to blunt the impact of reforms, and as long as people see a bottom line profit, albeit small, they do not feel the pressure to take serious actions. In family controlled companies there is an overriding desire to hang on. "This company will not be sold on my watch."

The hope is that persistence will pay off, that tomorrow will be better, that somehow there is a road to survival. If not, it will be a problem for the next generation. Although family managers actually own a small portion of their firm's equity, they behave like owners. Other shareholders like the banks which would love to convert their shares into cash, will not initiate a sale until they get a go sign from the family.

Finally, foreign companies which might benefit from an acquisition talk but do not act. They either believe better deals will come to those who wait or have the notion it does not make economic sense to buy problems. My suspicion is that both reasons mask an underlying ignorance of the Japanese market.

A Japanese writer would add to the above list the rationale that merged companies cannot achieve economies of scale by laying-off redundant employees. This argument suggests a firm does not exist for its shareholders, but for its employees. A social organism designed to provide secure employment.

A growing list of companies in Japan are facing a different reality and are in a race to see who can downsize the fastest. Hardly a day goes by that the newspaper does not report lay-offs or early retirements. So-called lifetime employment is a myth, not a reality.

Attitudes are changing rapidly. No doubt the pharmaceutical industry will reinvent itself to cope with the new realities of Japan's healthcare system. Some companies will become global players; other will stay home but prosper within defined areas.

Others will seek out compatible partners and merge. No one will go out of business, and at no time will the process be described as a mania or craze. Investment bankers will be politely asked to take their discounted cash flow analyses elsewhere.

Pharma Japan 1641, March 1999

Chapter X

Foreign Firms Struggle to Compete

The simple fact is foreign companies do not compete as effectively in Japan as they do in other markets. Why not is a question we returned to throughout the 1990s. The door is open, yet many continue to believe it is closed. There are no unique restrictions, yet many see barriers instead of bridges. Japan is different, but changes. Presence is not denied, nor is it guaranteed without extraordinary commitment, patience, and consistency of purpose.

Too Much Rice

Foreigners working in Japan, or those who observe and comment on the country from afar, are labeled according to their attitudes toward the Japanese. Labels have connotations that are neither a realistic nor an objective evaluation of intelligence or effectiveness. The typecasting game is played with a vengeance by those who interact with Japan.

Is there any other kind of basher than a Japan basher? There are only Japan revisionists and Japan apologists. A native English speaker who learns to speak French is considered cultured. The same person speaking Japanese is labeled weird. Japanese investments abroad are labeled invasions. No one ever wrote about Britain, Inc.

My own label, one I acquired long before writing this commentary, is one who has been eating too much rice. When I ask what this means, my question is answered by another question—whose side are you on anyway?

As a young graduate student, I spent one year in New Zealand doing biochemistry research in the medical school of Otago University. During two separate three-week holidays, I spoke to every Rotary Club on the South Island of New Zealand. The link with Rotary was through their Foundation, which financially supported my studies.

Upon returning to Pennsylvania, I gave enthusiastic speeches on what I viewed as the virtues of the "Land of the Long White Cloud," and the amicable "Kiwis" who lived there. Maybe people thought I had eaten too much lamb, but no one ever mentioned it.

A wide variety of people come to Japan: students, academics, military, government, tourists, maids, laborers, missionaries, athletes, trainees, and, of course, businessmen. Fortunately or unfortunately, my key relationships have been with businessmen, more specifically with those in the pharmaceutical business. All have played a role in the never-ending drama of, as a recent book title states, *Cracking the Japanese Market*.

Before most of us came to Japan, we didn't know much about the country, or people, or how to be effective managers in this culture. However, after one month everyone became an expert. As time went on, particularly among those of us who stayed here longer than five years, there was a steady downward slope on the knowledge curve. That is, just when you thought you knew everything, you realized there was so much more to learn.

Expatriate businessmen move from generalizations to specifics, from unity to diversity. Not all Japanese work hard, not all companies are benevolent, not all executives are long-term thinkers, and not all Tokyo University graduates are smart. Don't talk about THE JAPANESE, talk about individual people.

At first, generalizations are useful protective mechanisms to coat the psyche from the abuse of being different, of not being able to read simple signs like exit or entrance, of being led rather than leading, of not being capable of ordering a meal without pointing. Damn it, why does everything work in reverse?

The process is insidious. At first, you see only politeness, then only rudeness— shoving, pushing; at first, the decision-making process is interesting and challenging, then it appears time consuming and mysterious; at first you feel in charge, then you fear you are the last to know what is going on.

For some, there is a period of "Why Worry, Be Happy," and they pray each night for a transfer. Others get involved and achieve results in unexpected ways. Some never get over the "Remember Pearl Harbor'" syndrome.

Most executives represent their companies with distinction after they learn to use the system rather than fight it. After they appreciate that in matters of influence and persuasion, emotionality dominates rationality; the heart dominates the head.

These latter words are not mine, they come from Harold J. Leavitt, Professor of Organizational Behavior and Psychology at the Stanford Graduate School of Business. In an article entitled, Shaping the MBA of the Future, he added:

"Understanding human emotions is not only the key to effective influence; it is also the key in matters of teamwork, cooperation, and coordination of human effort. Project teams, task forces, alliances, mergers all stand or fall as much on the stability of their emotional and relational foundations as on their technical or financial ones. To get the world's work done, people have to get along with one another, and getting along requires empathy, sensitivity, and feelings of bondedness and membership."

I like rice, but some is better than others. If you think all rice is the same, you haven't been in Japan long enough. As to the question, "Whose side are you on anyway?" Professor Leavitt has some advice that is relevant:

"Traditional authoritarian hierarchies are just about dead. It was those hierarchies that sheltered many managers from their emotional and interpersonal incompetence."

Or as President Bush said in Pearl Harbor last December, "The war is over."

Pharma Japan 1290, February 10, 1992

Don't Agree or Disagree—Absorb

Readers familiar with me know I have three girls at home, a condition that prompts me to prefer luncheon meetings rather than dinner meetings. I like to go home at night. In Tokyo this policy effectively limits the number of people I get to meet. My favorite girl would not want her age reported, so let's just say she was born in Yamagata. Our favorite girls are four and six years old.

Everyday the children must cope with two cultures. How they cope is a constant source of marvel, and sometimes amusement. For example, dealing with two languages is easier than learning to eat with chopsticks instead of forks. This proves the brain is a more adaptable organ than the hand; or software is more readily assimilated than hardware.

You may wonder what this has to do with the pharmaceutical industry. Bear with me; I will get to the point very soon.

Our children attend the International School of the Sacred Heart, and there I have observed other bicultural kids, who, by the way, are not half American or half Japanese, they are "doubles." It struck me that these kids do not need books to learn about living in Japan. They are not sent to orientation seminars in Hawaii, or the Japan Society in New York to learn how to survive in Japan.

What these kids do is so simple. They do not prejudge; they do not agree or disagree; they absorb. They soak up what is going on, and they go with what works for them. This is coping; this is being effective; this is a no-stress, I-can-do-it existence.

Pharmaceutical executives would be wise to absorb what works in Japan or the United States before making judgments or fulfilling the insatiable urge to disagree. I am reminded of three examples.

We brought a very talented and effective marketing executive to Japan. Upon arrival he demanded a closed office which he equated with status and power. As it happened, we did not have the space; furthermore, I argued he would be more effective sitting with his people. My rationale was not convincing, so an autocratic decision was made—he would use a desk in the open office.

Months later we were able to find space for a closed office and I was delighted to satisfy his original request. You guessed it, he refused the office because he learned there was no way he could be as effective walled off from the action, out of sight, out of mind.

Second, many companies have delayed establishing facilities in Japan to manufacture a finished product. They disagree with customer complaints about the quality of tablet coatings or packaging, claiming they are examples of non-tariff trade barriers. In reality they would rather maximize exports from some other country, or increase utilization of another facility. Unsatisfied customers then switch to a competitor.

The competitive advantage of satisfying customers is not a unique Japanese phenomenon, but it is practiced here with a vengeance. Recently, after returning home from shopping at a Tokyo supermarket, my wife called the store to complain about an impolite employee. Within an hour the manager visited our house to apologize, and brought with him two large boxes of their most expensive strawberries as a gift. Disagreeing with customer expectations is not good business.

Finally, I am reminded of the Japanese enclave in Fort Lee, New Jersey. Pharmaceutical executives posted to New York return there at night after dining with their colleagues in a sushi restaurant. During the day their kids attend a Japanese school and their wives shop at Yaohan department store.

This is not internationalization. No one ever found the real spirit of America at a sushi bar in mid-Manhattan. Nor can one absorb the U.S. culture in Fort Lee. Maybe we must wait for third culture kids and doubles to grow us and show us how to really be effective in another business culture. Meanwhile, it is more productive to absorb than to agree or disagree.

Pharma Japan 1302, May 4 and 11, 1992

The Dreaded C Word

No one can guarantee a cure for the problem. Researchers believe there are a variety of factors that trigger its onset, including those in the environment. Yet, exposed to similar conditions certain people are afflicted, others are not. Personality traits alter the outcome. Those with the problem are often not told about it directly; when they find out, the first reaction is denial, followed by a tendency to blame others.

New hardware technology promised a cure, only to prove enormously expensive and disappointing. No nationality is immune; it strikes young and old alike: It can cut short a promising career. Those who have been cured never forget the experience, and live in fear it will return.

People posted abroad are the most susceptible to this problem: communication with the home office. Yes, communication is the C word. Every expatriate will tell you their biggest problem is communicating, read this as being understood, with the home office.

I thought about this during the Pharma Delegates Healthcare Seminar entitled, "The Role of Information Technology in the Pharmaceutical Industry." The venue was Shimoda, the home and office of America's first Consul General to Japan, Townsend Harris.

Consul Harris had it made. Right? His home office in Washington could not send a fax; no E-mail; no telephone calls in the middle of the night; no airplanes to fly in visiting firemen for an impromptu budget review. He only had two directives: to establish a consular office and to negotiate a trade treaty. His mission was to open Japan! Lots of people have the same objectives today.

Fourteen months after arriving in Japan, Harris received his first letters. In his diary he wrote:

"I received in all twenty-eight letters, but not one word from the Department of State about my Treaty with Siam, or one word in answer to some of mine that it was important to me to receive answers."

The State Department mail was a disappointment: all the letters, except one, were printed circulars. There was no word of praise or advice of reward for his Siam Treaty, and he learned from other letters that he had almost been fired. This diary entry was dated Tuesday, October 20, 1857. Lots of people have the same problem today.

Fast forward to the present. A Japanese executive was sent to America to build a manufacturing facility in Texas. His home office expected him to provide a large parking area for bicycles, an assembly area for all employees to gather for group exercises before work, meeting rooms for quality circles after work, and uniforms for everyone during work. He had complete freedom to spend money for what the home office considered important, but his request for a modest donation to a local charity was denied.

Information technology, or IT in the parlance of its practitioners, has made enormous strides. PCs are now as ubiquitous as multipurpose phones; and fax machines in hotel rooms as common as people with a phone in their ear in hotel restaurants.

More awesome are the software packages that bring data to life in living color at the click of a mouse. Sales results by district or hospital? No problem—do you want it annually, semi-annually, or monthly? In yen, dollars or by package size?

Home office executives have the technology to know more about a subsidiary than ever before, without taking an airplane ride. Oddly, their appetite is not sated; IT specialists are being asked to provide more data in different formats. One might speculate that the more honchos know the less they understand. But knowledge is power, and those who have it can use it or abuse it.

The communication problem is not going to be solved by smothering it with technology. Pictures on a screen are better than paper print-outs, but two people looking at the same picture often see different things. If you want to praise a man or do him in, the same information will suffice. Data can motivate or depress a man; it depends on how it is used. Some use it to tear down, others use it to build. Those who build do not have a communication problem.

Pharma Japan 1311, July 13, 1992

Get In by Getting Out

Because of what I do in Japan, it is necessary to call presidents of pharmaceutical companies, both foreign and Japanese. There are three possible responses to a phone call: the president is in and free to talk; he is in but unavailable; or he is out. The latter response can be subdivided into out of Japan, or out of the office but in Japan.

My theory is that a direct correlation can be made between phone responses and managerial competence. If proven, this simple test could save companies an enormous amount of time and money. They could trash performance reviews and management by objectives. Phone calls are cheap and responses are received in less than three minutes.

Actually, it is a bit more complicated. Take the "in and free to talk'" response. There are at least three conclusions.

1. The president is a good delegator of responsibility, thus reserving his time to answer outside phone calls. Maybe a headhunter will call; unfortunately it is usually the home office.
2. The president is only free for me because he knows I always have something important to say. HA.
3. The president has nothing to do except answer the phone because his organization ignores him.

The "in but unavailable" response can be evaluated somewhat more easily, depending upon the length of time it takes to respond. There are two categories of presidents:

1. Those that spend endless time in internal meetings, thus preempting time to stay personally connected to the outside world.
2. Those that devote their internal time efficiently to exercise leadership on a personal basis, but delegate details of implementation to others. Their responses to phone calls are made within an hour.

The "he is out" response is my favorite, with one qualification. If the president is working for a foreign company it is not OK to be out of Japan.

Effective presidents spend time with their customers, regulators, and field personnel. By customers I mean wholesalers. There are now 344 wholesalers who employ approximately 35,000 medical salespeople. Most manufacturers have their own medical representatives assigned to cover the 120,000 doctors in hospitals with more than 100 beds. Wholesale salespeople are the prime source of product information for the 80,000 doctors who work in smaller hospitals and clinics.

Given changes in the role of wholesalers to conduct all price negotiations with providers of health care; given their coverage of the entire market; and given their data base of product sales to the trade, these guys are definitely worth spending time with. A president once told me he was not concerned about wholesalers. He said, "If our people convince doctors to prescribe, wholesalers will supply." This president was always available for a phone call.

A quick read on the effectiveness of a president is to ask him when he last visited Koseisho. Another way is to watch him at a reception where Koseisho officers are present. If he is exchanging name cards, it is a sure bet this is their first meeting.

Field personnel need to see their leader more frequently than at product launch meetings. *Kacho*, or district managers, are on the front line in the day to day grind of convincing doctors to favor one product over 10 others. They make you a winner or a loser through countless actions every hour. How many D.M.s does the president know by name?

Some presidents are always in; they have a bunker mentality and their organizations suffer the consequences. Some foreign presidents are always in because their home offices ask endless questions. The ones who deserve sympathy are those who must be on their home phone late at night. Or those who make the trip to Narita once a month.

Effective presidents know that real business does not happen inside their own offices. They get into it by getting out.

Pharma Japan 1330, November 30, 1992

Business Lessons from a Japanese Barbershop

The genes in my body do not appear to carry the code for baldness, or even a mechanism for slowing the growth of hair as my cells age. I do not sport hairstyles that feature a ponytail or an over the ear Prince Valiant look. Hair growth on the neck reminds me of an age of civilization when men used their metal working skills to make swords rather than scissors.

As a result, I am a regular visitor to a barbershop, in fact, the same establishment in the Azabu section of Tokyo for 19 years. This small shop has more to offer than just a haircut, or an opportunity to look at risqué pictures in magazines I would never buy at kiosks outside railway stations. With a modicum of observation and a rudimentary understanding of Japanese, you can save the cost of "How To Do Business In Japan" books, and the fees for seminars with fancy titles, but address the same issues. There are many business lessons to learn in a Japanese barbershop. Consider a few of the more obvious.

Know Your Customer

My barbershop, simply named Barbershop Tanaka, is owned and operated by Mr. and Mrs. Tanaka, and was previously run by Mr. Tanaka's father and mother. It is a neighborhood institution. The fathers and grandfathers of present day customers are known to the Tanaka's. Each customer is more than a head of hair that needs to be cut, shampooed, and styled; the customer has a life.

In my case, Mr. Tanaka cut the hair of my two sons, my father's hair on his one and only visit to Japan, attended my wedding party, gave the first haircuts to my two daughters, and cuts the hair of several friends. He probably knows more about me than anyone except my wife, and never forgets any part of it. He knows my hobbies, my taste in music, my interest in sports, particularly sumo, and always discusses one facet of these interests during a haircut.

The current fad with MR qualification systems emphasizes product and scientific knowledge. Business schools turn out men and women who are experts at writing resumes extolling their personal skills, particularly those related to quantitative analysis. People thus trained and qualified love to tell customers how good they are—to demonstrate their skills and product knowledge—so eager to talk about themselves they fail to sense customer needs.

I happen to know Mr. Tanaka acts as a judge at contest organized by barber schools. I presume his skills as a barber are well respected by the people who organize these events, but not once has he told me how good he is.

"Know your customer," "The customer comes first," are often mere slogans printed on signs posted in sales offices or used as copy in media advertising. To Mr. Tanaka, knowing the customer is a way of life. Relationships are constantly renewed and nurtured. The customer feels comfortable, unhassled, and relaxed. I could go to a discount barbershop in another section of Tokyo and get a haircut for half the price, but do not for the simple reason I would be a non-person on an assembly line where barbers cut hair—period.

Be There

Did you ever call a business to place an order and no one answered the phone? Did you call back? Showing-up probably accounts for 90 percent of business success. The Barbershop Tanaka is open daily except Monday and the third Tuesday of each month. Every time I needed a haircut for 19 years Mr. Tanaka was there.

Absentee managers or owners are rarely serious competitors to managers who have a stake in the business. The same may be said of research. Innovative research in the United States is blossoming in small, research intensive firms, where all employees own part of the business. On a larger scale, consider research productivity in firms who have research centers in several countries outside their home base. It appears discoveries of new molecules are primarily made in the home country, whether it is Switzerland, Germany, Britain, or the United States.

This relationship can be expressed on a graph with the vertical axis representing the number of new chemical entities discovered, and the horizontal axis representing the distance from the company's central research laboratories. The resulting straight line goes down as the distance increases.

More discoveries are made closer to home because that is where the senior research managers show up. As stakeholders in the firm, they have the most to lose or gain from research productivity.

Attention to Detail

After my father had his haircut at Barbershop Tanaka, he described his experience by saying, "The barber used two hot towers on my head and at least six on my face; I think he cut every hair on my head individually; I know he clipped single hairs from may ears and nose; gave me a massage that almost put me sleep; then brushed me off like a dry cleaner."

A foreign pharmaceutical company executive in Tokyo for 10 years recently told me he has learned much about his home country by living in Japan. He said,

"My home office colleagues are great strategists, can see the big picture, conceive of synergistic deals, but are beaten by the Japanese because they cannot execute the details."

Research comes to mind again. The Japanese lead the world in the discovery of NCEs. Practically all of these are minor modifications of breakthrough drugs discovered outside Japan. Small step innovation is productive because it requires fanatical attention to detail. A non-Japanese probably invented the phrase, "God is in the details," but the Japanese put the phrase into actual practice.

Mr. Tanaka is so dedicated to a specific routine that you always get your 50 minutes in the chair whether his customer waiting area is full and empty. A negative of this system is its infexibility. A quick trim is not done. The advantage of the system is its predictability and reliability. Inflexibility is the most frequent frustration Westerners face in Japan. Those who adapt to do well, but end up fighting with their home office colleagues, a definite career negative. As flexibility in a system increases, its predictability goes down. The Japanese emphasize order and harmony in their business environment at the expense of flexibility.

Insiders Always Beat Outsiders

In our area of Tokyo there is an association of barbers and their wives. Mr. Tanaka joins the group for night outings in Tokyo, or day trips to hot spring resorts. The wives sometimes join in, but also run their own ladies program of events.

I presume group discussions over sake or in the communal bath relate to the price list for barbershop services and the possible entry of outsiders into their territory. An outsider unaware of the dynamics of this group is at a distinct disadvantage in establishing a new business.

Contrary to wishful thinking, there is no such thing as a level playing field. Demanding one is akin to throwing fluff into a gale and not expecting it to fly back into your face. There are exceptions, but the system works to expel outsiders as furiously as the immune system works to expel a foreign organ. Agents that work to suppress rejection are required, but they too may have unwelcome side effects.

The only way to compete effectively is to get inside the system without triggering rejection mechanisms. Join the association, make friends, take over an ailing business and strengthen its infrastructure that already is in place. Use the system to your advantage rather than fighting it.

Mr. Tanaka is not against change. He has relocated twice and changed the equipment and décor of his shop three times since I met him. He is beginning to talk about wanting more free time, but son did not become a barber. Here-in lies an opportunity for an outsider. It is hard to imagine Tanaka merging with another shop, too much pride and independence based upon a lifetime of competing with his association friends. Harmony and order are important, but business is business.

A foreign pharmaceutical executive I know is expanding his company's presence in Japan at a torrid pace. "Nothing fancy," he said," "just basic business principles executed in a step by step fashion." He went on to say, "I get my reward from small victories, one at a time." Well said, and as far as I know he does not have his hair cut by Mr. Tanaka, but the two would get along.

Analogies to Explain the Enigma

At a private dinner party I was reminded that conversations between foreigners haven't changed in 28 years. The initial get-to-know you routine includes classic questions such as, "Who are you with?" "How long have you been here?" "How long do you expect to stay?" These questions are preliminaries to the main event of analyzing the culture and mores of their unfamiliar environment. Each person, regardless of educational background, is transformed into an anthropologist.

The Japanese may be the most analyzed and least understood people on this side of the Pacific. There must be something therapeutic about the process, like talking to your shrink or priest.

Pharma execs face challenges that go beyond learning how to order and eat sushi. Building a business in Japan requires resource allocation decisions approved by home office people who live in a different world. The key to their support is a sympathetic ear and an open mind to how this market works.

There are different strategies to educate corporate visitors. Some guys lean toward the Kyoto/Nara "This is the soul of Japan" tour, complete with a session on Zen. Others see enlightenment through club hopping in Roppongi. Once upon a time I escorted every visitor to a *ryokan* for a steaming bath. Hard to be pretentious in the buff.

Alas, in an age of e-mail and sound bytes there is no time for quiet contemplation. People demand a quick way to describe the enigma of Japan's healthcare system and pharmaceutical market. Below are a few analogies to help explain Japan's complex structures and healthcare system to three minute managers over a power breakfast at the Hotel Okura.

Delivery and Reimbursement of Healthcare

The healthcare system is like a packaged tour that Japanese are fond of using on trips inside and outside Japan. A leader, carrying a flag (Koseisho) organizes and sets the prices for services provided by medical facilities. Participants organize themselves by their company affiliation, avocation, or profession and contribute monthly toward the cost of the trip. Travel agencies (insurance societies) contract with hotels and transportation companies to provide services at fixed rates determined by the leader.

Everyone on the tour is treated equally and all destinations are accessible if you are part of the group. In fact, service establishments love the business because they can provide standardized meals and other amenities without catering to individual tastes. This keeps costs relatively low while maintaining acceptable, but not exceptional quality.

The system, with minor adjustments, has worked well since 1961. To reduce costs, the leader periodically revised the prices at which service providers were paid for meals, transportation, and lodging. However, this enticed more people to travel so the absolute costs escalated. The leader is now considering how to cut the demand for travel.

Meanwhile, many people would like to avail themselves of the transportation fares in the tour package but prefer to make their own arrangements after arriving at their destination. In other words, the all inclusive tour package does not suit more discriminating and educated users of the system. The leader is reluctant to comply with these requests for fear of losing his flag.

Supplier companies ritually complain to the tour leader about the prices they can charge for the supplies used by the service providers. The leader is sensitive to this criticism because he has a part time responsibility to foster an innovative and productive industry.

The leader recently recommended a flat-sum payment for supplies used on certain tours. He also proposed a reference price for similar supplies offered on all tours. These proposals, if adopted, will strengthen the leaders' power to set standardized rates at a time when less regulation and more choice is desirable.

Pharmaceutical Company Restructuring

Up to the present, Japanese pharmaceutical companies were like guests invited to a buffet at the Hotel Okura. There was plenty of food to feed everyone, even those who arrived after the speeches. No one went hungry, and when the party was over there was still food on the table.

We are now entering an era when there will not be enough food to feed everyone, particularly those who arrive late. The guest lists will be pruned.

The reimbursement system provided enough money for all companies to survive. No one went out of business. The new reality is quite different. Every company must restructure. But for some, restructuring alone will not ensure survival.

Each company was like a department store, providing something for everyone and plenty of service personnel to bow at the doors and elevators. The restructuring process will convert some of these stores into special shops that focus on a core competence internally and on specific, targeted customers externally.

Their personnel policies will change from the old escalator system whereby new employees expected seniority raises in pay and age related promotions throughout their careers. Not all made it to the top, but the ride up to retirement was smooth and steady.

The new system will be more like stairs in a castle. One stairway will not lead directly to the top, some passageways will lead to dead ends, and others to the dungeon below.

People recruited by the firm will not be like mixed juice, a little of everything but no distinguishing taste. There will be distinct flavors that satisfy different needs.

Foreign Companies in Japan

Entry strategies by foreign pharmaceutical firms resembled a man who preferred many girl friends over one wife. Drugs were licensed-out to various companies. Some had several joint venture partners, plus licensees. Their resources were diluted to the point of exhaustion due to the stress of maintaining many relationships. Someone else's bed always looked enticing.

Building a large home on a strong foundation is slow, expensive work before the structure rises above ground. The risk of total commitment was considered too onerous to marry and get on with the work.

Going forward foreign firms will appreciate that casual relationships do not lead to control over outcomes. A shared relationship with long term commitments cannot be contractually guaranteed. A good pre-nuptial agreement does not lead to a successful marriage.

A Final Thought

At the party, no one said Japan was easy, but all were inquisitive because things in Japan do not work like you expect them to, but they work. Finding out why they work is a great adventure. It beats trying to change the system. Competition is fierce, but can be won if you remember a final analogy. Never eat rice from another person's rice bowl.

Pharma Japan, February 1999

Superficial Savvy Is Obnoxious

American visitors to Japan now witness the Japanese eating a variety of Western foods, sleeping on beds instead of in *futon*, walking on carpets instead of on *tatami*, speaking English without an accent. They leave with the impression that Japan is changing, that the Japanese are becoming more like us. They are right and they are wrong.

Right, Japan is changing. This is a dynamic society. Just look around. Tokyo seems to be simultaneously tearing itself down and rebuilding. In 1967, drugs were approved without any local clinical trials if they had been approved in the United States or Europe. In 1977, everyone complained about stringent Koseisho requirements. By 1987, the Koseisho was approving more new drugs at a faster rate than either the United States or any country in Europe.

Wrong, Japan is not becoming more like us. We like regulations defined by law. Koseisho likes guidelines defined by administrative guidance. We like transparency defined in terms of black and white. Koseisho likes consultation defined in shades of grey.

One of the current buzzwords in our business is "harmonization." International experts gather at a multitude of symposia to talk about harmonizing regulatory requirements between Japan, the United States, and Europe. To some, harmony means "your regulations should be like mine." To others, harmony can be achieved by combining all the regulations, everywhere, into one package.

These are worthy endeavors because the world is becoming more integrated every day. By definition, we are a global industry because disease itself does not recognize political or racial boundaries. Cancer can strike anyone, anywhere, at anytime. The genetic material that regulates cell growth is common to all, irrespective of where we might have been born.

Nevertheless, harmony is an elusive goal. Progress toward its definitive rewards is hampered by a lack of understanding. More detrimental is a superficial understanding of the current regulations within a single political entity. Japan is more susceptible to this problem for two reasons.

First is the reluctance or inability of many Japanese to describe their regulations and procedures in terms that can be understood by non-Japanese. Too often a question that begins with "Why . . . ?" is answered with, "Because Japan is different." This is a statement that says virtually nothing.

Second is the propensity of Westerners to believe Japan is becoming more like us. Having made this assumption, it is easy to believe Western practices and procedures will prevail. When they don't, the end result is frustration and suspicion.

Superficial savvy is obnoxious. However, there may be a middle ground to help us move forward. Plato said it in *The Republic* a long time ago:

"Between knowledge of what really exists and ignorance of what does not exist lies the domain of opinion. It is more obscure than knowledge, but clearer than ignorance."

Pharma Japan 1186, December 25, 1989

Never Be Surprised

There appears to be no end to the number of articles and books about how to do business in Japan. In fact, my own contribution to the literature on this subject was recently published by Simul Press in Japanese. The English-speaking reader will not be denied, Japan Times will publish an English version in November.

For a long time, almost 20 years, I have never passed up a book that might help me understand why the twain should not meet. I am such a junkie on the subject that my library has outgrown the small capacity of my typical Tokyo bedroom which serves as a den. On a cost per space basis, it should be capable of housing your average small town library.

As this is the season when many new residents begin their own Japan experience, allow me the audacity to suggest a bottom line, golden rule to a successful tour of duty. All the advice, in all the books can be condensed into three words, NEVER BE SURPRISED.

Consider the case of a friend in the food industry. He was the chief representative of the foreign parent in a joint venture. He had succeeded in convincing his Japanese colleagues to launch a caramel wrapped in a delicious chocolate. They went to work and prepared all the necessary procedures from manufacturing to advertising. At a very special dinner party in Kyoto, they presented him and his home office bosses with the finished product and full launch campaign. They had an impressive program—all built around the trade name CRAP. I leave you with your imagination to think how he got out of that one.

Never be surprised in an easy concept to understand. Achieving the goal is a bit more difficult. Would you appoint a man to manage your U.S. operations if he couldn't read English? Would you entrust your sales in the United States to a man who couldn't speak English to your customers? But most business executives are not sent to Japan to learn Japanese; that is a mission reserved for career foreign service officers and priests. Fortunately, businessmen are provided with ample resources to interpret what is going on.

For the really effective ex-pat, never be surprised means knowing and trusting your people. It means that you don't kill the messenger and you look beyond the process to focus on results.

Take as a simplistic example the barbershop. In the United States, they give you a shampoo before cutting your hair, in Japan, after. In the United States, you lay backward with your head in the sink; in Japan, you lean forward. Which is more effective? Who cares if the haircut is satisfactory?

Trust your people, listen to what they want to say, back them with a long-term commitment of adequate resources. Concentrate on results, not how you are supposed to get them. All this takes patience and humility. An example worth emulating is illustrated by the following story.

It is said that in ancient Japan three warriors were brought together to decide who should rule the entire country. Each was asked a simple question, "If you held a nightingale in your hand and it did not sing, what would you do?"

The first said, "If it did not sing, I would kill it."
The second said, "If it did not sing, I would make it sing."
The third said, "If it did not sing, I would wait for it to sing."

The third warrior was reputed to be Iyeyasu, the founder of the Tokugawa regime. He and his descendants ruled Japan for 200 years.

What Foreigners Should Know—But Don't

Bob (not his real name) was transferred to Japan as president of his company's operations, a major promotion certain to propel him into a senior corporate position. In other jobs during his fast track to the top, he mastered the art of personally delivering results. He knew the right buttons to push at the right time. He was on top of each business within six months, controlling information up and down the corporate hierarchy.

The first three months in Japan were exhilarating, at times inspirational. Bob joined a club, participated in trade association meetings, traveled to regional offices, was wined and dined, and frequently used his newly acquired Japanese language skills. He bubbled over with new ideas to increase sales and lower expenses. His staff gave every indication that they agreed to implement all his suggestions.

Sometime around the ninth month I met Bob, and he was not his usual jubilant self. The aura of self-confidence was gone. His trips to the home office were more frequent than those to Osaka. I politely inquired, "How is business?" His response was sharp and to the point. "I don't know what the hell is going on."

Many careers have been short circuited in Japan because of the frustration of not knowing what is going to happen next. One obvious explanation relates to language skills. Would you send an executive to St. Louis to run your U.S. operations if he did not speak, read, or write English? But this is only the tip of the iceberg. Some (most?) foreigners who speak, read, and write Japanese are not qualified to run a business in this country.

There are three ways to cope with the knowledge-gap frustration syndrome. First, avoid everything that is Japanese. Socialize with foreigners, schedule frequent planning meetings outside Japan; send your family abroad during the summer, Christmas/New Year, and spring break—chances are, you can conveniently join them as part of a business trip; insist everyone speak to you in English; do not travel alone in Japan. I know a foreigner who has this avoidance response down to such a fine art that he can spend two hours in a sushi shop without eating one piece of raw fish.

Second, try to be Japanese. Study the language, culture, art, and crafts intensely; send your kids to Japanese schools; eat rice twice a day and learn to love *natto*; insist everyone speak to you in Japanese; never write a letter or utter a thought without prefacing it with an apology. These people make very good missionaries, scholars, and career diplomats.

Third, focus on results, not the process. Bob knew the output, but was frustrated because he could not participate in every aspect of influencing inputs. He wanted to interview prospective salesmen, but his instincts were all wrong. Personal attributes that he considered vital for success in his home country did not match what it takes to establish rapport with a doctor in Japan.

Foreign marketing managers get enamored with the process of designing promotion pieces and educational material for doctors. They relate well with market research firms who survey 50 doctors at a cost of 120,000 yen per interview, then extrapolate the data to 5,000 doctors. Meanwhile, they fail to analyze the results of specific doctor calls to target a message. Everyone knows what a doctor prescribes and dispenses, but no one asks the question: WHY?

A foreign executive could not convince his sales managers to use less than 100 wholesalers to distribute their products because sales volume will decrease, relationships will suffer, and competitors will gain market share. He solicited advice from the president of a Japanese firm that was using half the number of wholesalers. The president replied, "You have the wrong guys."

Irrational distribution leads to excess costs. Too many orders increase shipping costs; expensive personnel maintain relationships which are unnecessary Sales do not directly correlate with wholesaler margins and rebates are not specifcally allocated to special promotion programs. A false sense of security exists that rebates directly infuence sales, when in fact, they may be lowering net effective selling prices—a certain formula for lower reimbursement prices at the time of price revisions.

A corollary strategy to focusing on results is, never be surprised by the results. During Bob's sixth month in Japan, he was surprised at the reimbursement price reductions imposed on his most important products. His staff blamed Koseisho's untransparent price survey and their bias against foreign-owned companies. In reality, district managers were given wide latitude to approve discounts to ostensively achieve sales targets.

"Blame Koseisho" is an easy out for not investing the time required to understand what is going on in the ministry on a daily basis. Some Japanese company employees spend every working day roaming the halls of Koseisho to gather information and keep their new product reviews on track. The people who blame Koseisho go there only when called.

At the end of Bob's second year, he was concentrating on issues where he could make a difference. More importantly, he found a few good men he could communicate with, men who knew the business and could mentally cope with a question beginning with two words, i.e., "What if . . . ?" Japanese managers who prefaced every response with, "Yes, but Japan is different," were given window jobs. Bob realized he had a lot to learn and did not unilaterally impose home office ideas on this staff. Many areas needed improvement, but step-by-step, he was getting the results he expected.

Nine months later, Bob was transferred to a staff position in the home office. Last I heard he was searching for a more "challenging" position. He deserves one because his company does not deserve him.

Pharma Japan 1472, October 1995

Process, Not Goals, Matters

Senior corporate executives who visit Japan usually get the standard orientation tour meetings and dinners with old and new partners to cement relationships, review plans, set goals, and sign contracts. Internal meetings for presentations on accomplishments and progress toward short- and long-range targets; the emphasis is on measurable results, on doing something.

I have been through many of these exercises, and at the time each one was critically important. Family outings were postponed and friends were neglected. I only saw my children sleeping. Everyone understood the oft-used phrase, "I have visitors from the home office." In retrospect, I cannot remember why the visits were important.

An exception, there is always one, was a president who wanted to learn more about Japan than our market share. He had the discipline to not be disciplined, to deny the feeling that he was wasting his time to learn how things got done in Japan, not what was done.

We went to Kyoto where there were no factories, offices, or partners. We arranged for discussions with a history professor and an anthropologist-cum-psychologist. But the highlight was a visit with a Zen priest at his home/temple, followed by dinner.

Our conversation turned to why the monks were diligently sweeping the temple grounds although, with the exception of a few leaves, there was nothing to sweep. The point, he said, was the process, not the goal. Every life ends the same way, I understood him to say, so why be in such a hurry to get to the finish line?

This was a bit too much for my president. He argued there must be a reason for sweeping. The satisfaction of a clean garden, the discipline of a routine. There must be a goal or there is no rationale for the process.

The evening ended in a neutral truce and I assumed our president was unconvinced. A couple of years later I was frustrated with our progress to consummate the acquisition of Banyu. We were involved in endless negotiations over details that were irrelevant to the business. One inconclusive meeting led to another. At a home office meeting I pressed for a "drop dead" date, for specific milestones to be met, or else.

The president took me aside. I knew he was as anxious as I was to close the deal. We were treading water in Japan until we could focus our resources on a unified organizational structure. His advice indicated that the Kyoto experience was not forgotten. He said, "Fasty, fasty monkey scratch, slowly, slowly, monkey catch." The phrase is not Zen, but he understood the process of making a deal is as important as the deal.

Last year Koseisho initiated quarterly meetings with representatives of the Japanese, European, and U.S. pharmaceutical industry. As I reported these meetings to my American friends I could see their eyes glaze over and roll skyward. They were polite not to criticize directly, but the vibrations came through loud and clear. No results, no specific agenda, no answers, no timetable for action. What was agreed? Why didn't the industry respond more forcefully? Why didn't we push for results?

Process matters. Talking is better than not talking. No one can argue things do not get done in Japan. How they got done is a study which is never learned by those frustrated with the system and the people who are paid to represent them. Some of us try to learn with varying degrees of success.

Recently I read a comment by someone who is on the right track. "Having my nose to the grindstone, my ear to the ground, and my shoulder to the wheel for long periods is not the most comfortable position. Sometimes lying in the bathtub is."

Pharma Japan 1345, March 22, 1993

Entry Advice

This is the season when foreigners enter Japanese subsidiaries, a time of enthusiasm and great expectations. It follows the entry of Japanese employees in April, who enter foreign companies with a mixture of enthusiasm and anxiety over their choice of a company and a career. Yes, the two are mutually intertwined, most often a one-time decision. Switching careers or companies in Japan is risky business.

The foreigner's perspective is quite different. He already changed jobs and/or companies more than once. The Japan assignment is a promotion and an opportunity to fill out the résumé with international experience, a valuable commodity for future career advancement. The Japanese freshman is thinking about the next 35 years, the foreigner is thinking about the next three years.

A foreigner wants to hit the ground running, make his mark in the shortest possible time. He is highly visible to the home office and is expected to work the same kind of miracles as were done in his last job. There is an intense desire to get things done and get out.

I am not a cross-cultural adaptation specialist. Academics who write, lecture, and conduct seminars on cultural shock must know of which they speak, but the subject matter leaves me cold. Is Japan really so different? Do we do justice to our psyche by looking for differences?

Hey, I was born, raised and lived in Pennsylvania until the age of 23. My only forays out of the state were confined to a 500-mile radius. My first sales territory with Eli Lilly was in North Carolina. Many of the doctor offices I called on had two entrances, one in front, and one on the side. The front door was for the white folk, the side door was for blacks. A buyer at the local wholesaler also served as the county coroner, and he offered to take me on his runs to record and identify dead bodies. I learned about fatal gunshot and stab wounds. The blacks who were laid out on tables in the cold room were labeled and quietly forgotten. That was cultural shock.

Since I am not a cultural expert, I can offer entry advice without peer review. You can take it or leave it and neither one of us will know the difference.

- Learn enough Japanese so you know the difference between a "no" response to your proposal and a serious "yes." It is amazing how many people do business in this country without knowing when they get rejected. Even Mr. Clinton advised Mr. Yeltsin that the Japanese often mean no when they say yes. The word "*hai*" means I am listening, I am interested in what you have to say, but it does not necessarily follow that I agree with you.
- Put any Japanese who says, "Japan is different" in a window job, that is, in a position where he can no longer influence policy. Better yet, put him in a closet and throw away the key. "Japan is different" says absolutely nothing and is a guise for not wanting to take action.
- Stop using "The Japanese" generalization as soon as possible. There are Japanese who work hard, others goof off all time; some work late because they have something meaningful to do, others don't want to go home to a small apartment with two young children; some are inscrutable, others show their emotions readily. Generalizations are not helpful, not even true.

- Take a morning and evening subway ride that is typical of your employee's daily routine. Do it in August or during the rainy season to appreciate the amount of effort expended just to show up at work every day.
- Never kill the messenger. It is easy to be out of the loop, and berating the bearer of bad news will ensure that you rarely hear anything of importance. When you finish a meeting, figure the time spent listening and talking. If the total elapsed time was more of the latter, you are in trouble.
- See Japan beyond Roppongi. This relates to the first point above. If you know enough Japanese to wander around, you are on your way to understanding that all Japanese are not the same, and the twain can meet. The first step is to stop your wife from planning trips outside Japan during every short break in the school calendar.
- Finally, good or bad, the Japan experience will never be forgotten. It leaves an indelible mark on one's personal and business life. For some, it will be the high point of an otherwise ordinary career. For others, it will be the low point of a previously successful rise up the corporate ladder. At least there is no danger of falling asleep during the time you are here.

Pharma Japan 1354, May 31, 1993

Japan Can Be Frustrating

A pharmaceutical executive friend in Japan for 20 years told me he went through three phases in his business outlook since arriving:

1. The first three years he was expected to know what was going on in the company and in the market. He knew he had very few answers.
2. The next three years he thought he knew everything.
3. Since then he admits to not knowing everything, but is willing to show his ignorance by asking for advice from people who have the answers.

Newcomers on these shores would be wise to recognize the rites of passage my friend described. There are worse outcomes. Consider some of the most nauseating.

1. The home office visitors who hold court at the Park Hyatt Hotel and know all there is to know about Japan because they come here once each quarter.

2. The guy with a Japanese surname and Western first name, e.g., Gary Tanaka, who lives in the United States or Britain, and claims to know all the key people in Japan.
3. The type who knows he will be here less than three years and intends to change everything before he leaves.
4. The five-year resident who will tell you everything that is wrong with the Japanese. He loves Japan; it's the Japanese he can't stand.
5. The association junkie who believes the ACCJ and the American Embassy should solve all his problems with Koseisho.
6. The traveler who finds every excuse to spend as much time as possible outside Japan.
7. The night owl who actually believes hostesses are sincere in telling him he knows all the answers.
8. The guy who goes home at night but sticks a phone in his ear to talk endlessly with the home office.
9. The language arts type who bores everyone with his analysis of kanji; an exercise as interesting as talking about the proper way to spell androgynous.
10. The husband who says he loves it here, but his wife can't cope. Everyone familiar with his wife knows she is at the top of her game.

I hope incoming expats were not told this is a slam dunk assignment. It can be frustrating. If it was easy, foreign companies would have pounded their Japanese competitors into submission a long time ago. The reason you are here, Mr. Newcomer, is your company has a way to go before the locals respect your company's threat as a serious competitor. One way to get a head start is to recognize the frustrations and deal with them. Some of the more frequent are:

1. The fact that you are different. No amount of time at the American Club will eliminate the reality of your minority status.
2. Unless you are a missionary or linguist, you will need to rely on people to tell you what is said or written. Dependence on others for basic information is not your style, but it is the path of least resistance to knowledge, if not peace of mind.
3. You know, and your staff knows, you will not be here forever. Thus, loyalty in both directions is difficult to imbue in your relationships. Take one day at a time.
4. There is an inverse relationship between your effectiveness in Japan and your status in the corporate pecking order. As you learn how to operate

effectively here, your mentors back home will accuse you of eating too much rice.

5. You want to think from your head—conceptualize; your staff will act from their gut, proceeding on the basis of past experience. This is why Japanese are great with hardware, but lousy with software.

6. The employees you believe are winners are often considered losers by your colleagues. Your judgments of people seem to be completely reverse of the norm.

7. Your colleagues insist on telling you what will not work, rather than suggesting what will work.

8. Your straight from the heart motivational speech loses a lot in the translation.

9. In meetings, the conversation is around the point rather than to the point.

10. Finally, if you are a baseball fan, the television channel will cut off the game at 9:20 p.m.—right in the middle of the crucial ninth inning with two men on base and two outs. Check out *The Japan Times* the next day for the final score.

The song, "No One Knows/the Trouble I've Seen," is an apt description of the initiation into Japan. But as my friend understands, life does get better. Why else stay for 20 years?

Keep in mind this pharmaceutical market is larger than any other single country market except the United States. It is changing so fast the local players are despairing at their own ability to cope. New thinking is required, and you are not mired in the old ways of doing business. You can do things a Japanese cannot do because of cultural limitations. You can change the status quo. Hey—isn't that why you were transferred here?

Pharma Japan 1565, September 1997

Inverse Relationships

Some people associated with Japan for a long time are fond of helping newcomers adapt to the business culture. Their enthusiasm for telling others what the Japanese are really like never wanes. They can wax eloquently about the proper use of a business card, and never lose their fascination for kanji—which is akin to talking to a six-year old about the proper way to spell English words.

Bless these people; they must serve a very useful purpose. You find them at *Living in Japan* seminars, at cocktail parties, and in every foreign company. Many Japanese love to play this game; you spot them in restaurants showing foreigners how to eat with chopsticks. It is amazing that otherwise normal people are intellectually stimulated by spending their waking hours telling others one plus one equals two.

It is a fact that newcomers need help. I am meeting more than my share lately and they are definitely characterized by a general aura of being up tight. All the instincts that served them well during a rapid run up the corporate ladder appear to be useless here. They are, for the first time in their lives, in a minority racial position. Most cannot read the local newspaper or speak to the natives. All begin by following rather than leading. No wonder the Sunday champagne brunch at Trader Vics is packed with foreigners steeling themselves with enough confidence to face another week.

I do not profess to have a better answer to the "how to understand Japan" challenge. My natural tendency is to avoid newcomers; and I recognize I am over the hill because my New York friends accuse me of assuming Japanese mannerisms like uttering HAI, HAI or other guttural sounds after their one line statements. But I have learned a survival rule of thumb, which is so simple it must be good: Everything in Japan is the reverse of what you think it should be. Here are a few examples.

- The best English speaking Japanese guy across the table is not the most powerful or the smartest person in the room.
- The most enthusiastic responder to your brilliant new idea will not be your ally. He may be the first guy to object.
- When a Japanese colleague approaches you with a big grin on his face, he has bad news.
- When you know everything is going well with a deal, it is bound to be in trouble.
- The girl in a club who showers you with the most compliments about your Hollywood good looks is the least interested.
- A Japanese job applicant with a very impressive résumé is the least attractive candidate.
- You are convinced the Japanese are becoming more "Western." Forget it.
- Everything you heard tonight over ample quantities of sake should be repeated tomorrow in a formal management meeting.

- The Japanese are long-term thinkers; therefore they will enthusiastically work with you on the five-year strategic plan. Drop it. Talk about what you will do today.
- Individual self interest rules, therefore the sales director will love your new incentive/commission plan. He cares about the self interest of the group—not the individual.
- Your secretary would make a great manager of public relations. This is definitely lose/lose. You lose a great secretary and get a lousy manager.
- Every decision must be made by consensus. Learn that power is faster.

This is so much fun it is a shame to stop, but I am running out of space. Let's close with the inevitable direct relationship. Just when you are relaxed in the business culture; when there are few surprises; you are leading not following; your minority status gives you special privileges; the difference between *toro* and *taco* at your favorite sushi bar is a no brainer; you have developed a new set of instincts; say HAI over the telephone have an excellent file system for your collection of *meishi*; and don't hang out with newcomers—guess what, the company transfers you to New Jersey.

Pharma Japan, June 1992

Everything You Need To Know

If you don't know anything about the Japanese pharmaceutical market before coming here, do not despair. After three months, you will have an opinion on everything. After one year, you will be convinced you know all there is to know. After two years, the learning curve peaks and begins its inevitable and consistent downward slope. In other words, you will realize you know less and less, or conversely, what you know is minuscule compared to what you should know. This is a good time to leave Japan, and most expatriates go after three years.

Those who stay for five years get so enamored by the challenge of learning more that they will do almost anything to prolong their stay. It is a weird pattern that all of you who arrived this summer should be aware of, your career may depend on it. Corporate promotions are not given to people who walk around mumbling how much they don't know about this market, they go to people who boast about how much they know.

To help you succeed, I succumbed to the bad habit of every writer, which is to compile a top ten list of things you need to know to crack the pharmaceutical market. In the style of a U.S. talk show host, David Letterman, let's start with number 10 and work our way up to the number one thing you need to know.

10. Business is business. Relationships are important, but do not become so captivated by them that you make bad business decisions because of past relationships. Your Japanese partners will sing the song of "our good relationship" to extract benefits they neither deserve nor earn.

9. Put it in writing. Take notes to build an institutional memory bank, woefully lacking in foreign firms but honed to a fine art in Japanese firms. A statement whispered confidentially at a table in a club on the Ginza at 11:00 p.m. is "table talk," well meaning but not to be taken seriously unless repeated at 9:00 a.m. in a company conference room the next morning while you take notes.

8. Recognize good management, not just good English. Many people succeed by virtue of their command of the English language, but have absolutely no business sense. It is much easier to teach a good manager English than it is to make a good manager out of someone who's only skill is good English.

7. Learn some Japanese. An effective missionary must know how to talk to his flock in Japanese, but you were sent here to do business, not preach. Many fluent Japanese speakers do not know a debit from a credit or an asset from a liability. But, you need to know enough to order lunch without pointing in the window or playing charades. It's also nice to have some idea of what the hell is going on without waiting for the translation.

6. Don't be surprised. Open your door, or better yet, sit in an open office. Never kill the messenger or you will be cut off from all news except the announcement of a dire emergency.

5. Similarities are more important than differences. Newcomers delight in swapping stories about "THE Japanese," and your business associates will preface every fifth phase with "WE Japanese." Both statements are intended to highlight the gap between them and us. Reality is there are more intraracial differences than interracial differences. Focus on how we think alike.

4. Good manners and common sense work. If you try to learn all the politically correct mannerisms of this society, you will go nuts and look foolish in the process. A sincere handshake is better than an awkward bow. But if you must ask for a fork in a sushi restaurant, get reservations on the next flight out of here.

3. Forget the Madam Butterfly myths. Women in this country are not the docile, subservient creatures that have been idolized in Hollywood or personal classified ads. Nor should they be relegated to serving tea. They are a reservoir of talent waiting to be effectively utilized.

2. Get out of town. Meet customers on their turf, visit branch offices, meet doctors and wholesalers where they work. Don't let the home office tie you down to answering faxes three hours every day, and phone calls every night.

And finally, the number one thing you need to know to make your stay in Japan a memorable and rewarding experience.

1. Remember who you are. If you were not born a Japanese, it is highly unlikely you will ever become a Japanese. Don't Japanize your office. Learn what works instead of emulating every Japanese business practice. You run the risk of getting stuck with bad practices Japanese companies would like to eliminate. The old saw about "When in Rome, etc." may have been great for the Romans, but they were not aware of the existence of Japan.

Enjoy yourself, and try to stay on the right side of the Shinkansen tracks. Moving in the opposite direction of the flow is costly in terms of time, and the clock is ticking rapidly toward the three-year cutoff point for your next promotion.

Pharma Japan 1515, September 1996

911 or 119: Which One Is Backwards?

The curse for foreigners living and working in Japan is the necessity to think in terms diametrically opposed to what is assumed to be normal behavior. The paradigm for achieving results is upside down and yet, things work, stuff gets done, customers are satisfied, and Japanese products compete fiercely around the world.

How many Japanese systems are considered inefficient, doomed to fail, or at least are behind the curve of change in the West, destined to catch up or face extinction? Foreigners who believe this spend their time trying to change local behavior to "normal." They live a frustrating existence.

In every day life the situations are so numerous it is an interesting hobby to catalogue them for reference. They make excellent conversation topics on home leave. The premise is you must put your head on backwards to understand Japan.

The most frequently cited example is the use of the word "yes" when the Japanese clearly mean "no." The word "difficult" to an English speaking executive implies a challenge that can be overcome. In Japan the real meaning is "no way."

Bad news, like the death of close relative, is delivered with a smile, even a nervous laugh; good news comes with a frown, or an apology that the good fortune was undeserved or just luck. Results are of secondary importance to process. Management by objectives (MBO), a U.S. management craze before the era of reengineering, was DOA (dead on arrival) when corporate human resource (HR) people arrived in Japan to preach the gospel of MBO.

An analogy might be the old, endless song about a bear that climbed a mountain, and what do you think he saw? He saw another mountain; he saw another mountain, etc. Rewards in Japan do not hinge on reaching the top, the climb itself is the raison d'être.

How many corporate marketing executives truly understand the dynamics of pricing in the Japanese pharmaceutical market? Who can blame them for not believing the lowest volume customers, i.e., small dispensing clinics, get the highest discounts? That a low priced generic must offer a larger percentage discount than a high priced proprietary drug? That dispensers prefer a high price drug over a low price drug? That more, not less patient days in a hospital are preferred by administrators?

Who, in their right mind, can believe medical representatives (MR) visit their doctors once a week? Or that wholesaler salesmen (MS) visit the same doctors' office every other day? Western marketing effectiveness experts beg for a rational explanation of this behavior. Sales executives are baffled by explanations to justify a desk in an office for every MR. Why can't they work from their homes? Individual sales targets and incentives are shunned in favor of group or section goals, rewarding poor performers with the same bonuses as the "stars."

HR people go nuts reviewing salary scales that do not reward performance, but look like escalators based on age. Annual review reports focus more on an employee's ability to get along with others rather than on their ability to do a job. Career planning exercises have a very short time frame, and succession planning, if done at all, is carried out in secrecy only the CIA would admire.

Who understands the logic of assigning highly qualified women to serving tea, or to a lower pay scale than less qualified men, or exclusion from certain sections, e.g., sales?

QC people fail to understand the passion of Japanese customers for the outside appearance of a product when it is the inside active ingredient at work in the patient. A chipped vial or tablet provokes a major crisis.

A star athlete in the West would not understand the remark by Hideki Matsui, the Yomiuri Giants outfielder who batted .314 and knocked in 38 homers and 99 RBIs while playing every game for the third straight season in 1996. Although his salary was doubled to 160 million yen for the 1997 season; it will be less than half that paid to one of the Giants pitchers. Matsui accepted his new salary saying, "The team officials told me I'm actually worth more than my salary but they had to keep it low in line with those of the other players." George Steinbrenner, owner of the New York Yankees, would love players with this attitude.

Who knows why the emergency telephone number in Japan is 119, the reverse of 911 used in America. But neither number is wrong if it achieves the desired response. Results count, how you get them is irrelevant. Flashy presentations or beautiful business plans are often prepared by people who have no responsibility for achieving results. What they plan to do is far less important than what they do. Foreigners who learn these lessons become impatient with corporate strategic thinkers; the big picture guys who have great ideas but no clue how to execute them in Japan.

Pharma Japan, February 1997

Wouldn't It Be Lovely . . .

If home office personnel:

- Would call at a time convenient for you instead of the time convenient for them.
- Would stop being jealous of your perceived expensive life style in exotic Japan.
- Would approve the cost of Japanese lessons as a necessary business expense.
- Would appreciate the flight from Tokyo to headquarters for a meeting requires more energy than a drive in from the suburbs.
- Would leave their ideas of power breakfast meetings at home, and not expect to go out every night during their stay in Japan.
- Would learn that the MOSS agreements were not about protecting the green growth on the leeward side of trees.

If your Japanese employees:

- Would enthusiastically welcome just one of your new ideas.
- Would not believe you enjoy those frequent mileage bonuses for flying back to the home office every six weeks.
- Would stop saying "Japan is different."
- Would get tough with distributors who always want a higher margin but never commit to higher sales.
- Would, just once, give you a reason why something will work instead of 10 reasons why it will not work.
- Would speak up in a meeting as forcefully and passionately as they sang "I Left My Heart in San Francisco" at the karaoke bar last night.

If your Japanese partner:

- Freely offered to promote your products with the same enthusiasm as his own products.
- Came to you first with his new product for marketing outside Japan.
- Introduced you to his friends in Koseisho as frequently as he introduces you to his "friends" on the Ginza.
- Stopped hinting to the home office that you are creating disharmony in a fine relationship carefully built on trust and good will.
- Would give you at least one good person instead of the 10 he speaks highly of but doesn't know what to do with.

If your wife:

- Stopped questioning why your company doesn't offer all the wonderful perks enjoyed by her friends in the flower-arranging class.
- Would plan a trip in Japan rather than to all the lush resorts in Asia.
- Would not convert your home into a Japanese antique shop or a woodblock print gallery.
- Would understand that all the late nights are important business meetings. Well, that might be going too far—she knows better, but bless her patience.

If:

- The profit plan could be finalized after you know the 1994 price reductions.
- You weren't complimented on your wonderful Japanese ability after uttering *domo arigato*.

- You could attend a concert without ordering tickets six months in advance.
- You could buy a box of cereal for less than six dollars. Damn the home office people who think you are living like a king because they must pay $10,000 per month for your apartment.
- Every place was not so crowded you might actually enjoy living here.

On second thoughts, if everything was so lovely, there would be nothing to complain about, nothing to laugh about with fellow expats, and nothing to write home about. Anyway, it sounds like the home office is not a great place to be these days, your Japanese employees get stuff done on time, your partners exceeded plan, yen sales look 20 percent better in dollars, your wife loves the flowers, there is more to life than corn flakes in the morning, crowds can be avoided, and you get more attention than most movie actors. Tell the boss the company can benefit from continuity—meaning you.

Pharma Japan 1380, December 6, 1993

Concentrate on What Is Possible

There is nothing more painful, or boring, than having to listen through all the reasons why you can't do something. The process begins at an early age. Remember the admonition, "Don't walk in the water." Kids love to walk in the water. They will go out of their way to find a puddle on an otherwise dry sidewalk It's fun.

As we get older we cannot escape those who delight in telling us what we cannot do. Don't smoke; don't eat foods that taste good, they give you high cholesterol and make you fat; don't stay out late; don't work too hard. The list is endless.

I suppose it is a lot easier for most people to think of all the reasons why something cannot be done because it protects the status quo, the familiar, the procedures we are comfortable with. Change, in any form, is stressful. But for others, there is a temptation to ask the simple question. "Why not?"

There are a few "why not" questions that seem appropriate in our pharmaceutical world. Why not . . .

- harmonize pre-clinical and clinical regulatory requirements between Japan, Europe and the United States?
- change this price reimbursement system that practically guarantees regular price reductions? Who benefits?

• build a dedicated sales training facility?
• hire women to do more than serve tea?
• eliminate the economic incentives for dispensing drugs?

Sometimes, unfortunately too often, the answer is "Because Japan is different." This is a statement that says virtually nothing. I recommend you put the people who are fond of this response behind desks next to windows which look out into blank walls. Their capacity for creative thought is severely limited.

How refreshing it is to listen to a person tell us what is possible, what can be done. Such people are invaluable in any organization. You only need a few.

Get one in regulatory affairs to tell you what can be approved by Koseisho instead of what they will not accept. Get one responsible for negotiating a price Koseisho will accept instead of the one that gives you no premium. Get one in personnel who won't always tell you why foreign companies cannot hire good people. Get one in sales who finds reasons why your products are much better than the competition. Get one who can help you convince your home office colleagues what is really possible in Japan.

There are two wood block prints on my office wall by Clifton Karhu, the American artist who lives and works in Kyoto. They tell it better than my poor choice of words. One reads:

"You become good at what you like to do."

The other says:
"What one can do ninety-nine cannot, and the other way around."

It's worth thinking about. You can make a difference, and it won't take many more like you to blow away the competition.

Pharma Japan 1189, January 22, 1990

The Least Publicized Secret of Success

For more than two years, and in well over 100 articles, I have failed to mention the most important key to success for a foreign company in Japan. Everyone keeps it a secret; no one ever talks about it.

Get a group of pharmaceutical guys in a room and ask them the key to success in Japan's pharmaceutical market, and what do you think they say? I had the opportunity to do this in Tokyo and San Francisco recently. The favorite response was "new products." Then, in a quiet voice they added, "At high prices."

Would you disagree that new products drive sales and earnings in this business? There is absolutely no substitute for good science. I fall asleep listening to analysts predict a zillion dollar market for generics. Can you imagine devoting a career to developing and marketing old technology? Sure—there is money to be made; particularly when single-source products have such a high price, only fools would not rush in.

Fortunately, many dedicated people in this business believe there is more to innovation than a lower price. Where would we be if the researchers of this world stopped looking for new antihypertensive medicines after they found reserpine and the diuretics? What if the only cure for an infection was good cheap penicillin? I remember waiting for my father to be released from a Philadelphia hospital after having two-thirds of his stomach removed because of an ulcer. Before the operation, he was told to eat crackers and drink milk. Now, we know that prescription was like pouring oil on a fire. Today, the mail-order pharmacy people and smart MBAs in hospital buying groups say we only need one cheap H_2 antagonist.

Give me a break; no generic company will ever find a cure for AIDS, or cancer, or schizophrenia. Old technology has a limited useful life, and companies that embrace it will also have a limited life. In 50 years, no one will remember the companies who bet on generic products in 1993.

Another key to success mentioned in Tokyo and San Francisco was good people. Everyone agreed it was much easier to recruit good people in the United States, maybe more so now that every company is restructuring, a Harvard B-school euphemism for involuntary layoffs.

Again, no one will disagree that good people make the difference between mediocrity and a first-class operation. Yet, we often neglect the influence of internal politics on the performance of good people. It is distressing to think of the many good men who came to Japan and would have succeeded had it not been for destructive politics behind their backs at the home office.

New products, good people, a solid commitment to building a presence in Japan have been written about ad nauseam. But rarely does anyone pay tribute to the real key to success for foreign companies in Japan. It is without doubt the bilingual, Japanese ladies who act as secretaries. The word secretary does not begin to describe their role or unwritten job descriptions. Interpreter, tour guide, confidante, fixer, assistant, hostess, meeting planner, visitor arranger, public relations, accountant, personnel liaison, etc., etc.

And think of the indignities they silently suffer. Wives are jealous (sometimes for good reason), long hours coping with a foreign language in various accents, translating direct (sometimes rude) statements into polite, indirect Japanese, patiently explaining simple directions, serving tea to disrespectable males, etc., etc.

I know it will never happen, but think of this fantasy. A man is posted to Japan and does well enough to earn a promotion back to the home office. At the Hotel Okura sayonara party, he stands in the receiving line with his secretary and tells every guest, "This person was the key to my success." And everyone marvels at the ice carving which is a perfect likeness of the secretary.

Thank you, ladies, without you foreign business in Japan would grind to a bumbling, glacial pace. There is a special place in heaven reserved for all of you. And I have it on good authority that your former bosses will be employed there as tea servers.

Pharma Japan 1365, August 23, 1993

The Ideal Home Office Visitor Itinerary

Years of diligent research at great expense produced the first ideal itinerary for a visitor from the home office. A consultant could retire on the value of this advice, but I share it freely with the humanitarian goal of easing the stress of local executives who entertain more visitors to these shores than the JTB (Japan Travel Bureau).

Before plunging into the details, a few assumptions must be understood. In other words, what is the profile of a typical visitor?

1. Practically all visitors are male because home offices have the uninformed opinion that females cannot operate effectively in Japan. Little do they realize this is a matriarchal society. It is common for a mother to retain a small piece of the umbilical cord from the birth of a son to forever remind him of the ties that bind them together.
2. Visitors usually arrive on Sunday or Monday and leave on Friday. This ensures minimum disruption of their family weekends; and given the political intrigue in most home offices, everyone wants to stay close to the big bosses.

3. Visitors expect to be entertained every night on the local operation budget. This practice keeps their own expense accounts clean and above suspicion.
4. All visitors need an interpreter except within the confines of their first class hotel.
5. Unlike normal people, visitors have two mouths and one ear. They talk twice as much as they listen.
6. Visitors evaluate Japanese staff on the basis of their ability to speak English.
7. Visitors love to come to Japan because they can accumulate more airline mileage points than most other destinations.
8. Visitors are impatient with explanations that suggest results in Japan can be obtained with methods unknown in the West.
9. Bean counting visitors (financial staff) have two objectives: raise transfer prices to Japan and lower expenses in Japan.
10. The best conversation with every visitor begins with the word "Sayonara" on Friday afternoon.

Here is the itinerary every home office visitor should follow.

Sunday: Arrival at Narita
Be sure to tell the customs officer you work for a DRUG company.

Take a taxi to the hotel. This is your first lesson in the cost of doing business in Japan.

After check-in call the gaijin manager of your local affiliate to suggest changes in your itinerary. This will ensure he spends the next two hours on the telephone, disrupting the one night he planned to spend alone with his wife.

Monday
5:00 a.m.: Emulate the former CEO of Merck, Dr. Roy Vagelos, who jogged out of his hotel to the Imperial Palace but got lost on the return trip. He hailed a taxi for the unexpected one-minute ride to the hotel, then realized he had no money to pay the 650-yen fare.

All day: Go over in exquisite detail the objectives of your visit that must be accomplished without fail by Friday noon. The staff will listen politely and respond with the words "Hai, Hai," signifying they agree with your plan.

Evening: Dinner at a sushi restaurant in Tsukiji where raw fish and sake are the only menu options. Go to a "second place" where the hostesses are convinced you are a movie star.

Return to the hotel and order a massage from the phone number prominently displayed on a card in the bathroom next to the disposable shower cap.

Tuesday

5:00 a.m.: Skip the jogging for a taxi ride to Tsukiji to get your feet soaked and listen to people yell unintelligibly around huge slabs of fish.

All day: Meet with the staff to answer questions about the objectives of your visit. You will hear loud sucking noises of air through clenched teeth, signifying your colleagues have a few problems with your plans.

Evening: Dinner at a yakitori restaurant with the top people in the department you are visiting. The noise will preempt a heart-to-heart discussion but the food will be cooked. Go to a "second place" where the hostesses know your colleagues are important and you are neglected.

Wednesday

5:00 a.m.: Try to go back to sleep but the curtains will not restrain the light. Get up and go to the health club for a regimented exercise routine.

All day: Visit the offices of your Japanese partners where everyone will listen to your plans and express their sincere interest in implementing them. Patiently listen to all the difficulties of doing business in Japan.

Evening: Go to a restaurant on the Ginza where you will be welcomed by a bevy of older women dressed in Kimono. Dine seated on the floor, legs crossed, and glass in hand to receive refills from the lady who is assigned exclusively to you for this task. Go to a "second place" where an English speaking hostess will complain about the Japanese customers who insist on fondling unmentionable places. Return to the hotel and collapse, forgetting to go on line for important E-mail messages.

Thursday

AM: Oversleep. Answer messages by convincing the home office you are working night and day.

All day: Visit a branch office, hospital, pharmacy, wholesaler, and clinic. Eat a bento for lunch. Return to the hotel convinced you understood no more than 10 percent of what was said during the day.

Evening: Dinner at a French restaurant with an English speaking outside consultant who completely understands your objectives and assures you they can be implemented. Return to the hotel and prepare your trip report.

Friday
AM: Check out of the hotel and pray your American Express card will not be rejected.

Wrap up: Meet with the staff to confirm milestones and assignments. Have a working lunch ordered from the Subway sandwich shop down the street.

Farewell: Take an early train to Narita so you do not miss the plane.

P. Reed Maurer's itinerary brought him to Japan in 1970. He has a spouse visa and welcomes visitors to his consulting firm International Alliances Limited (IAL).

Pharma Japan 1554, June 1997

Pharma Primer for Visitors

Coincident with the blooming of cherry blossoms is an increase of visitors from the home office. Most of them deserve and appreciate the efforts made on their behalf by the local staff who thought they were hired by a pharmaceutical company but their job descriptions could have been written by the Japan Travel Bureau. Some visitors expect treatment reserved for a head of state. These are the same people who write critical reports when they return to their cubicles in the home office.

I have the pleasure of meeting with visiting executives every week, but count my blessings I am not responsible for their schedules. Furthermore, I enforce some basic ground rules, like no power breakfasts at the Hotel Okura. A recent fax requested me to meet the visitor with a tight schedule for lunch on Sunday at a hotel in Ikebukuro. I passed.

Many, no all of the questions I am asked could be answered by the local staff, but an outsider can give answers unexpected by the boss. I do not call myself an "expert" as an "ex" is a has been, and a "spurt" is a drip under pressure.

So, what kinds of questions are asked? To break the ice, the general economy is a good place to start. Surprising how many people come here and expect to see bread lines and general idleness of the unemployed. Show, not tell is good advice. A local guy took his boss to Shibuya at 6:00 p.m. for a walk around. The visitor's eyes saw what the brain could not compute, so the question to me was, "What about conditions in the countryside?"

Somehow, people want to believe Japan's economic miracle is a 40-year-old fluke, a house built on sand. They view Japan's positive trade imbalance with the United States as a reflection of barriers into this market rather than competitive advantage. No one seems concerned that U.S. trade negotiators focus on apples, rice tariffs, flat glass, and hot rolled steel.

The next question invariably concerns reimbursement pricing in general and reference prices specifically. I have reams of opinions on these subjects but personally do not talk about them. Until decisions are made, it is more productive to talk about how to operate within the present system. Associations discuss "What if?" questions; businessmen are better off concentrating on what is. However, a number of reasonable bets can be made about the outcomes of healthcare reform:

1. The government will reward and encourage innovation. Old technology will not be protected or encouraged.
2. Insurers will not deny access to therapy. Approved drugs and procedures will not be restricted.
3. Before scandals shook up Koseisho, NDAs were approved in Japan faster than in the United States and Europe. It was also the first launch country for most new drugs. In both categories Japan is now the laggard, but will get its act together.
4. More options for healthcare will be available. This will lead to less regulation. Quality of care is the issue.

Getting down to the pharma industry, most questions relate to the future viability of Japanese companies. Frequent comments include: "They missed the boat in genomics." "They are not international and foreign companies are increasing share in Japan." "Their presidents are too old."

All of the above contain elements of truth, but it's an old story. Japanese firms, at least the better ones, are reinventing themselves to cope with a new set of realities. For every Shionogi who is a mere shadow of its former power, there is a Yamanouchi on a roll. Generalizing about the "industry" gets you nowhere. Better to talk about individual companies.

Questions about people are always a favorite subject. Not too long ago the issue was how to find a warm body that would accept an offer of employment in a foreign firm. Now companies are swamped with applications so the issue is outplacement or early retirement. No one ever gets fired in Japan.

Some topics never change. How to negotiate the beginning or end of a relationship is an example. Alliances are not forever, they serve useful and profitable purposes for both sides then end or are revised. People agonize over and procrastinate what should be unemotional business decisions. Many foreign companies forfeited a presence in the market because the emotional aspects of a relationship got in the way of a rational decision.

An undercurrent to all of the above subjects is a sense that visitors are not in control. Some of the blustering and table pounding is a cover-up for insecurity. Companies cede control because of fear or ignorance on how to operate in this environment. People sitting on the other side of the table eagerly but politely take the control they are offered. The result is an imbalance in the sharing of rewards. Control should be paid for. It is not a gift that comes with the cultural territory.

Visitors do not need a lesson on how to do business in Japan, a tour of temples and shrines, or a cultural immersion class. Good business practices and decent manners travel well across national boundaries.

What helps visitors most is a long corporate memory. Who did what to who in the past should be required reading of every new guy. A fresh perspective is great, but if you've been there, done that, the conversation is boring. Unfortunately there are too many people making the same old mistakes.

Pharma Japan 1645, April 1989

Explaining Japan

An American executive of a U.S. pharmaceutical company stationed in Japan wrote me a letter suggesting a topic for an article. He then went on to say, "After three years, I'm fed up explaining to new employees and reminding old ones at the home offce that things are different here. I think it would save a lot of *gaijin* time if one could simply respond: see Maurer article number X in Pharma Japan vol. Y."

The implied compliment was appreciated, but citing Maurer to his home office and 500 yen will not buy a cup of coffee in Roppongi. "Think globally, act locally" is a great slogan for corporate advertisements, but is a rare commodity inside an organization. Think like us and act accordingly is the more common operative dictum for corporate staffers.

Explaining what works in Japan is a constant problem for expatriates who are sent here to get results. Jeffery Pfeffer, who teaches organizational behavior at the Graduate School of Business at Stanford University, gives practical advice in a recently published book entitled *Managing with Power: Politics and Influence in Organizations*. He maintains, "It is essential to assume not everyone in the organization is going to be our friend, or agree with us, or even that preferences are uniformly distributed."

Pfeffer says, "It is all too easy to assume that those with a different perspective are somehow not as smart as we are, not as informed, not as perceptive. If that is our belief, we may act contemptuously toward those who disagree with us—after all, if they aren't as competent or as insightful as we are, why should we take them seriously? If we think people are misinformed, we are likely to try to inform them, or to try to convince them with facts and analysis. This usually does not work because their disagreement may not be based on a lack of information; it may, instead, arise from a different perspective on what our information means."

As the title to Pfeffer's book suggests, the answer to this problem is to get power ". . . more power than those whose opposition you must overcome. It is not enough to do our best, work hard, be nice, and believe things will work out for the best." Getting things done requires power.

This book should be required reading for anyone assigned to Japan. I am reminded of one nice, hardworking manager of a U.S. firm who advocated an independent sales force and distribution capability for their Japan subsidiary. Naturally, the Japanese partner objected and went straight to the home office to voice concern and dismay. In the power struggle that ensued, the local manager was fired—of course, in a nice way. He has since become head of another country subsidiary for a different company.

A few years later his successor proposed exactly the same strategy, which was enthusiastically supported by the home office. The new man is a hero and considers this strategy his original idea. We may sympathize with the nice guy, but must respect the power player for getting things done. Power, not an explanation, was more productive.

There is one problem with this scenario. Power in the hands of someone who implements the wrong strategy can lead to organizational failure. It is important to know what will work in Japan. Take the guy who comes here intent on carrying out a plan solely devised by the home office, one that is incorrect. Any attempt to explain Japan will erode his power—cut him off from the people who can thwart his ambitions for moving up the corporate ladder. He drives forward.

Mistakes in a marketing plan can be corrected. A botched clinical trial program may delay approval but result in a product profile that receives a favorable price. One factor that deserves an explanation of Japan is personnel policy. Generous out placement programs eagerly accepted by mobile, independent U.S. employees may have disastrous morale implications in Japan. Conversely, staffing up by hiring outside senior managers may demoralize loyal insiders.

Power players like fast, decisive actions they know will appeal to those above them in the chain of command. This is admirable so long as they realize getting a decision implemented requires cooperation by people outside the purview of their authority or understanding. For example, employees who do not speak English but have lots of intelligent things to say about what really works

Pharma Japan 1313, July 1992

Back to the ABCs

Always nice at the beginning of a new year to believe we can start over, shed old habits, change our state of mind, and do all the right things. That is a good trick anywhere, but if you live and work in Japan the odds of getting past January 15 with this attitude are pretty slim.

But what if you could change the Japan operations of your company without objections from the home office, your colleagues, or partners? A clean slate, anything you wanted to do without being told Japan is different, or headcount is limited, or expenses are restricted. Anything, except as a prudent businessman you will be expected to generate a market return on the money invested, grow sales faster than the market, and meet or exceed the objectives you set for yourself. Hey—nobody gets a free ride. So, what would you do?

A good place to start is to model your actions on what is working in Japan, not in your native country. To start with, don't read any book about doing business in Japan more than two years old, particularly chapters on personnel management. They are out of date because models of success are changing rapidly. It seems like yesterday when the Osaka companies were feared and admired. Now Shionogi, Fujisawa, Tanabe, and Dainippon look like basket cases. On the other hand, Takeda is reinventing itself from top to bottom—restructuring its personnel system, focusing on an enviable new product portfolio, and streamlining its supply chain. Modeling the number one company is a good bet.

Get the Fundamentals Right

Before you make the plunge into massive restructuring, it might be helpful to quietly contemplate the ABCs, or basics of what it takes to succeed in this pharmaceutical market. Most games are won by executing fundamentals better than the competition. You may have some flashy plays in mind, but they will not give you a sustainable basis for outperforming your rivals.

1. Know Your Customer

This is so basic I am embarrassed to mention it except so many people violate the rule. How many companies isolate themselves from customers by entrusting the development and marketing of their drugs to licensees? The financial advantages may be obvious, but a lack of presence relegates licensors to a remote seat in the stadium, unable to see the players and cheers of encouragement go unheeded on the field.

If you sell direct to wholesalers, the typical mistake is to use too many. Takeda is down to 50 and they have a long history of close relations with many more. Companies with limited resources should be down to 30 or fewer wholesalers. In our company, NPP, we achieve nationwide coverage with 12. The more you have, the less you know about these customers.

A fact of life in Japan is the high intensity of doctor visits. This will change, but remember you are not going to change Japan and meet your objectives. Go with the flow, but execute better than others. This means you should look very closely at your territory allocation of doctors. No doubt you will find at least 20 percent of doctors called-on are not prime targets for your drugs. By eliminating these and substituting the right doctors you can increase the productivity of your MRs by 20 percent without adding a single person.

2. Know Your Employees

People are your biggest expense. A knee jerk reaction is to downsize and become an overnight hero with the home office. Resist the temptation, but get the right people in the right jobs. How many are in wrong positions simply because they speak English, or were transferred from your partner, or have a good friend in the home office? Remove people who always know why you cannot do something. They start every sentence with, "Japan is different." This is not an easy task, but you can't move forward while these people throw up roadblocks.

Promote from within and recruit outside for entry-level jobs. The devil you know is better than the devil you do not know. Filling middle management jobs from outside is a time consuming, expensive process.

Do not be shy about bringing capable foreigners into key positions. If they don't work out, you can have them on the next plane home. But give them the tools to succeed. Before they set foot in the Japan office, send them through an intensive language program.

3. Know the Regulators

Much of your success will be driven by the timely approval of new products. It is damn difficult to re-launch old products in this market. Like it or not, Koseisho is the doorkeeper and you need to know their house rules to tilt the odds in your favor. You can try to change the rules, but it is a long, frustrating process. Far better to meet the decision-makers on a regular basis. When was the last time you met a Koseisho official? If it wasn't this week or last, you are out of sight and out of mind.

4. Bring Commitment and Passion to the Task

Companies often fail to optimize their potential in spite of good products and access to good people. One reason is their gut belief that Japan is not for real. They believe the market will decline, prices will be cut, local companies will get all the goodies, everyone hides information, and the system works to exclude outsiders except when needed to provide new technology. These people lead a life of suspicion rather than inquisitiveness. They fail to recognize you win more games by scoring points (offense) versus stopping competitors from scoring (defense).

Learn quickly that the ABCs cannot be implemented by sitting in your office with a daily schedule of meetings around your coffee table. Getting out to wholesalers, hospitals, branch offices and Koseisho requires a high level of commitment, not to mention stamina. It's tough on the ego to be led rather than lead, to be where you are the only round eyed person in the room, to not make your points forcefully in your native tongue, to not be in control.

You can always stuff the New Year's resolutions and go back to following orders, making presentations to corporate visitors, and planning your next home leave. Your local competitors expect that to occur—why not surprise them for a change.

Pharma Japan 1631, January 1999

20 Stupid Assumptions

I will not waste your time with a long introduction into a list of stupid assumptions. Then why bother at all? Because some people believe this nonsense and make life difficult for the rest of us.

1. All Japanese company employees work hard, have reverent respect for their bosses, and want to stay with one company for a lifetime.
2. All foreigners play hard, disrespect authority, and are constantly searching for a new job.
3. All Japanese companies have long-term goals; salary systems based solely on seniority, and maintain rigid quality standards.
4. Every foreign company has short-term goals, salary systems based solely on performance, and a low priority on quality.
5. Doctors in Japan make most of their income by dispensing high priced drugs.
6. Foreigners living in Japan understand Japanese doctors so well they know the standard of medicine is poor.
7. The total number of MRs should be cut by at least half.
8. Certification examinations will instill in the public and medical profession a high degree of respect for MRs.
9. Women and wholesaler MS cannot promote drugs to doctors.
10. Sales will decrease if we reduce the number of our wholesalers.
11. Generics will be a booming business in Japan because the government wants to cut costs.
12. OTC's will be a booming business because the government will force patients to self medicate.
13. Koseisho's industrial policy determines which companies get high prices for new drugs, and smaller price reductions on older drugs.
14. Japanese companies will consolidate because of government guidance.
15. Japanese companies will consolidate because mergers outside Japan demonstrated the value of "bigness" in the pharmaceutical industry.
16. The best way for a foreign company to do business in Japan is through a joint venture.
17. Japanese companies are not for sale.
18. The introduction of GCP in Japan will not occur during our lifetime.
19. Koseisho will never approve new drugs as fast as the FDA.
20. Foreign companies will only succeed in Japan if they "Japanize" their management and personnel practices.

When this theme first came to mind, I thought it would be difficult to come up with 20 stupid assumptions, but it was easy. More could have been added. If you have been here long enough to know the difference between the image and reality of Japan, you have your own favorites.

Untruths persist because they make life easier for the people who perpetuate them. Good examples relate to what Koseisho supposedly can do to control every facet of the pharmaceutical industry, and people believe this without ever talking to a single official. During the six years I represented the PMA (now PhRMA [Pharmaceutical Research and Manufacturers of America]) in Japan, I searched in vain for evidence of an industrial policy or deliberate actions that specifically discriminated against foreign companies. People with Koseisho problems are those who never enter the building. Some don't know where it is.

Other stupid assumptions are those espoused by Japan experts who live outside Japan. Or by Japanese who begin every statement with, "We Japanese . . ." It is as though they were given special dispensation to speak for the entire race. These characters prey upon newcomers, or appeal to executives who know they will not stay in Japan long and want to impress the home office with their grasp of the culture. Corporate types like one line generalizations.

Inherent in their advice is what you cannot do in Japan. The only way out of this trap is to talk with people who know what you can do. Folks like this are hard to find because they are not part of the crowd who show up at association meetings to complain about barriers. No, they quietly make money and are not eager to tell others how. It may be unfair, but who said insiders have an obligation to help outsiders?

Pharma Japan 1599, May 1998

Five Ways to Succeed in Japan

Guess I'm just lucky. Many people and their companies succeed in Japan, and it has been my good fortune to be part of the process, or close enough, to observe the results.

There are many roads to success, but one word is common to all, i.e., COMMITMENT. In successful companies, you notice it throughout the organization. It is so real you can feel it from the receptionist to the president. They know they will crack this market and have no doubt about the ultimate outcome. Discussions are not about the problems of doing business in Japan; the focus is on opportunities. These people do not say, "Japan is different." They believe Japan is predictable. They are confident and secure, eager to try new ideas, experiment, take risks. The antithesis of this attitude was evident in the voice of a man who told me, "I don't know what I am doing—or why—but I am really, really busy."

The successful people and companies I am lucky to meet attribute their success to several factors. There are five recurring themes. Listen to what these people say.

1. Don't organize Japan as part of a region, e.g., Asia/Pacific. It is a region. If the person responsible for Japan is sitting in a home office location, he is in the wrong place. If he sits in Japan but has responsibility for everything south to Australia and west to Bangladesh, he is never in Japan at the right time

In 1994, Japan accounted for 23 percent of the world pharmaceutical market; all of Europe, 29 percent; and North America, 31 percent. The people responsible for these three regions must report directly to the top of the organization. If the Japan guy is just another country manager, commitment is diluted to a meaningless phrase. Japanese partners and staff are not fooled. Real decisions are made elsewhere. The Japan president, or whatever the title may be, is a messenger. How many organizational layers does your head of Japanese operations go through to the CEO? If it is over two, he is spending more time educating his bosses than motivating this staff.

2. Establish a presence in Japan, which you control, to develop, promote, and distribute your products. These are the minimum strategic necessities. Without them you forfeit customer contact, knowledge of key players, and value-added margins. You are dependent on others to build relationships, which is OK only as long as "others" do not have conflicting business interests. As a Japanese president recently told me, "Relationships are fine, but business is business."

"Critical mass" is the phrase most often used. There are several ways to get it. In Merck, in 1983, we achieved it through acquisition of Banyu and Torii. Today, companies are getting it through internal growth. A company I know had 20,000 inquiries for 30 job openings. They intensively interviewed 110 and selected the cream of the crop. Another company hired 100 MRs this year and are convinced they did not compromise their high standards in the selection process.

3. Utilize partners to supplement weakness, but do not believe they will help you build strength or critical mass.

Non-committed organizations love the prefix "co" in front of the strategic necessities: develop, promote, and distribute. Most, if not an, co-agreements place your own organization in a subservient role. Additional sales may be generated, but invariably the incremental income is not reinvested in growing the Japan business. The local manager spends half his life negotiating transfer prices and the percentage of detail time allocated by his co-partner, but rarely gets credit for the results.

The exception, and a good one, is an alliance that results in a product swap—a product that is very important for the organization outside Japan. Nevertheless, do not expect your Japanese partner to offer an exclusive license—they never exclude themselves, and neither should you.

4. Access discovery research in Japan. When I came to Japan in 1970, there was essentially no discovery research, except to discover new ways of making drugs discovered elsewhere. When product patent laws were enacted in the mid-1970s, the research emphasis shifted to discovering something new—anything new. The results were incredible. Today, the productivity of Japanese research in terms of NCEs exceeds every other country.

Companies not committed to Japan have missed this revolution, or argue that Japanese NCEs are not innovative, or are unsuitable for Western medical practices—whatever that means. Successful companies are establishing basic research facilities in Japan, or forming research alliances with Japanese institutes and institutions.

5. Use the distribution system for competitive advantage. Foreign companies have been slow to assume control over distribution, preferring to rely on Japanese partners. Or should I say, forced to distribute through former partners. How many home office-bound executives don't want to upset the status quo?

This is understandable in the context of other markets where distribution is the mere act of physically moving merchandise. It does not have strategic implications. Furthermore, when Japan had over one thousand wholesalers, distribution was a black hole.

Much has changed and successful companies inside Japan work very hard at wholesaler relations. They know, or are learning, how to use fewer wholesalers, select the winners or survivors, and shorten their access to customers who both prescribe and dispense. Forty-eight percent of Japan's pharmaceutical market is generated by doctors working in small hospitals and clinics, and they typically buy the drugs they prescribe. Wholesalers do not.

My successful friends are the first to admit they do not have all five keys to success under control. But they don't complain. They know what they are doing and are really, really busy.

What Foreign Companies Need

A swift kick in the behind? A manager who stays here long enough to find his way across town without an interpreter? Japanese staffs who want to compete in Japan more than they want to take trips out of Japan? Regulatory affairs people who talk with rather than about Koseisho officials? What do foreign companies need to succeed in Japan's pharmaceutical market?

The fact that this question must be asked is a sad commentary on the presence of foreign companies in Japan. No company has achieved a market share in this country commensurate with their global share. A few examples below confirm this status:

Company	Sales % Japan	Sales % Global
Novartis	2.6	4.2
Merck	2.9	4.2
Pfizer	2.4	3.9
Bayer	1.5	2.1
Roche	0.95	3.0

Source: IMS 1998

Not a single Japanese company is ranked in the global top 20, yet they dominate the same ranking in Japan. Why?

A knee-jerk explanation is the market is closed to foreign investment. In reality, it has been completely open for 25 years. Doctors are not known as ultranationalists who prefer Made In Japan drugs. Accusing Koseisho of discrimination against foreign origin products is an excuse for incompetence. There is no alibi or escape from the reality that foreign companies managed their Japan businesses poorly relative to their own internal global standards. What went wrong and how can it be made right?

Good People

Answers must begin with an analysis of the people employed to operate the business. When restrictions to entry were eliminated in the mid 1970s, good people did not consider a career in a foreign company a wise decision; or if they did, their family and professors convinced them otherwise. While it was easy to cite these cultural biases as a barrier to entry, companies were not creative in overcoming them.

Few took the time and effort to approach professors for student recommendations. Those who did had the bad habit of accepting candidates on an inconsistent basis. One year they were adding people, the next year they were not.

Another common mistake was to judge people on the basis of their ability to speak English. The linguists should have been recruited by a travel agency rather than a drug company.

Although good people are hard to find in any country, Japan ceased to be a special case 15 years ago. Unfortunately, recruiting qualified personnel is still neglected by many foreign firms.

Marketing Control

A second area of non-commitment is marketing. No U.S. company built a presence in Europe by licensing-out its drugs to European companies. No European company became a major factor in the U.S. market by licensing-out its drugs to a U.S. company. Yet both justify to themselves the value of a licensing-out strategy in Japan.

Across a wide range of industries successful companies are those who control their products through the supply chain. They do not forfeit distribution. They do not restrict themselves to market research and promotion. They sell to users. They are in touch with their customers on a daily basis with their own people.

Manufacturing Is Not a Necessity

In the past I considered it critical to manufacture finished products in Japan as offshore facilities could not meet the quality standards demanded by Japanese customers. It appears that by and large this is not an issue today. A pharmaceutical manufacturing presence in Japan is a luxury rather than a strategic necessity. Japanese firms are moving abroad to take advantage of lower energy costs, tax incentives, and less intensive anti-pollution requirements.

Research Debatable—Development a Must

The need to do basic research in Japan continues to be a debatable question. An undeniable fact is new drugs are discovered in Europe, the United States and Japan. This argues for a presence within the research community that comes from having an infrastructure to do research. Those who elect not to do discovery research in

Japan often base their decisions on short term expense limitations rather than long term strategic reasons.

Few argue against the need for a development capability, no matter the outcome of harmonization and acceptance of foreign data. Hard to imagine asking medical representatives to detail doctors in Osaka with clinical data from Baltimore.

A common theme in all of the above factors is the necessity for a presence proportionate to the size of this market. Presence is a function of people and money. No company is or will be a competitive threat in Japan if it forfeits a presence. A joint venture or licensing partner will not provide it because their own interests come first. Japanese companies are learning this same principal applies to their licensees in the United States and Europe.

Resource Limitations

This is not a good time for Japan based executives to argue with their corporate colleagues for additional resources. The U.S. market is on a roll and Europe is beginning to act like a single market, at least in currency and regulatory approvals. Meanwhile, conditions in Japan are portrayed as deteriorating.

But this is precisely why foreign companies are relatively weak in Japan. There was always an excuse not to invest. First because it was considered a closed market, second because there was a downward price spiral, and now because of health care reform measures. If you don't want to be a serious competitor, there is always a reason not to make the effort.

In essence, foreign companies need to make commitments that go beyond philosophical statements or profit plan hype. Achieving a top 10 position in Australia, Taiwan or Brazil may be commendable, but failing to do so will not hurt a company. Failure to succeed in Japan is a strategic disaster completely avoidable.

Pharma Japan 1651, June 1999

Continuity and Commitment

Continuity: An uninterrupted succession
Commitment: To do, perform, or perpetuate

These two words are the most often abused and used words in the English language that foreigners use when speaking of their company operations in Japan.

These speeches usually reach a crescendo in the Spring of every year. Why this is I haven't figured out, but it may relate to ancient tribal customs in northern climates where people emerged from caves after long winters, determined to change the way arrowheads were made.

As soon as I hear the word continuity, I make a silent bet that what will follow is an announcement of management change. As soon as I hear that Joe (not related to present company) has done a great job in Japan, I bet Joe is going to be replaced. Who ever said? "Joe is doing a great job in Japan, and we want continuity of purpose and mission. Therefore, Joe will be staying in Japan for at least five more years."

Wall Street investment houses are a classic example. One firm has 40 foreigners in their Ark Hills office. Amazing! The entire U.S. pharmaceutical industry in Japan employs over 15,000 Japanese nationals and only 57 foreigners. In Ark Hills, foreigners come and go so fast they don't even have time to join the American Club. Continuity equates to quantity, not longevity.

Occasionally one hears truth, "Joe is OK in Japan but we need him in the home office." This is a rare revelation that jobs in the home office are more important than managing the business in Japan.

Those expatriates that recognize Japan for what it is do well in the career path roulette game. Japan is important, visible, and a stepping-stone to a corporate job. These people appreciate it is not necessary to understand Japan, it is enough to maintain harmony, speak of commitment and be an industry spokesman in the ACCJ.

Others believe it is important to get inside Japan. They study the language, stay in *ryokan*s instead of hotels, and go to *nomiya*s after work with their Japanese colleagues. But they lose their visibility and credibility. Home office visitors ask, "Who is Joe working for?" Joe's final embarrassment is to introduce a hotshot successor in the name of continuity.

Is there a compatible middle ground? The man who knows Japan, and is visible and credible? I have known a few. Bill Anderson comes to mind. He managed NCR Japan from the inside, then went on to be Chairman of the corporation. But the exceptions prove the rule of incompatibility between really knowing Japan and maintaining credibility at home.

Commitment also has double meanings. When I hear a commitment speech, I make a silent bet the company is about to close their joint venture, or appoint a new distributor, or cut their head count, or stop recruiting. Every company is committed, but only if Japan contributes to EPS growth. Bean counters hate commitments that penalize short-term earnings.

All Japanese understand the words *tatemae* and *honne*. The first describes a professed position; the second describes one's real intention. Many have mastered the art of *tatemae*. Continuity and commitment pronouncements are a form of *tatemae* and this is OK as long as no one takes them seriously.

A person or a company that is 100 percent *tatemae* is bound to fail. Believe it or not, *honne*, real commitment and true continuity is good business. *Honne* persons get a good night's sleep. *Tatemae* persons return to their caves without creating lasting value. That is, a new arrowhead maker—same lousy arrows.

Pharma Japan 1306, June 8, 1992

Strategic Necessities: Commitment and Presence

Westerners have contemplated how to crack the Japanese market since some Portuguese sailors were blown ashore at Tanegashima, an island off the southern tip of Kyushu, in 1542. Coincidentally, today Tanegashima is the home of Japan's Space Center where satellites are launched into space. Is there a message in this juxtaposition of roles?

After Westerners had been in Japan for 150 years, a high Japanese official commented, "With the exception of medicines, we can dispense with everything that is brought us from abroad." Modern day trade negotiators probably agree not much has changed in the last 300 years. Fortunately for most readers of this paper, the official did make an exception.

Why were medicines so important regardless of origin? Two reasons may be cited. The first is re-enacted NHK samurai dramas aired in prime time. The most revered samurai either engage in the art of inflicting wounds or the art of healing them. High court appointments were reserved for masters of both.

A second reason is the singular veneration Japanese people hold for medicine. Patient visits to a doctor average 13 times per year (the U.S. number is 5), primarily to receive medicine. In preparing for a trip, the first item packed in a suitcase is not clean underwear, it is a bag of medicine. The first Europeans were amazed at this pursuit of effective medicines. A Jesuit priest in a report form Japan in 1585 noted, "Amongst us pearls are used for personal ornamentation, in Japan they serve for nothing more than to be ground to make medicine."

The Japanese pharmaceutical market is now equal to West Germany, Italy, France, and Britain combined. Japanese companies dominate the top 20 ranking in terms of sales, and although Japan represents 22 percent of the world market for drugs, no U.S. or European pharmaceutical companies I know report more than 10 percent of their total sales as originating in Japan. Not that foreign companies need to be reminded of this gap, many smart people meet regularly in planning sessions to plot elaborate strategies for increasing sales in Japan.

Meanwhile, Japanese executives have their own problems as they contemplate expanding into the U.S. market and try to understand disease management, HMO's PBMs, and other acronyms. Europe, with its mosaic of cultures, languages, and regulations, is a mystery. Japan imports 2.5 times more medicines than it exports. A comparison of 20 leading U.S. and 20 leading Japanese companies indicates U.S. company sales are two times the Japanese level, but their international sales are 10 times higher.

Someone listening in from another planet might be amused to hear a cacophony of board room voices saying, "How do we get into Japan?" And, "How do we get out of Japan?" One answer is to focus on two strategic necessities, i.e., commitment and presence. Foreign companies need both to come in, and Japanese companies need both to get out of Japan.

During the past 20 years Japanese industry has established a blitz of new international subsidiaries. One survey indicates there were 30 companies abroad in 1975, and 128 in 1993. My standard question in conversations with Japanese presidents is to ask if they are traveling much outside Japan. The typical response is eight times per year, stated in a satisfied, not apologetic voice.

On the other had foreign company CEOs visit Japan regularly, sometimes with their entire board of directors. Plenty of visits in both directions. The impression I get is lots of flag waving. Both sides would be better served if they empowered local people to implement specific objectives rather than organizing tours and speeches.

Another favorite exercise is to conduct studies. Corporate Planning Departments bulge with Japan studies and internationalization studies. Today they formulate an acquisition strategy, tomorrow an internal growth strategy. Today they plan serious recruiting efforts, tomorrow they restructure to reduce headcount.

The senior executives I worked under in Merck 15 years ago had an unwavering commitment to Japan. They galvanized the entire company to allocate resources to first build effective personnel resources, then to acquire two Japanese companies. The process was never easy, but the Chairman used a pithy saying to calm those who were impatient. He would say, "Fasty, fasty monkey scratch; slowly, slowly monkey catch." The results of Merck in Japan today attest to his commitment.

The chairman of a Japanese company I admire entered his company in the 1950s. He is not prone to take the advice of those who suggest he must rush into foreign markets before windows of opportunity close. His response, "Slowly,

slowly—but sure," is a statement that may not play well in a business school but it does convey a consistent commitment.

Presence

A fully integrated presence flows from commitments. At minimum, presence in product development, promotion, and distribution is required. A company without presence forfeits customer contacts, relationships, and value added margins.

Alliances, the buzzword of the nineties, supplement weaknesses but do not build strength. Low control alliances, e.g., licensing-out, are short-term strategies favored by financial bean counters that generate cash but do not build infrastructure.

The top four foreign companies in Japan have one thing in common—they each have an integrated presence. I am often asked, "What Japanese companies will become truly international (none are today)?" The answer must be to pick those who are building a presence in the United States and Europe rather than licensing-out their NCEs.

Overseas markets are difficult to crack, insiders have advantages over outsiders, the playing field is never level. Historical events have one lesson worth thinking about. Some companies do succeed and have enormous lasting influence. Commitment and presence make a difference. Tell that to the next guy who flies here for three days to review your strategic plan numbers.

Pharma Japan 1444, March 1996

Foreign Companies Should Not Localize

The phrase, "Think globally, act locally," is a sign makers dream. Posted on office walls and engraved on paperweights, it looks good and sounds good, but who can fathom how to apply it to the practical realities of running a business? Foreign pharmaceutical companies in Japan should think and act globally unless they intend to move their corporate headquarters to Tokyo. My reasons for this opinion follow.

Sales and Marketing

Sales strategies in Japan emphasize "push" selling by males. They must call on as many doctors as possible when not confined to an office filing reports and listening to motivational speeches by sales managers who rarely visit doctors themselves.

There is certain inevitability to the notion that higher sales are the result of more representatives (MR) making more calls on doctors more often. Over 80 percent of all calls made by 50,000 MRs are directed toward 130,000 doctors working in hospitals with more than 100 beds, who represent 52 percent of the pharmaceutical market. The numbers demonstrate an intensive, "wet" relationship between MRs and doctors.

To supplement this effort, wholesalers are offered rebates for a variety of mundane tasks, all designed to stock drugs in hospital pharmacies. Sales are physically made through a manufacturer to wholesaler to pharmacy channel. There are 300 wholesalers but 100 have more than a 90 percent share of the market. It does not require a post-graduate education to forecast the demise of 200 wholesalers in a relatively short time frame.

Manufacturers have not kept pace with consolidation in the wholesale industry. Twenty years ago there were 1000 wholesalers, all characterized as local and most identified with a major Japanese manufacturer. Companies typically utilized 150 wholesalers, or 15 percent of the total to distribute their products.

Today there are 300 wholesalers, 20 of whom have regional influence, and most are independent from any single manufacturer. Leading companies use 80 wholesalers, or 27 percent of the total, for distribution. A more appropriate number would be under 50, but relationships of the past are difficult to break by acting locally.

Act globally to slash distribution costs. This means more business with fewer wholesalers and fewer orders with higher quantities in each order. Reduce shipping costs, order processing time, and the number of people responsible for wholesaler relations. Margins are improved and more importantly, the manufacturer gets closer to the local needs of customers.

Act globally by hiring female MRs and reduce the time all MRs spend on administrative tasks. Use marketing activities to "pull through" sales. Call on the right doctor at the right time with the right message for his patients' needs. Recognize that the global empowerment of patients for their healthcare needs will influence the delivery of health care in Japan.

Personnel

Mighty Toyota has stated publicly it intends to reward individual ability and break the tradition of seniority-based wage systems. Japan Airlines hires contract stewardesses on an annual basis. Companies downsize and do not have problems with the union. Unemployment is stuck at 3.4 percent—an all time high.

Act locally and you have too many people doing unproductive work. Recruit by emphasizing your global strengths rather than portraying yourself as a Japanized company.

Foreign companies are recruiting the cream of the crop for entry-level positions by selling their uniqueness and willingness to reward stars, people who like to stand out rather than stand in.

Development

Good Clinical Practice (GCP) guidelines, harmonization, and reimbursement prices that reward innovation are revolutionizing the development process. Acting locally is definitely out of step with reality. Global clinical trial standards, including informed consent, will be adopted in Japan.

Production

If acting locally implies basic manufacturing in Japan, forget it. Anything energy intensive, pollution intensive, or requiring large amounts of space is not welcome in Japan. Acting globally implies production facilities in countries with favorable tax rates and assistance in procuring infrastructure needs by local authorities.

Use What Works

I could go on but I think you get the point. Emulating Japanese pharmaceutical company practices puts the foreign company at a serious competitive disadvantage. In the first place, Japanese companies have been here longer and know how to implement local practices better than a foreign company ever will. Second, there is danger of adopting local policies the Japanese are in the process of discarding.

A word of caution with the home office guy from St. Louis who preaches a global thought process. He may be asking you to implement U.S. practices in the name of globalization. There are more ways to skin a cat than what is taught at the Harvard Business School. Every foreign company in Japan should be learning as well as teaching. Results are what count. There are many roads to success. What's important is to be able to read the direction signs, and many are not written in English.

Pharma Japan 1487, February 1996

Foreign Company Blunders Taint Everyone

In a relatively closed society, club, or association, outsiders are judged harshly if not unfairly. They are held to higher standards than insiders. I suppose this is a basic trait of human nature and will be with us for a long time irrespective of international harmonization.

The situation for foreigners is particularly acute in homogeneous Japan. Indeed, native Japanese who stray too far from the norm are under a lot of pressure to conform. One of the greatest weaknesses of this country is the stigma attached to failure. Young people in particular learn early to play it safe by avoiding risky ventures. Everyone is responsible but no one is accountable.

More Japanese than the Japanese

For the most part, executives of foreign pharmaceutical companies in Japan demonstrate a high degree of sensitivity to local customs. At times they act more Japanese than the Japanese. Consider a few examples.

A major multinational is assuming direct control over distribution previously carried out by its former joint venture partner. Rather than expressing an attitude of "good riddance," every public statement praises the Japanese firm for its support, patience and good will.

At a large reception to announce a major move into Japan, a foreign company CEO did not say he wanted to crush local competition. Rather, he humbly asked for support from his old partners and friends.

A company executive visited Koseisho and spoke in a more deferential tone than he would ever use in talking with government officials in his native country. An acquiring company executive praised the acquired company management as visionaries and partners in a global vision.

All of the above men were well schooled in the importance of images in Japan. They know confrontation is a losing strategy. In delicate situations, they use the word difficult rather than saying, "No way, Jose!" They know what goes around comes around, and good manners are effective negotiating tools in this culture.

People who bluster into Japan with table-pounding ultimatums generally leave empty-handed. How easy it is to stonewall a guy who must catch a plane out of here before the weekend. Few of us have the patience of a saint, but it's an objective worth striving for, and planes do fly on Sundays.

How Not to Do Business

With so many good guys around, the stupidity exhibited by a few is damaging to all. Two recent events will not make headlines but are case studies on how not to do business in Japan.

A relatively small Japanese company bet its future on a new delivery system licensed from a foreign company. The development program was impressive and Koseisho approved the product quickly. A respectable NHI price was granted by the authorities and plans were made for launch.

At this juncture, unbelievably and without precedence in my experience, the foreign company terminated the license and refused to supply the product. Negotiations did not resolve the issue, so the case ended up in arbitration.

Irrespective of the outcome, if I were a Koseisho official, I would not look kindly upon future product applications by this foreign company, and would not worry for one minute about those who criticized my actions as unfair or nontransparent.

The second case involves a product deletion because of an unwillingness to invest in production capacity. Although substitute products exist, this action will inconvenience hospitals and dealers in the supply chain. No doubt, there will be a long memory amongst users as to the reliability of this company specifically, and other foreign companies generally. It will be easy for insiders to cast a wide net over foreigners by saying, "A Japanese company would not act in such a manner."

These two unrelated acts reminded me how much Japanese must learn before they can compete effectively abroad. Japanese act to avoid confrontation while in many places abroad it is expected behavior. If confrontation is avoided, the other side is given a license to take advantage of the outsider. A willingness to compromise is taken as a weakness to be exploited.

Second, Japanese must appreciate the power of return on investment decisions versus judgment related to the value of service and long-term presence in a market. For the bean counters, it's all about money.

Building Goodwill

A *Wall Street Journal* article reported the United States and Japan are working on a report about how to improve the foreign investment environment in Japan. A U.S. official said the final report will focus on ways to develop the mergers-and-acquisition market, decrease restrictions on land availability and use, and improve labor market mobility.

Wonderful. But I suspect we would all be better off if actions by the good guys were given government recognition, and the few bad guys were denied a passport to travel abroad.

I know a man, a large man, from Montana. He was a Marine in the Pacific War and entered Nagasaki when hostilities ceased. He and an equally large friend were invited into a Japanese home to share a meal with a family who said they would serve meat as the main course. The single, small piece of meat on the table was sliced thinly so everyone could share.

Back home in Montana for the rest of his life, he spoke kindly about his hosts who opened their hearts to a former enemy. He could have made fun of the meager meal. The fact that he did not helped to build a bridge of understanding many have traveled over since. Too bad some people are chipping away at the foundations.

Pharma Japan 1657, July 1999

Classic Mistakes

It is difficult for me to deal with the young, energetic upward mobile, single men posted to Japan. They are smart, have a clear set of objectives, know where they will go from here, and have no doubt they will succeed. Such confidence deserves respect, and they are more fun to talk with than the guys who are sour on Japan. I guess my problem is envy, thinking of them as kids let loose in a candy store.

One such person lives in an apartment which I view from my own balcony, down and off to an angle, about 200 meters away. He does not close his curtains as no other building fronts his own unobstructed view. I spend a lot of time on the balcony because I am a *hotaru-zoku*. In other words, I am not allowed to smoke inside the house.

Since I have never met the young man, I have no idea what he does for a living. He works long hours during the week, and upon returning home, spends a lot of time with a portable phone in his ear. Weekends are different; he entertains. Suffice it to say, even from my distant post I can see his taste is first rate. My guess is he does not complain to the home office about a cultural adjustment to Japan.

Alas, the point of this commentary is to focus on the pharmaceutical industry. The young men I do meet in this industry know the right questions to ask. A good one posed to me recently was direct and to the point, "What is the classic mistake made by most foreign companies in Japan?"

I know some people who would love to answer this question. I have wasted more late nights with Japanese and foreign old hands who like to tell dumb *gaijin* stories. We all have our favorites.

But give me a break. Foreign pharmaceutical companies have penetrated this market better than any other industry (McDonald's is not an industry.). The U.S. pharmaceutical industry is the number one success story in Japan, bar none. There may have been many classic mistakes over the years, but on balance the results have been positive.

These young men, however, want to do better and not repeat the mistakes of the past. They are impatient with trite answers to serious questions.

In my view, classic mistakes have been made in two areas. First, failure to retain ownership to the fruits of research. Licensing-out was an easy game to play. No risk and high ROI returns. No presence, but the bottom line looked great. Bean counters love up-front money, milestone payments, royalties, and a good price on raw material sourced out of tax-free production sites. Many executives made a handsome bonus on deals done with only the expense of a few trips to Japan.

Sadly, these guys forfeited ownership and the opportunity to build a business. In the old days, Merck licensed-out the production of streptomycin which made Meiji a world-class fermenter of antibiotics. Presently, there are others intent on optimizing short-term returns which will compromise their long-term future.

Second, failure to move faster into distribution and sales. Companies forfeited contact with their customers by giving away sole distribution rights for a commission. Content to sit back and collect a fee, rather than invest in people who could sell, they didn't get to know their customers. This deserves a failing grade in Business 101.

Japan is a candy store. New products are rewarded with high prices; there are no formulary restrictions; distribution is not a mystery; pricing policy is transparent; good people can be recruited; regulatory procedures are efficient; success is not guaranteed, but neither is it denied.

That's why I envy these young men. They have more opportunities to succeed than at any time in the past. And they don't need to close the curtains; no one will deny them the opportunity to score.

Prescription for Foreign Success in Japan

Losers cry to their government for protection. "Raise tariffs, a minivan is not a car, it is a truck." "We need negotiators who can guarantee us a specific share of the Japanese market." Losers bash the Japanese. Winners quietly smile all the way to the bank. The media likes failures. The U.S. side serves them up as proof that Japan is a closed market or plays by different rules. The Japanese view them as examples of "not trying," or a lack of "spirit."

Overlooked in the babel of charges and countercharges is the success story of foreign pharmaceutical companies in Japan. The story has three ingredients: experience based upon long-term commitments; the buildup of critical mass; and consistent efforts to remain on the leading edge of technology. Describing each is relatively simple.

The Japanese market was effectively closed to majority or wholly-owned foreign affiliated companies until 1975. This did not stop the foreigners. They entered into agreements with local partners that turned into win-win situations for both sides. Joint venture companies expanded to develop new drugs, to manufacture, to do market research, and to promote directly to doctors.

After liberalization, the foreigners took control, usually in a friendly manner. Now joint ventures are passe, but strong distribution alliances persist. Internal growth drove integration along the spectrum of basic research, development, manufacturing, and sales. In a few cases, acquisitions accelerated internal growth.

What emerged is a commitment to an integrated presence in Japan. There is a pervading recognition that customer contact cannot be relegated to third parties, that development cannot be forfeited to licensees, that a presence cannot be defined by proxy. The key factor is controlled by critical mass in all phases of the business.

Critical mass is not a function of bricks and mortar—it is people-related. This is not a capital-intensive business; rather, success is based upon the ideas of people. It is not surprising that foreigners focused on building critical mass in the development and marketing functions. Basic research was largely concentrated at home, but the hits of research must be developed and marketed in Japan.

Local development enhances a firm's knowledge of medical practices, thus positioning a product for optimum sales. Salient features of different dosage strengths and delivery systems go unnoticed by those who insist that what is good enough for a foreign market is good enough for Japan.

Now we are witnessing the buildup of critical mass in basic research. People in a local research center become knowledgeable of Japanese competitors' research strengths, and interact with university and government researchers. They enhance the firms' competitiveness locally and internationally.

Manufacturing operations have also been expanded. There are two reasons. The first is to satisfy Japan's quality crazy customers with an unchipped tablet, a foreign particle-free ampoule, or a granule with consistent size and color. The quality of the package is as important as the effectiveness of the ingredients.

Second is the reverse flow of technology. For example, learning about machines that feed and run themselves, then check the quality of their own output. As in the case of research, presence enhances worldwide competitiveness.

Integration forward into distribution is intensifying because of wholesaler concentration. Fewer, stronger, regional, full-line wholesalers cannot be controlled by leading Japanese manufacturers. In the past, a manufacturer would decide which wholesalers handled his product. Now wholesalers decide which products they promote and sell.

Too bad this exciting story does not make headlines. There is no bashing of Koseisho officials. There is no lack of spirit or innovativeness. Rather, there is confidence based upon long-term experience, a willingness to invest in people, and a passion to stay on the leading edge of technology.

Are you sitting there thinking I must be talking about a company other than your own? Then look around, lots of foreign companies are increasing their market share and making shareholders happy. The story is not titillating—it is the kind that ends: "And they lived happily ever after."

Pharma Japan 1338, February 1, 1993

Who Is Bashing Who?

It is becoming fashionable for Japanese businessmen to criticize Americans for their poor performance in Japan. Recently, two pharmaceutical executives have joined the club. One via a speech in Los Angeles as reported in *The Japan Times*, and one with an article in *Nikkei Business*. In case you missed their words of wisdom, let me give you a short summary.

American businessmen are:

Unknowledgeable about Japan
Send "losers" to manage their Japan operations

    Short-term thinkers
    Incapable of hiring high-caliber Japanese employees
    Only concerned with their own benefit

American businesses:

    Treat people as objects, like money and products
    Do not train employees
    Should appoint Japanese managers and leave them alone
    Are no longer competitive
    Perceive all difficulties as trade barriers

This is pretty strong stuff from two gentlemen who have each worked for outstanding American companies for more than ten years. It makes me wonder what happened to the old-fashioned Japanese sense of loyalty.

Some of us believe that there are great strengths in each of our systems and would like to see cooperation instead of confrontation. Bashing each other is a no-win game for both sides.

The American business system has unleashed more creative endeavors than any other in history. Today, and I suspect it will be true tomorrow, there are a lot more people trying to get in for a piece of the action than are leaving. This includes a significant number of Japanese. Check out the number of Japanese nationals enrolled in U.S. business schools, most sent there by bastions of Japanese industry.

Japan has proved to the world its system is capable of a productive capacity other competitors find difficult to emulate. Attention to the details of development have lowered costs and provided quality products for consumers all over the globe.

Now we need to take a good look in the mirror and admit that neither system is perfect. A good dose of humility might permit us to concentrate on combining our strengths to create a system better than either could do alone. Those that recognize and accept this challenge will make immeasurable contributions to mankind. Those that sit around crapping about the other's weaknesses will miss out on the greatest opportunity of our, and our children's, lifetime.

Pharma Japan, October 2, 1989